Big Data

FOR

DUMMIES®

A Wiley Brand

by Judith Hurwitz, Alan Nugent, Dr. Fern Halper, and Marcia Kaufman

Big Data For Dummies®

Published by
John Wiley & Sons, Inc.
111 River Street
Hoboken, NJ 07030-5774

www.wiley.com

About the Authors

Judith S. Hurwitz is President and CEO of Hurwitz & Associates, a research and consulting firm focused on emerging technology, including cloud computing, big data, analytics, software development, service management, and security and governance. She is a technology strategist, thought leader, and author. A pioneer in anticipating technology innovation and adoption, she has served as a trusted advisor to many industry leaders over the years. Judith has helped these companies make the transition to a new business model focused on the business value of emerging platforms. She was the founder of Hurwitz Group. She has worked in various corporations, including Apollo Computer and John Hancock. She has written extensively about all aspects of distributed software. In 2011 she authored *Smart or Lucky? How Technology Leaders Turn Chance into Success* (Jossey Bass, 2011). Judith is a co-author on five retail *For Dummies* titles including *Hybrid Cloud For Dummies* (John Wiley & Sons, Inc., 2012), *Cloud Computing For Dummies* (John Wiley & Sons, Inc., 2010), *Service Management For Dummies,* and *Service Oriented Architecture For Dummies,* 2nd Edition (both John Wiley & Sons, Inc., 2009). She is also a co-author on many custom published *For Dummies* titles including *Platform as a Service For Dummies,* CloudBees Special Edition (John Wiley & Sons, Inc., 2012), *Cloud For Dummies,* IBM Midsize Company Limited Edition (John Wiley & Sons, Inc., 2011), *Private Cloud For Dummies,* IBM Limited Edition (2011), and *Information on Demand For Dummies,* IBM Limited Edition (2008) (both John Wiley & Sons, Inc.).

Judith holds BS and MS degrees from Boston University, serves on several advisory boards of emerging companies, and was named a distinguished alumnus of Boston University's College of Arts & Sciences in 2005. She serves on Boston University's Alumni Council. She is also a recipient of the 2005 Massachusetts Technology Leadership Council award.

Alan F. Nugent is a Principal Consultant with Hurwitz & Associates. Al is an experienced technology leader and industry veteran of more than three decades. Most recently, he was the Chief Executive and Chief Technology Officer at Mzinga, Inc., a leader in the development and delivery of cloud-based solutions for big data, real-time analytics, social intelligence, and community management. Prior to Mzinga, he was executive vice president and Chief Technology Officer at CA, Inc. where he was responsible for setting the strategic technology direction for the company. He joined CA as senior vice president and general manager of CA's Enterprise Systems Management (ESM) business unit and managed the product portfolio for infrastructure and data management. Prior to joining CA in April of 2005, Al was senior vice president and CTO of Novell, where he was the innovator behind the company's moves into open source and identity-driven solutions. As consulting CTO for BellSouth he led the corporate initiative to consolidate and transform all of BellSouth's disparate customer and operational data into a single data instance.

Al is the independent member of the Board of Directors of Adaptive Computing in Provo, UT, chairman of the advisory board of SpaceCurve in Seattle, WA, and a member of the advisory board of N-of-one in Waltham, MA. He is a frequent writer on business and technology topics and has shared his thoughts and expertise at many industry events throughout the years.

He is an instrument rated private pilot and has played professional poker for the past three decades. In his sparse spare time he enjoys rebuilding older American muscle cars and motorcycles, collecting antiquarian books, epicurean cooking, and has passion for cellaring American and Italian wines.

Fern Halper, PhD, is a Fellow with Hurwitz & Associates and Director of TDWI Research for Advanced Analytics. She has more than 20 years of experience in data analysis, business analysis, and strategy development. Fern has published numerous articles on data analysis and advanced analytics. She has done extensive research, writing, and speaking on the topic of predictive analytics and text analytics. Fern publishes a regular technology blog. She has held key positions at AT&T Bell Laboratories and Lucent Technologies, where she was responsible for developing innovative data analysis systems as well as developing strategy and product-line plans for Internet businesses. Fern has taught courses in information technology at several universities. She received her BA from Colgate University and her PhD from Texas A&M University.

Fern is a co-author on four retail *For Dummies* titles including *Hybrid Cloud For Dummies* (John Wiley & Sons, Inc., 2012), *Cloud Computing For Dummies* (John Wiley & Sons, Inc., 2010), *Service Oriented Architecture For Dummies,* 2nd Edition, and *Service Management For Dummies* (both John Wiley & Sons, Inc., 2009). She is also a co-author on many custom published *For Dummies* titles including *Cloud For Dummies,* IBM Midsize Company Limited Edition (John Wiley & Sons, Inc., 2011), *Platform as a Service For Dummies,* CloudBees Special Edition (John Wiley & Sons, Inc., 2012), and *Information on Demand For Dummies,* IBM Limited Edition (John Wiley & Sons, Inc., 2008).

Marcia A. Kaufman is a founding Partner and COO of Hurwitz & Associates, a research and consulting firm focused on emerging technology, including cloud computing, big data, analytics, software development, service management, and security and governance. She has written extensively on the business value of virtualization and cloud computing, with an emphasis on evolving cloud infrastructure and business models, data-encryption and end-point security, and online transaction processing in cloud environments. Marcia has more than 20 years of experience in business strategy, industry research, distributed software, software quality, information management, and analytics. Marcia has worked within the financial services, manufacturing, and services industries. During her tenure at Data Resources, Inc. (DRI), she developed sophisticated industry models and forecasts. She holds an AB from Connecticut College in mathematics and economics and an MBA from Boston University.

Marcia is a co-author on five retail *For Dummies* titles including *Hybrid Cloud For Dummies* (John Wiley & Sons, Inc., 2012), *Cloud Computing For Dummies* (John Wiley & Sons, Inc., 2010), *Service Oriented Architecture For Dummies,* 2nd Edition, and *Service Management For Dummies* (both John Wiley & Sons, Inc., 2009). She is also a co-author on many custom published *For Dummies* titles including *Platform as a Service For Dummies,* CloudBees Special Edition (John Wiley & Sons, Inc., 2012), *Cloud For Dummies,* IBM Midsize Company Limited Edition (John Wiley & Sons, Inc., 2011), *Private Cloud For Dummies,* IBM Limited Edition (2011), and *Information on Demand For Dummies* (2008) (both John Wiley & Sons, Inc.).

Dedication

Judith dedicates this book to her husband, Warren, her children, Sara and David, and her mother, Elaine. She also dedicates this book in memory of her father, David.

Alan dedicates this book to his wife Jane for all her love and support; his three children Chris, Jeff, and Greg; and the memory of his parents who started him on this journey.

Fern dedicates this book to her husband, Clay, daughters, Katie and Lindsay, and her sister Adrienne.

Marcia dedicates this book to her husband, Matthew, her children, Sara and Emily, and her parents, Gloria and Larry.

Authors' Acknowledgments

We heartily thank our friends at Wiley, most especially our editor, Nicole Sholly. In addition, we would like to thank our technical editor, Brenda Michelson, for her insightful contributions.

The authors would like to acknowledge the contribution of the following technology industry thought leaders who graciously offered their time to share their technical and business knowledge on a wide range of issues related to hybrid cloud. Their assistance was provided in many ways, including technology briefings, sharing of research, case study examples, and reviewing content. We thank the following people and their organizations for their valuable assistance:

Context Relevant: Forrest Carman

Dell: Matt Walken

Epsilon: Bob Zurek

IBM: Rick Clements, David Corrigan, Phil Francisco, Stephen Gold, Glen Hintze, Jeff Jones, Nancy Kop, Dave Lindquist, Angel Luis Diaz, Bill Mathews, Kim Minor, Tracey Mustacchio, Bob Palmer, Craig Rhinehart, Jan Shauer, Brian Vile, Glen Zimmerman

Kognitio: Michael Hiskey, Steve Millard

Opera Solutions: Jacob Spoelstra

RainStor: Ramon Chen, Deidre Mahon

SAS Institute: Malcom Alexander, Michael Ames

VMware: Chris Keene

Xtremedata: Michael Lamble

Publisher's Acknowledgments

We're proud of this book; please send us your comments at http://dummies.custhelp.com. For other comments, please contact our Customer Care Department within the U.S. at 877-762-2974, outside the U.S. at 317-572-3993, or fax 317-572-4002.

Some of the people who helped bring this book to market include the following:

Acquisitions, Editorial

Senior Project Editor: Nicole Sholly

Project Editor: Dean Miller

Acquisitions Editor: Constance Santisteban

Copy Editor: John Edwards

Technical Editor: Brenda Michelson

Editorial Manager: Kevin Kirschner

Editorial Assistant: Anne Sullivan

Sr. Editorial Assistant: Cherie Case

Cover Photo: © Baris Simsek / iStockphoto

Composition Services

Project Coordinator: Sheree Montgomery

Layout and Graphics: Jennifer Creasey, Joyce Haughey

Proofreaders: Debbye Butler, Lauren Mandelbaum

Indexer: Valerie Haynes Perry

Publishing and Editorial for Technology Dummies

   Richard Swadley, Vice President and Executive Group Publisher

   Andy Cummings, Vice President and Publisher

   Mary Bednarek, Executive Acquisitions Director

   Mary C. Corder, Editorial Director

Publishing for Consumer Dummies

   Kathleen Nebenhaus, Vice President and Executive Publisher

Composition Services

   Debbie Stailey, Director of Composition Services

Contents at a Glance

Table of Contents

Chapter 13: Understanding Text Analytics and Big Data 153

Chapter 14: Customized Approaches for Analysis of Big Data 167

Part V: Big Data Implementation............................... 179

Chapter 15: Integrating Data Sources. 181

Introduction

Welcome to *Big Data For Dummies*. Big data is becoming one of the most important technology trends that has the potential for dramatically changing the way organizations use information to enhance the customer experience and transform their business models. How does a company go about using data to the best advantage? What does it mean to transform massive amounts of data into knowledge? In this book, we provide you with insights into how technology transitions in software, hardware, and delivery models are changing the way that data can be used in new ways.

Big data is not a single market. Rather, it is a combination of data-management technologies that have evolved over time. Big data enables organizations to store, manage, and manipulate vast amounts of data at the right speed and at the right time to gain the right insights. The key to understanding big data is that data has to be managed so that it can meet the business requirement a given solution is designed to support. Most companies are at an early stage with their big data journey. Many companies are experimenting with techniques that allow them to collect massive amounts of data to determine whether hidden patterns exist within that data that might be an early indication of an important change. Some data may indicate that customer buying patterns are changing or that new elements are in the business that need to be addressed before it is too late.

As companies begin to evaluate new types of big data solutions, many new opportunities will unfold. For example, manufacturing companies may be able to monitor data coming from machine sensors to determine how processes need to be modified before a catastrophic event happens. It will be possible for retailers to monitor data in real time to upsell customers related products as they are executing a transaction. Big data solutions can be used in healthcare to determine the cause of an illness and provide a physician with guidance on treatment options.

Big data is not an isolated solution, however. Implementing a big data solution requires that the infrastructure be in place to support the scalability, distribution, and management of that data. Therefore, it is important to put both a business and technical strategy in place to make use of this important technology trend.

For many important reasons, we think that it is important for you to understand big data technologies and know the ways that companies are using emerging technologies such as Hadoop, MapReduce, and new database engines to transform the value of their data. We wrote this book to provide a perspective on what big data is and how it's changing the way that organizations can leverage more data than was possible in the past. We think that this book will give you the context to make informed decisions.

About This Book

Big data is new to many people, so it requires some investigation and understanding of both the technical and business requirements. Many different people need knowledge about big data. Some of you want to delve into the technical details, while others want to understand the economic implications of making use of big data technologies. Other executives need to know enough to be able to understand how big data can affect business decisions. Implementing a big data environment requires both an architectural and a business approach — and lots of planning.

No matter what your goal is in reading this book, we address the following issues to help you understand big data and the impact it can have on your business:

- ✔ What is the architecture for big data? How can you manage huge volumes of data without causing major disruptions in your data center?
- ✔ When should you integrate the outcome of your big data analysis with your data warehouse?
- ✔ What are the implications of security and governance on the use of big data? How can you keep your company safe?
- ✔ What is the value of different data technologies, and when should you consider them as part of your big data strategy?
- ✔ What types of data sources can you take advantage of with big data analytics? How can you apply different types of analytics to business problems?

Foolish Assumptions

Try as we might to be all things to all people, when it came to writing this book, we had to pick who we thought would be most interested in *Big Data For Dummies*. Here's who we think you are:

- ✔ **You're smart.** You're no dummy, yet the topic of big data gives you an uneasy feeling. You can't quite get your head around it, and if you're pressed for a definition, you might try to change the subject.

✔ **You're a businessperson who wants little or nothing to do with technology.** But you live in the 21st century, so you can't escape it. People are saying, "It's all about big data," so you think that you better find out what they're talking about.

✔ **You're an IT person who knows a heck of a lot about technology.** The thing is, you're new to big data. Everybody says it's something different. Once and for all, you want the whole picture.

Whoever you are, welcome. We're here to help.

How This Book Is Organized

We divided our book into seven parts for easy reading. Feel free to skip about.

Part I: Getting Started with Big Data

In this part, we explain the basic concepts you need for a full understanding of big data, from both a technical and a business perspective. We also introduce you to the major concepts and components so that you can hold your own in any meaningful conversation about big data.

Part II: Technology Foundations for Big Data

Part II is for both technical and business professionals who need to understand the different types of big data components and the underlying technology concepts that support big data. In this section, we give you an understanding about the type of infrastructure that will make big data more practical.

Part III: Big Data Management

Part III is for both technical and business professionals, but it gets into a lot more of the details of different database options and emerging technologies such as MapReduce and Hadoop. Understanding these underlying technologies can help you understand what is behind this important trend.

Part IV: Analytics and Big Data

How do you analyze the massive amounts of data that become part of your big data infrastructure? In this part of the book, we go deeper into the different types of analytics that are helpful in getting real meaning from your data. This part helps you think about ways that you can turn big data into action for your business.

Part V: Big Data Implementation

This part gets to the details of what it means to actually manage data, including issues such as operationalizing your data and protecting the security and privacy of that data. This section gives you plenty to think about in this critical area.

Part VI: Big Data Solutions in the Real World

In this section, you get an understanding of how companies are beginning to use big data to transform their business operations. If you want to get a peek into the future at what you might be able to do with data, this section is for you.

Part VII: The Part of Tens

If you're new to the *For Dummies* treasure-trove, you're no doubt unfamiliar with The Part of Tens. In this section, Wiley editors torture *For Dummies* authors into creating useful bits of information that are easily accessible in lists containing ten (or so) elucidating elements. We started these chapters kicking and screaming but are ultimately very glad that they're here. After you read through the big data best practices, and the do's and don'ts we provide in The Part of Tens, we think you'll be glad, too.

Glossary

We include a glossary of terms frequently used when people discuss big data. Although we strive to define terms as we introduce them in this book, we think you'll find the glossary a useful resource.

Icons Used in This Book

Pay attention. The bother you save may be your own.

You may be sorry if this little tidbit slips your mind.

With this icon, we mark particularly useful points to pay attention to.

Here you find tidbits for the more technically inclined.

Where to Go from Here

We've created an overview of big data and introduced you to all its significant components. We recommend that you read the first four chapters to give you the context for what big data is about and what technologies are in place to make implementations a reality. The next two chapters introduce you to some of the underlying infrastructure issues that are important to understand. The following eight chapters get into a lot more detail about the different types of data structures that are foundational to big data.

You can read the book from cover to cover, but if you're not that kind of person, we've tried to adhere to the *For Dummies* style of keeping chapters self-contained so that you can go straight to the topics that interest you most. Wherever you start, we wish you well.

Many of these chapters could be expanded into full-length books of their own. Big data and the emerging technology landscape are a big focus for us at Hurwitz & Associates, and we invite you to visit our website and read our blogs and insights at www.hurwitz.com.

Occasionally, John Wiley & Sons, Inc., has updates to its technology books. If this book has technical updates, they will be posted at www.dummies.com/go/bigdatafdupdates.

Part I

getting started with **Big Data**

Visit www.dummies.com for more great *Dummies* content online.

In this part . . .

- ✔ Trace the evolution of data management.
- ✔ Define big data and its technology components.
- ✔ Understand the different types of big data.
- ✔ Integrate structured and unstructured data.
- ✔ Understand the difference between real-time and non-real-time data.
- ✔ Scale your big data operation with distributed computing.

Chapter 1

Grasping the Fundamentals of Big Data

In This Chapter

▶ Looking at a history of data management

▶ Understanding why big data matters to business

▶ Applying big data to business effectiveness

▶ Defining the foundational elements of big data

▶ Examining big data's role in the future

Managing and analyzing data have always offered the greatest benefits and the greatest challenges for organizations of all sizes and across all industries. Businesses have long struggled with finding a pragmatic approach to capturing information about their customers, products, and services. When a company only had a handful of customers who all bought the same product in the same way, things were pretty straightforward and simple. But over time, companies and the markets they participate in have grown more complicated. To survive or gain a competitive advantage with customers, these companies added more product lines and diversified how they deliver their product. Data struggles are not limited to business. Research and development (R&D) organizations, for example, have struggled to get enough computing power to run sophisticated models or to process images and other sources of scientific data.

Indeed, we are dealing with a lot of complexity when it comes to data. Some data is structured and stored in a traditional relational database, while other data, including documents, customer service records, and even pictures and videos, is unstructured. Companies also have to consider new sources of data generated by machines such as sensors. Other new information sources are human generated, such as data from social media and the click-stream data generated from website interactions. In addition, the availability and adoption of newer, more powerful mobile devices, coupled with ubiquitous access to global networks will drive the creation of new sources for data.

Although each data source can be independently managed and searched, the challenge today is how companies can make sense of the intersection of all these different types of data. When you are dealing with so much information in so many different forms, it is impossible to think about data management in traditional ways. Although we have always had a lot of data, the difference today is that significantly more of it exists, and it varies in type and timeliness. Organizations are also finding more ways to make use of this information than ever before. Therefore, you have to think about managing data differently. That is the opportunity and challenge of big data. In this chapter, we provide you a context for what the evolution of the movement to big data is all about and what it means to your organization.

The Evolution of Data Management

It would be nice to think that each new innovation in data management is a fresh start and disconnected from the past. However, whether revolutionary or incremental, most new stages or waves of data management build on their predecessors. Although data management is typically viewed through a software lens, it actually has to be viewed from a holistic perspective. Data management has to include technology advances in hardware, storage, networking, and computing models such as virtualization and cloud computing. The convergence of emerging technologies and reduction in costs for everything from storage to compute cycles have transformed the data landscape and made new opportunities possible.

As all these technology factors converge, it is transforming the way we manage and leverage data. Big data is the latest trend to emerge because of these factors. So, what is big data and why is it so important? Later in the book, we provide a more comprehensive definition. To get you started, big data is defined as any kind of data source that has at least three shared characteristics:

- ✔ Extremely large *Volumes* of data
- ✔ Extremely high *Velocity* of data
- ✔ Extremely wide *Variety* of data

Big data is important because it enables organizations to gather, store, manage, and manipulate vast amounts data at the right speed, at the right time, to gain the right insights. But before we delve into the details of big data, it is important to look at the evolution of data management and how it has led to big data. Big data is not a stand-alone technology; rather, it is a combination of the last 50 years of technology evolution.

Organizations today are at a tipping point in data management. We have moved from the era where the technology was designed to support a specific business need, such as determining how many items were sold to how many customers, to a time when organizations have more data from more sources than ever before. All this data looks like a potential gold mine, but like a gold mine, you only have a little gold and lot more of everything else. The technology challenges are "How do you make sense of that data when you can't easily recognize the patterns that are the most meaningful for your business decisions? How does your organization deal with massive amounts of data in a meaningful way?" Before we get into the options, we take a look at the evolution of data management and see how these waves are connected.

Understanding the Waves of Managing Data

Each data management wave is born out of the necessity to try and solve a specific type of data management problem. Each of these waves or phases evolved because of cause and effect. When a new technology solution came to market, it required the discovery of new approaches. When the relational database came to market, it needed a set of tools to allow managers to study the relationship between data elements. When companies started storing unstructured data, analysts needed new capabilities such as natural language–based analysis tools to gain insights that would be useful to business. If you were a search engine company leader, you began to realize that you had access to immense amounts of data that could be monetized. To gain value from that data required new innovative tools and approaches.

The data management waves over the past five decades have culminated in where we are today: the initiation of the big data era. So, to understand big data, you have to understand the underpinning of these previous waves. You also need to understand that as we move from one wave to another, we don't throw away the tools and technology and practices that we have been using to address a different set of problems.

Wave 1: Creating manageable data structures

As computing moved into the commercial market in the late 1960s, data was stored in flat files that imposed no structure. When companies needed to get to a level of detailed understanding about customers, they had to apply brute-force methods, including very detailed programming models to create some value. Later in the 1970s, things changed with the invention of the relational data model and the relational database management system (RDBMS) that imposed structure and a method for improving performance. Most importantly, the relational model added a level of abstraction (the structured query language [SQL], report generators, and data management tools) so that it was easier for programmers to satisfy the growing business demands to extract value from data.

The relational model offered an ecosystem of tools from a large number of emerging software companies. It filled a growing need to help companies better organize their data and be able to compare transactions from one geography to another. In addition, it helped business managers who wanted to be able to examine information such as inventory and compare it to customer order information for decision-making purposes. But a problem emerged from this exploding demand for answers: Storing this growing volume of data was expensive and accessing it was slow. Making matters worse, lots of data duplication existed, and the actual business value of that data was hard to measure.

At this stage, an urgent need existed to find a new set of technologies to support the relational model. The Entity-Relationship (ER) model emerged, which added additional abstraction to increase the usability of the data. In this model, each item was defined independently of its use. Therefore, developers could create new relationships between data sources without complex programming. It was a huge advance at the time, and it enabled developers to push the boundaries of the technology and create more complex models requiring complex techniques for joining entities together. The market for relational databases exploded and remains vibrant today. It is especially important for transactional data management of highly structured data.

When the volume of data that organizations needed to manage grew out of control, the data warehouse provided a solution. The data warehouse enabled the IT organization to select a subset of the data being stored so that it would be easier for the business to try to gain insights. The data warehouse was intended to help companies deal with increasingly large amounts of structured data that they needed to be able to analyze by reducing the volume of the data to something smaller and more focused on a particular area of the business. It filled the need to separate operational decision support processing and decision support — for performance reasons. In addition, warehouses often store data from prior years for understanding organizational performance, identifying trends, and helping to expose patterns of behavior. It also provided an integrated source of information from across various data sources that could be used for analysis. Data warehouses were commercialized in the 1990s, and today, both content management systems and data warehouses are able to take advantage of improvements in scalability of hardware, virtualization technologies, and the ability to create integrated hardware and software systems, also known as appliances.

Sometimes these data warehouses themselves were too complex and large and didn't offer the speed and agility that the business required. The answer was a further refinement of the data being managed through data marts. These data marts were focused on specific business issues and were much more streamlined and supported the business need for speedy queries than the more massive data warehouses. Like any wave of data management, the warehouse has evolved to support emerging technologies such as integrated systems and data appliances.

Data warehouses and data marts solved many problems for companies needing a consistent way to manage massive transactional data. But when it came to managing huge volumes of unstructured or semi-structured data, the warehouse was not able to evolve enough to meet changing demands. To complicate matters, data warehouses are typically fed in batch intervals, usually weekly or daily. This is fine for planning, financial reporting, and traditional marketing campaigns, but is too slow for increasingly real-time business and consumer environments.

How would companies be able to transform their traditional data management approaches to handle the expanding volume of unstructured data elements? The solution did not emerge overnight. As companies began to store unstructured data, vendors began to add capabilities such as *BLOBs (binary large objects)*. In essence, an unstructured data element would be stored in a relational database as one contiguous chunk of data. This object could be labeled (that is, a customer inquiry) but you couldn't see what was inside that object. Clearly, this wasn't going to solve changing customer or business needs.

Enter the object database management system (ODBMS). The object database stored the BLOB as an addressable set of pieces so that we could see what was in there. Unlike the BLOB, which was an independent unit appended to a traditional relational database, the object database provided a unified approach for dealing with unstructured data. Object databases include a programming language and a structure for the data elements so that it is easier to manipulate various data objects without programming and complex joins. The object databases introduced a new level of innovation that helped lead to the second wave of data management.

Wave 2: Web and content management

It's no secret that most data available in the world today is unstructured. Paradoxically, companies have focused their investments in the systems with structured data that were most closely associated with revenue: line-of-business transactional systems. Enterprise Content Management systems evolved in the 1980s to provide businesses with the capability to better manage unstructured data, mostly documents. In the 1990s with the rise of the web, organizations wanted to move beyond documents and store and manage web content, images, audio, and video.

The market evolved from a set of disconnected solutions to a more unified model that brought together these elements into a platform that incorporated business process management, version control, information recognition, text management, and collaboration. This new generation of systems added metadata (information about the organization and characteristics of the stored information). These solutions remain incredibly important for companies needing to manage all this data in a logical manner. But at the same time, a new generation of requirements has begun to emerge that drive us to the next wave. These new requirements have been driven, in large part, by a convergence of factors including the web, virtualization, and cloud computing. In this new wave, organizations are beginning to understand that they need to manage a new generation of data sources with an unprecedented amount and variety of data that needs to be processed at an unheard-of speed.

Wave 3: Managing big data

Is big data really new or is it an evolution in the data management journey? The answer is yes — it is actually both. As with other waves in data management, big data is built on top of the evolution of data management practices over the past five decades. What is new is that for the first time, the cost of computing cycles and storage has reached a tipping point. Why is this important? Only a few years ago, organizations typically would compromise by storing snapshots or subsets of important information because the cost of storage and processing limitations prohibited them from storing everything they wanted to analyze.

In many situations, this compromise worked fine. For example, a manufacturing company might have collected machine data every two minutes to determine the health of systems. However, there could be situations where the snapshot would not contain information about a new type of defect and that might go unnoticed for months.

With big data, it is now possible to virtualize data so that it can be stored efficiently and, utilizing cloud-based storage, more cost-effectively as well. In addition, improvements in network speed and reliability have removed other physical limitations of being able to manage massive amounts of data at an acceptable pace. Add to this the impact of changes in the price and sophistication of computer memory. With all these technology transitions, it is now possible to imagine ways that companies can leverage data that would have been inconceivable only five years ago.

But no technology transition happens in isolation; it happens when an important need exists that can be met by the availability and maturation of technology. Many of the technologies at the heart of big data, such as virtualization, parallel processing, distributed file systems, and in-memory databases, have been around for decades. Advanced analytics have also been around for decades, although they have not always been practical. Other technologies such as Hadoop and MapReduce have been on the scene for only a few years. This combination of technology advances can now address significant business problems. Businesses want to be able to gain insights and actionable results from many different kinds of data at the right speed — no matter how much data is involved.

If companies can analyze petabytes of data (equivalent to 20 million four-drawer file cabinets filled with text files or 13.3 years of HDTV content) with acceptable performance to discern patterns and anomalies, businesses can begin to make sense of data in new ways. The move to big data is not just about businesses. Science, research, and government activities have also helped to drive it forward. Just think about analyzing the human genome or dealing with all the astronomical data collected at observatories to advance our understanding of the world around us. Consider the amount of data the government collects in its antiterrorist activities as well, and you get the idea that big data is not just about business.

Different approaches to handling data exist based on whether it is data in motion or data at rest. Here's a quick example of each. Data in motion would be used if a company is able to analyze the quality of its products during the manufacturing process to avoid costly errors. Data at rest would be used by a business analyst to better understand customers' current buying patterns based on all aspects of the customer relationship, including sales, social media data, and customer service interactions.

Keep in mind that we are still at an early stage of leveraging huge volumes of data to gain a 360-degree view of the business and anticipate shifts and changes in customer expectations. The technologies required to get the answers the business needs are still isolated from each other. To get to the desired end state, the technologies from all three waves will have to come together. As you will see as you read this book, big data is not simply about one tool or one technology. It is about how all these technologies come together to give the right insights, at the right time, based on the right data — whether it is generated by people, machines, or the web.

Defining Big Data

Big data is not a single technology but a combination of old and new technologies that helps companies gain actionable insight. Therefore, big data is the capability to manage a huge volume of disparate data, at the right speed, and within the right time frame to allow real-time analysis and reaction. As we note earlier in this chapter, big data is typically broken down by three characteristics:

- ✔ **Volume:** How much data
- ✔ **Velocity:** How fast that data is processed
- ✔ **Variety:** The various types of data

 Although it's convenient to simplify big data into the three *V*s, it can be misleading and overly simplistic. For example, you may be managing a relatively small amount of very disparate, complex data or you may be processing a huge volume of very simple data. That simple data may be all structured or all unstructured. Even more important is the fourth *V*: veracity. How accurate is that data in predicting business value? Do the results of a big data analysis actually make sense?

It is critical that you don't underestimate the task at hand. Data must be able to be verified based on both accuracy and context. An innovative business may want to be able to analyze massive amounts of data in real time to quickly assess the value of that customer and the potential to provide additional offers to that customer. It is necessary to identify the right amount and types of data that can be analyzed to impact business outcomes. Big data incorporates all data, including structured data and unstructured data from e-mail, social media, text streams, and more. This kind of data management requires that companies leverage both their structured and unstructured data.

Building a Successful Big Data Management Architecture

We have moved from an era where an organization could implement a database to meet a specific project need and be done. But as data has become the fuel of growth and innovation, it is more important than ever to have an underlying architecture to support growing requirements.

Beginning with capture, organize, integrate, analyze, and act

Before we delve into the architecture, it is important to take into account the functional requirements for big data. Figure 1-1 illustrates that data must first be captured, and then organized and integrated. After this phase is successfully implemented, data can be analyzed based on the problem being addressed. Finally, management takes action based on the outcome of that analysis. For example, Amazon.com might recommend a book based on a past purchase or a customer might receive a coupon for a discount for a future purchase of a related product to one that was just purchased.

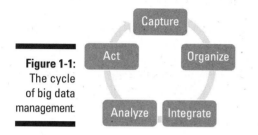

Figure 1-1:
The cycle
of big data
management.

Although this sounds straightforward, certain nuances of these functions are complicated. Validation is a particularly important issue. If your organization is combining data sources, it is critical that you have the ability to validate that these sources make sense when combined. Also, certain data sources may contain sensitive information, so you must implement sufficient levels of security and governance. We cover data management in more detail in Chapter 7.

Of course, any foray into big data first needs to start with the problem you're trying to solve. That will dictate the kind of data that you need and what the architecture might look like.

Setting the architectural foundation

In addition to supporting the functional requirements, it is important to support the required performance. Your needs will depend on the nature of the analysis you are supporting. You will need the right amount of computational power and speed. While some of the analysis you will do will be performed in real time, you will inevitably be storing some amount of data as well. Your architecture also has to have the right amount of redundancy so that you are protected from unanticipated latency and downtime.

Your organization and its needs will determine how much attention you have to pay to these performance issues. So, start out by asking yourself the following questions:

- How much data will my organization need to manage today and in the future?

- How often will my organization need to manage data in real time or near real time?

✔ How much risk can my organization afford? Is my industry subject to strict security, compliance, and governance requirements?

✔ How important is speed to my need to manage data?

✔ How certain or precise does the data need to be?

To understand big data, it helps to lay out the components of the architecture. A big data management architecture must include a variety of services that enable companies to make use of myriad data sources in a fast and effective manner. To help you make sense of this, we put the components into a diagram (see Figure 1-2) that will help you see what's there and the relationship between the components. In the next section, we explain each component and describe how these components are related to each other.

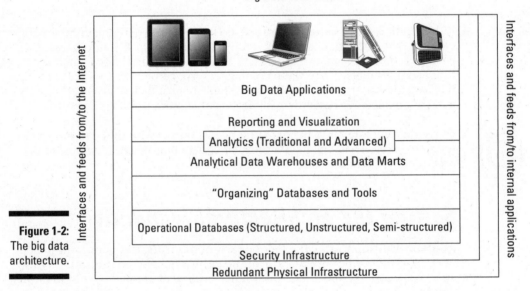

Figure 1-2: The big data architecture.

Interfaces and feeds

Before we get into the nitty-gritty of the big data technology stack itself, we'd like you to notice that on either side of the diagram are indications of interfaces and feeds into and out of both internally managed data and data feeds from external sources. To understand how big data works in the real world, it is important to start by understanding this necessity. In fact, what makes big data big is the fact that it relies on picking up lots of data from lots of sources. Therefore, open application programming interfaces (APIs) will be core to any big data architecture. In addition, keep in mind that interfaces exist at every level and between every layer of the stack. Without integration services, big data can't happen.

Redundant physical infrastructure

The supporting physical infrastructure is fundamental to the operation and scalability of a big data architecture. In fact, without the availability of robust physical infrastructures, big data would probably not have emerged as such an important trend. To support an unanticipated or unpredictable volume of data, a physical infrastructure for big data has to be different than that for traditional data. The physical infrastructure is based on a distributed computing model. This means that data may be physically stored in many different locations and can be linked together through networks, the use of a distributed file system, and various big data analytic tools and applications.

Redundancy is important because we are dealing with so much data from so many different sources. Redundancy comes in many forms. If your company has created a private cloud, you will want to have redundancy built within the private environment so that it can scale out to support changing workloads. If your company wants to contain internal IT growth, it may use external cloud services to augment its internal resources. In some cases, this redundancy may come in the form of a Software as a Service (SaaS) offering that allows companies to do sophisticated data analysis as a service. The SaaS approach offers lower costs, quicker startup, and seamless evolution of the underlying technology.

Security infrastructure

The more important big data analysis becomes to companies, the more important it will be to secure that data. For example, if you are a healthcare company, you will probably want to use big data applications to determine changes in demographics or shifts in patient needs. This data about your constituents needs to be protected both to meet compliance requirements and to protect the patients' privacy. You will need to take into account who is allowed to see the data and under what circumstances they are allowed to do so. You will need to be able to verify the identity of users as well as protect the identity of patients. These types of security requirements need to be part of the big data fabric from the outset and not an afterthought.

Operational data sources

When you think about big data, it is important to understand that you have to incorporate all the data sources that will give you a complete picture of your business and see how the data impacts the way you operate your business. Traditionally, an operational data source consisted of highly structured data managed by the line of business in a relational database. But as the world changes, it is important to understand that operational data now has to encompass a broader set of data sources, including unstructured sources such as customer and social media data in all its forms.

You find new emerging approaches to data management in the big data world, including document, graph, columnar, and geospatial database architectures. Collectively, these are referred to as *NoSQL*, or not only SQL, databases. In essence, you need to map the data architectures to the types of transactions. Doing so will help to ensure the *right* data is available when you need it. You also need data architectures that support complex unstructured content. You need to include both relational databases and nonrelational databases in your approach to harnessing big data. It is also necessary to include unstructured data sources, such as content management systems, so that you can get closer to that 360-degree business view.

All these operational data sources have several characteristics in common:

- ✔ They represent systems of record that keep track of the critical data required for real-time, day-to-day operation of the business.

- ✔ They are continually updated based on transactions happening within business units and from the web.

- ✔ For these sources to provide an accurate representation of the business, they must blend structured and unstructured data.

- ✔ These systems also must be able to scale to support thousands of users on a consistent basis. These might include transactional e-commerce systems, customer relationship management systems, or call center applications.

Performance matters

Your data architecture also needs to perform in concert with your organization's supporting infrastructure. For example, you might be interested in running models to determine whether it is safe to drill for oil in an offshore area given real-time data of temperature, salinity, sediment resuspension, and a host of other biological, chemical, and physical properties of the water column. It might take days to run this model using a traditional server configuration. However, using a distributed computing model, what took days might now take minutes.

Performance might also determine the kind of database you would use. For example, in some situations, you may want to understand how two very distinct data elements are related. What is the relationship between buzz on a social network and the growth in sales? This is not the typical query you could ask of a structured, relational database. A graphing database might be a better choice, as it is specifically designed to separate the "nodes" or entities from its "properties" or the information that defines that entity, and the "edge" or relationship between nodes and properties. Using the right database will also improve performance. Typically the graph database will be used in scientific and technical applications.

Other important operational database approaches include columnar databases that store information efficiently in columns rather than rows. This approach leads to faster performance because input/output is extremely fast. When geographic data storage is part of the equation, a spatial database is optimized to store and query data based on how objects are related in space.

Organizing data services and tools

Not all the data that organizations use is operational. A growing amount of data comes from a variety of sources that aren't quite as organized or straightforward, including data that comes from machines or sensors, and massive public and private data sources. In the past, most companies weren't able to either capture or store this vast amount of data. It was simply too expensive or too overwhelming. Even if companies were able to capture the data, they did not have the tools to do anything about it. Very few tools could make sense of these vast amounts of data. The tools that did exist were complex to use and did not produce results in a reasonable time frame. In the end, those who really wanted to go to the enormous effort of analyzing this data were forced to work with snapshots of data. This has the undesirable effect of missing important events because they were not in a particular snapshot.

MapReduce, Hadoop, and Big Table

With the evolution of computing technology, it is now possible to manage immense volumes of data that previously could have only been handled by supercomputers at great expense. Prices of systems have dropped, and as a result, new techniques for distributed computing are mainstream. The real breakthrough in big data happened as companies like Yahoo!, Google, and Facebook came to the realization that they needed help in monetizing the massive amounts of data their offerings were creating.

These emerging companies needed to find new technologies that would allow them to store, access, and analyze huge amounts of data in near real time so that they could monetize the benefits of owning this much data about participants in their networks. Their resulting solutions are transforming the data management market. In particular, the innovations MapReduce, Hadoop, and Big Table proved to be the sparks that led to a new generation of data management. These technologies address one of the most fundamental problems — the capability to process massive amounts of data efficiently, cost-effectively, and in a timely fashion.

MapReduce

MapReduce was designed by Google as a way of efficiently executing a set of functions against a large amount of data in batch mode. The "map" component distributes the programming problem or tasks across a large number of systems and handles the placement of the tasks in a way that balances the load and manages recovery from failures. After the distributed computation is completed, another function called "reduce" aggregates all the elements back together to provide a result. An example of MapReduce usage would be to determine how many pages of a book are written in each of 50 different languages.

Big Table

Big Table was developed by Google to be a distributed storage system intended to manage highly scalable structured data. Data is organized into tables with rows and columns. Unlike a traditional relational database model, Big Table is a sparse, distributed, persistent multidimensional sorted map. It is intended to store huge volumes of data across commodity servers.

Hadoop

Hadoop is an Apache-managed software framework derived from MapReduce and Big Table. Hadoop allows applications based on MapReduce to run on large clusters of commodity hardware. The project is the foundation for the computing architecture supporting Yahoo!'s business. Hadoop is designed to parallelize data processing across computing nodes to speed computations and hide latency. Two major components of Hadoop exist: a massively scalable distributed file system that can support petabytes of data and a massively scalable MapReduce engine that computes results in batch.

Traditional and advanced analytics

What does your business now do with all the data in all its forms to try to make sense of it for the business? It requires many different approaches to analysis, depending on the problem being solved. Some analyses will use a traditional data warehouse, while other analyses will take advantage of advanced predictive analytics. Managing big data holistically requires many different approaches to help the business to successfully plan for the future.

Analytical data warehouses and data marts

After a company sorts through the massive amounts of data available, it is often pragmatic to take the subset of data that reveals patterns and put it into a form that's available to the business. These warehouses and marts provide compression, multilevel partitioning, and a massively parallel processing architecture.

Big data analytics

The capability to manage and analyze petabytes of data enables companies to deal with clusters of information that could have an impact on the business. This requires analytical engines that can manage this highly distributed data and provide results that can be optimized to solve a business problem. Analytics can get quite complex with big data. For example, some organizations are using predictive models that couple structured and unstructured data together to predict fraud. Social media analytics, text analytics, and new kinds of analytics are being utilized by organizations looking to gain insight into big data. Big data analytics are described in more detail in chapters 12, 13, and 14.

Reporting and visualization

Organizations have always relied on the capability to create reports to give them an understanding of what the data tells them about everything from monthly sales figures to projections of growth. Big data changes the way that data is managed and used. If a company can collect, manage, and analyze enough data, it can use a new generation of tools to help management truly understand the impact not just of a collection of data elements but also how these data elements offer context based on the business problem being addressed. With big data, reporting and data visualization become tools for looking at the context of how data is related and the impact of those relationships on the future.

Big data applications

Traditionally, the business expected that data would be used to answer questions about what to do and when to do it. Data was often integrated as fields into general-purpose business applications. With the advent of big data, this is changing. Now, we are seeing the development of applications that are designed specifically to take advantage of the unique characteristics of big data.

Some of the emerging applications are in areas such as healthcare, manufacturing management, traffic management, and so on. What do all these big data applications have in common? They rely on huge volumes, velocities, and varieties of data to transform the behavior of a market. In healthcare, a big data application might be able to monitor premature infants to determine when data indicates when intervention is needed. In manufacturing, a big data application can be used to prevent a machine from shutting down during a production run. A big data traffic management application can reduce the number of traffic jams on busy city highways to decrease accidents, save fuel, and reduce pollution.

The Big Data Journey

Companies have always had to deal with lots of data in lots of forms. The change that big data brings is what you can do with that information. If you have the right technology in place, you can use big data to anticipate and solve business problems and react to opportunities. With big data, you can analyze data patterns to change everything, from the way you manage cities, prevent failures, conduct experiments, manage traffic, improve customer satisfaction, or enhance product quality, just to name a few examples. The emerging technologies and tools that are the heart of this book can help you understand and unleash the tremendous power of big data, changing the world as we know it.

Chapter 2

Examining Big Data Types

*V*ariety is the spice of life, and variety is one of the principles of big data. In Chapter 1, we discuss the importance of being able to manage the variety of data types. Clearly, big data encompasses everything from dollar transactions to tweets to images to audio. Therefore, taking advantage of big data requires that all this information be integrated for analysis and data management. Doing this type of activity is harder than it sounds. In this chapter, we examine the two main types of data that make up big data — structured and unstructured — and provide you with definitions and examples of each.

Although data management has been around for a long time, two factors are new in the big data world:

✔ Some sources of big data are actually new like the data generated from sensors, smartphone, and tablets.

✔ Previously produced data hadn't been captured or stored and analyzed in a usable way. The main reason for this is that the technology wasn't there to do so. In other words, we didn't have a cost-effective way to deal with all that data.

You have many different ways to put big data to use to solve problems. For example, in some situations, you want to deal with data in real time, such as when you're monitoring traffic data. In other situations, real-time data management won't be necessary, such as when you're collecting massive amounts of data that you want to analyze in batch mode to determine an unsuspected pattern. Likewise, you sometimes need to integrate multiple sources of data as part of a big data solution, so we look at why you might want to integrate data sources. The bottom line is that what you want to do with your structured and unstructured data informs the technology purchases that you make.

Defining Structured Data

The term *structured data* generally refers to data that has a defined length and format. Examples of structured data include numbers, dates, and groups of words and numbers called *strings* (for example, a customer's name, address, and so on). Most experts agree that this kind of data accounts for about 20 percent of the data that is out there. Structured data is the data that you're probably used to dealing with. It's usually stored in a database. You can query it using a language like structured query language (SQL), which we discuss later in the "Defining Unstructured Data" section.

Your company may already be collecting structured data from "traditional" sources. These might include your customer relationship management (CRM) data, operational enterprise resource planning (ERP) data, and financial data. Often these data elements are integrated in a data warehouse for analysis.

Exploring sources of big structured data

Although this might seem like business as usual, in reality, structured data is taking on a new role in the world of big data. The evolution of technology provides newer sources of structured data being produced — often in real time and in large volumes. The sources of data are divided into two categories:

✔ **Computer- or machine-generated:** Machine-generated data generally refers to data that is created by a machine without human intervention.

✔ **Human-generated:** This is data that humans, in interaction with computers, supply.

Some experts argue that a third category exists that is a hybrid between machine and human. Here though, we're concerned with the first two categories.

Machine-generated structured data can include the following:

✔ **Sensor data:** Examples include radio frequency ID (RFID) tags, smart meters, medical devices, and Global Positioning System (GPS) data. For example, RFID is rapidly becoming a popular technology. It uses tiny computer chips to track items at a distance. An example of this is tracking containers of produce from one location to another. When information is transmitted from the receiver, it can go into a server and then be analyzed. Companies are interested in this for supply chain management and inventory control. Another example of sensor data is smartphones that contain sensors like GPS that can be used to understand customer behavior in new ways.

- **Web log data:** When servers, applications, networks, and so on operate, they capture all kinds of data about their activity. This can amount to huge volumes of data that can be useful, for example, to deal with service-level agreements or to predict security breaches.

- **Point-of-sale data:** When the cashier swipes the bar code of any product that you are purchasing, all that data associated with the product is generated. Just think of all the products across all the people who purchase them, and you can understand how big this data set can be.

- **Financial data:** Lots of financial systems are now programmatic; they are operated based on predefined rules that automate processes. Stock-trading data is a good example of this. It contains structured data such as the company symbol and dollar value. Some of this data is machine generated, and some is human generated.

Examples of structured human-generated data might include the following:

- **Input data:** This is any piece of data that a human might input into a computer, such as name, age, income, non-free-form survey responses, and so on. This data can be useful to understand basic customer behavior.

- **Click-stream data:** Data is generated every time you click a link on a website. This data can be analyzed to determine customer behavior and buying patterns.

- **Gaming-related data:** Every move you make in a game can be recorded. This can be useful in understanding how end users move through a gaming portfolio.

You get the idea. Some of this data may not be that big on its own, such as profile data. However, when taken together with millions of other users submitting the same information, the size is astronomical. Additionally, much of this data has a real-time component to it that can be useful for understanding patterns that have the potential of predicting outcomes. The bottom line is that this kind of information can be powerful and can be utilized for many purposes.

Understanding the role of relational databases in big data

Data persistence refers to how a database retains versions of itself when modified. The great granddaddy of persistent data stores is the *relational database management system (RDBMS)*. In its infancy, the computing industry used what are now considered primitive techniques for data persistence.

You may recall "flat files" or "network" data stores that were prevalent before 1980 or so. Although these mechanisms were useful, they were very difficult to master and always required system programmers to write custom programs to manipulate the data.

The relational model was invented by Edgar Codd, an IBM scientist, in the 1970s and was used by IBM, Oracle, Microsoft, and others. It is still in wide usage today and plays an important role in the evolution of big data. Understanding the relational database is important because other types of databases are used with big data. We contrast various kinds of databases used for big data throughout this book.

In a relational model, the data is stored in a table. This database would contain a *schema* — that is, a structural representation of what is in the database. For example, in a relational database, the schema defines the tables, the fields in the tables, and the relationships between the two. The data is stored in columns, one each for each specific attribute. The data is also stored in the rows. For instance, the two tables shown in Figure 2-1 represent the schema for a simple database. The first table stores product information; the second stores demographic information. Each has various attributes (customer ID, order number, purchase code for a product, and so on). Each table can be updated with new data, and data can be deleted, read, and updated. This is often accomplished in a relational model using a structured query language (SQL).

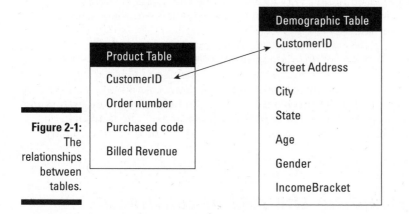

Figure 2-1:
The
relationships
between
tables.

Another aspect of the relational model using SQL is that tables can be queried using a common key (that is, the relationship). In Figure 2-1, the common key in the tables is CustomerID.

You can submit a query, for example, to determine the gender of customers who purchased a specific product. It might look something like this:

```
Select CustomerID, State, Gender, Product from
        "demographic table", "product table" where
        Product= XXYY
```

Although relational databases have ruled the roost for the last several decades, they can be difficult to use when you're dealing with huge streams of disparate data types. Relational database vendors are not standing still, however, and are starting to introduce relational databases designed for big data. In addition, new database models have evolved to help people manage big data. We talk a little bit about technologies like NoSQL, streaming databases, and others in Chapter 1. These data management systems are a subject unto themselves, so we devote all of Part III to them.

PostgresSQL (www.postgressql.org), a technology we talk about in Chapter 7, is the most widely used open source relational database available. Its extensibility and the fact that it is available on many varieties of mainframes make it a foundation technology for some relational big data databases.

Defining Unstructured Data

Unstructured data is data that does not follow a specified format. If 20 percent of the data available to enterprises is structured data, the other 80 percent is unstructured. Unstructured data is really most of the data that you will encounter. Until recently, however, the technology didn't really support doing much with it except storing it or analyzing it manually.

Exploring sources of unstructured data

Unstructured data is everywhere. In fact, most individuals and organizations conduct their lives around unstructured data. Just as with structured data, unstructured data is either machine generated or human generated.

Here are some examples of machine-generated unstructured data:

- ✓ **Satellite images:** This includes weather data or the data that the government captures in its satellite surveillance imagery. Just think about Google Earth, and you get the picture (pun intended).
- ✓ **Scientific data:** This includes seismic imagery, atmospheric data, and high energy physics.

- ✔ **Photographs and video:** This includes security, surveillance, and traffic video.

- ✔ **Radar or sonar data:** This includes vehicular, meteorological, and oceanographic seismic profiles.

The following list shows a few examples of human-generated unstructured data:

- ✔ **Text internal to your company:** Think of all the text within documents, logs, survey results, and e-mails. Enterprise information actually represents a large percent of the text information in the world today.

- ✔ **Social media data:** This data is generated from the social media platforms such as YouTube, Facebook, Twitter, LinkedIn, and Flickr.

- ✔ **Mobile data:** This includes data such as text messages and location information.

- ✔ **Website content:** This comes from any site delivering unstructured content, like YouTube, Flickr, or Instagram.

And the list goes on.

Some people believe that the term *unstructured data* is misleading because each document may contain its own specific structure or formatting based on the software that created it. However, what is internal to the document is truly unstructured.

By far, unstructured data is the largest piece of the data equation, and the use cases for unstructured data are rapidly expanding. On the text side alone, text analytics (a technology that we discuss in Chapter 13) can be used to analyze unstructured text and to extract relevant data and transform that data into structured information that can be used in various ways. For example, a popular big data use case is social media analytics for use with high-volume customer conversations. In addition, unstructured data from call center notes, e-mails, written comments in a survey, and other documents is analyzed to understand customer behavior. This can be combined with social media from tens of millions of sources to understand the customer experience.

Looking at semi-structured data

Semi-structured data is a kind of data that falls between structured and unstructured data. Semi-structured data does not necessarily conform to a fixed schema (that is, structure) but may be self-describing and may have simple label/value pairs. For example, label/value pairs might include: <family>=Jones, <mother>=Jane, and <daughter>=Sarah. Examples of semi-structured data include EDI, SWIFT, and XML. You can think of them as sort of payloads for processing complex events.

Understanding the role of a CMS in big data management

Organizations store some unstructured data in databases. However, they also utilize enterprise content management systems (CMSs) that can manage the complete life cycle of content. This can include web content, document content, and other forms media.

According to the Association for Information and Image Management (AIIM; www.aiim.org;), a nonprofit organization that provides education, research, and best practices, Enterprise Content Management (ECM) comprises the "strategies, methods, and tools used to capture, manage, store, preserve, and deliver content and documents related to organizational processes." The technologies included in ECM include document management, records management, imaging, workflow management, web content management, and collaboration.

A whole industry has grown up around managing content, and many content management vendors are scaling out their solutions to handle large volumes of unstructured data. However, new technologies are also evolving to help support unstructured data and the analysis of unstructured data. Some of these support both structured and unstructured data. Some support real-time streams. These include technologies like Hadoop, MapReduce, and streaming. These technologies each require chapters of their own, and we devote Chapters 8, 9, and 10 to them, respectively.

Systems that are designed to store content in the form of content management systems are no longer stand-alone solutions. Rather, they are likely to be part of an overall data management solution. For example, your organization may monitor Twitter feeds that can then programmatically trigger a CMS search. Now, the person who triggered the tweet (maybe looking for a solution to a problem) gets an answer back that offers a location where the individual can find the product that he or she might be looking for. The greatest benefit is when this type of interaction can happen in real time. It also illustrates the value of leveraging real-time unstructured, structured (customer data about the person who tweeted), and semi-structured (the actual content in the CMS) data.

The reality is that you will probably use a hybrid approach to solve your big data problems. For example, it doesn't make sense to move all your news content, for example, into Hadoop on your premises because it is supposed to help manage unstructured data.

Looking at Real-Time and Non-Real-Time Requirements

As we discuss in previous sections of this chapter, big data is often about doing things that weren't widely possible because the technology was not advanced enough or the cost of doing so was prohibitive. The big change that we are encountering with big data is the capability to leverage massive amounts of data without all the complex programming that was required in the past. Many organizations are at a tipping-point in terms of managing large volumes of complex data. Big data approaches will help keep things in balance so we don't go over the edge as the volume, variety, and velocity of data changes. Companies have had a difficult time managing increasing amounts of data that needs to be managed at high speeds. Organizations had to settle for analyzing small subsets of data which often lacked critical information to get a full picture that the data could reveal. As big data technologies evolve and get deployed, we will be able to more easily analyze the data and use it to make decisions or take actions.

The real-time aspects of big data can be revolutionary when companies need to solve significant problems. What is the impact when an organization can handle data that is streaming in real time? In general, this real-time approach is most relevant when the answer to a problem is time sensitive and business critical. This may be related to a threat to something important like detecting the performance of hospital equipment or anticipating a potential intrusion risk. The following list shows examples of when a company wants to leverage this real-time data to gain a quick advantage:

- Monitoring for an exception with a new piece of information, like fraud/intelligence
- Monitoring news feeds and social media to determine events that may impact financial markets, such as a customer reaction to a new product announcement
- Changing your ad placement during a big sporting event based on real-time Twitter streams
- Providing a coupon to a customer based on what he bought at the point of sale

Sometimes streaming data is coming in really fast and does not include a wide variety of sources, sometimes a wide variety exists, and sometimes it is a combination of the two. The question you need to ask yourself if you're moving to real time is this: Could this (problem) be solved with traditional information management capabilities or do we need newer capabilities? Is the sheer volume or velocity going to overwhelm our systems? Oftentimes it is a combination of the two.

So, if you need real-time capabilities, what are the requirements of the infrastructure to support this? We talk more about this in Chapter 3 when we discuss distributed computing. However, the following list highlights a few things you need to consider regarding a system's capability to ingest data, process it, and analyze it in real time:

- ✔ **Low latency:** Latency is the amount of time lag that enables a service to execute in an environment. Some applications require less latency, which means that they need to respond in real time. A real-time stream is going to require low latency. So you need to be thinking about compute power as well as network constraints.

- ✔ **Scalability:** Scalability is the capability to sustain a certain level of performance even under increasing loads.

- ✔ **Versatility:** The system must support both structured and unstructured data streams.

- ✔ **Native format:** Use the data in its native form. Transformation takes time and money. The capability to use the idea of processing complex interactions in the data that trigger events may be transformational.

The need to process continually increasing amounts of disparate data is one of the key factors driving the adoption of cloud services. The cloud model is large-scale and distributed. We talk more about the cloud in Chapter 6.

Putting Big Data Together

What you want to do with your structured and unstructured data indicates why you might choose one piece of technology over another one. It also determines the need to understand inbound data structures to put this data in the right place.

Managing different data types

Figure 2-2 shows a helpful table that outlines some of the characteristics of big data and the types of data management systems you might want to use to address each one. We don't expect you to know what these are yet; they are described in the chapters that follow.

	Batch	Streaming	Complex Query
Structured	Hadoop	Key/Value	RDBMS
Unstructured	Document	Graph Spatial	Columnar
Both	Hybrid	Hybrid	Hybrid

Figure 2-2: The characteristics of different data types.

Integrating data types into a big data environment

Another important aspect of big data is that you often don't need to own all the data that you will use. Many examples make the point. You may be leveraging social media data, data coming from third-party industry statistics, or even data coming from satellites. Just think about social media and you'll understand what we mean. Oftentimes, it becomes necessary to integrate different sources. This data may be coming from all internal systems, from both internal and external sources, or from entirely external sources. Much of this data may have been siloed before.

Data need not be coming to you in real time. You just may have a lot of it and it is disparate in nature. This could still qualify as a big data problem. Of course, you could also be faced with a scenario where you're seeing huge volumes of data, at high velocities, and it is disparate in nature. The point is that you won't get the business value if you deal with a variety of data sources as a set of disconnected silos of information.

Components you need include connectors and metadata, which we discuss next.

Connectors

You want to have some connectors that enable you to pull data in from various big data sources. Maybe you want a Twitter connector or a Facebook one. Maybe you need to integrate from your data warehouse with a big data source that's off your premises so that you can analyze both of these sources of data together. We discuss connectors in more detail in Chapter 15.

Metadata

A critical component to integrating all this data is the metadata. *Metadata* is the definitions, mappings, and other characteristics used to describe how to find, access, and use a company's data (and software) components. One example of metadata is data about an account number. This might include the number, description, data type, name, address, phone number, and privacy level.

Metadata can be used to help you organize your data stores and deal with new and changing sources of data. Although the idea of metadata is not new, it is changing and evolving in the context of big data. In the traditional metadata world, it is important to have a catalog that provides a single view of all data sources. But this catalog will have to be different when you don't control all these data sources. You may need an analytic tool that will help you understand the underlying metadata.

Chapter 3

Old Meets New: Distributed Computing

. . . .

In This Chapter

▶ Taking a look at distributed computing through the years

▶ Exploring the elements of distributed computing

▶ Putting distributed computing together with hardware and software advancements

. . . .

Distributed computing is not a new technology concept. It has been around for almost 50 years. Initially, the technology was used in computer science research as a way to scale computing tasks and attack complex problems without the expense of massive computing systems. One of the most successful early endeavors into distributed computing was a project funded by the U.S. Defense Advanced Research Project Agency (DARPA). The result of the organization's research was the development of the Internet, the first distributed computing network. You might say that it initiated a revolution that has led to a transformation of everything from commerce to healthcare, to transportation, and to human-to-human and machine-to-machine communications. In this chapter, we explain what distributed computing is and describe why it is the foundation for big data.

A Brief History of Distributed Computing

Behind all the most important trends over the past decade, including service orientation, cloud computing, virtualization, and big data, is a foundational technology called *distributed computing*. Simply put, without distributing computing, none of these advancements would be possible. Distributed computing is a technique that allows individual computers to be networked together across geographical areas as though they were a single environment, as shown in Figure 3-1. You find many different implementations of distributed computing. In some topologies, individual computing entities simply pass messages to each other. In other situations, a distributed computing environment may share resources ranging from memory to networks and storage. All distributed computing models have a common attribute: They are a group of networked computers that work together to execute a workload or process.

Giving thanks to DARPA

The most well-known distributed computing model, the Internet, is the foundation for everything from e-commerce to cloud computing to service management and virtualization. The Internet was conceived as a research project funded by the U.S. DARPA. It was designed to create an interconnecting networking system that would support noncommercial, collaborate research among scientists. In the early days of the Internet, these computers were often connected by telephone lines (see Figure 3-1)! Unless you experienced that frustration, you can only imagine how slow and fragile those connections were.

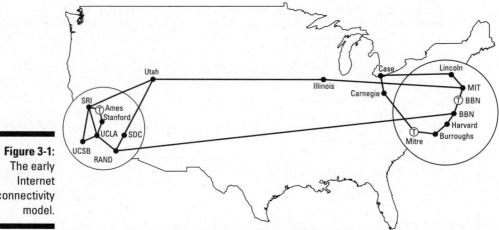

Figure 3-1:
The early
Internet
connectivity
model.

As the technology matured over the next decade, common protocols such as Transmission Control Protocol (TCP) helped to proliferate the technology and the network. When the Internet Protocol (IP) was added, the project moved from a closed network for a collection of scientists to a potentially commercial platform to transfer e-mail across the globe. Throughout the 1980s, new Internet-based services began to spring up in the market as a commercial alternative to the DARPA network. In 1992, the U.S. Congress passed the Scientific and Advanced-Technology Act that for the first time, allowed commercial use of this powerful networking technology. With its continued explosive growth, the Internet is truly a global distributed network and remains the best example of the power of distributed computing.

The value of a consistent model

What difference did this DARPA-led effort make in the movement to distributed computing? Before the commercialization of the Internet, there were hundreds of companies and organizations creating a software infrastructure intended to provide a common platform to support a highly distributed computing environment. However, each vendor or standards organization came up with its own remote procedures calls (RPCs) that all customers, commercial software developers, and partners would have to adopt and support. RPC is a primitive mechanism used to send work to a remote computer and usually requires waiting for the remote work to complete before other work can continue.

With vendors implementing proprietary RPCs, it became impractical to imagine that any one company would be able to create a universal standard for distributed computing. By the mid-1990s, the Internet protocols replaced these primitive approaches and became the foundation for what is distributed computing today. After this was settled, the uses of this approach to networked computing began to flourish. Today, we take it for granted that we can create a network of loosely coupled computers that can exchange information and communicate at the right speed at the right time, as shown in Figure 3-2.

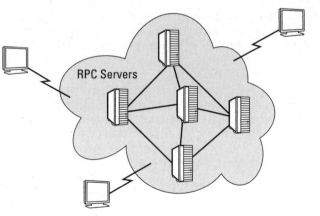

Figure 3-2: An example of how a Remote Procedure Call has been used in early distributed computing techniques.

RPC Servers

Understanding the Basics of Distributed Computing

There isn't a single distributed computing model because computing resources can be distributed in many ways. For example, you can distribute a set of programs on the same physical server and use messaging services to enable them to communicate and pass information. It is also possible to have many different systems or servers, each with its own memory, that can work together to solve one problem.

Why we need distributed computing for big data

Not all problems require distributed computing. If a big time constraint doesn't exist, complex processing can done via a specialized service remotely. When companies needed to do complex data analysis, IT would move data to an external service or entity where lots of spare resources were available for processing. It wasn't that companies wanted to wait to get the results they needed; it just wasn't economically feasible to buy enough computing resources to handle these emerging requirements. In many situations, organizations would capture only selections of data rather than try to capture all the data because of costs. Analysts wanted all the data but had to settle for snapshots, hoping that they captured the right data at the right time.

Key hardware and software breakthroughs revolutionized the data management industry. First, innovation and demand increased the power and decreased the price of hardware. New software emerged that understood how to take advantage of this hardware by automating processes like load balancing and optimization across a huge cluster of nodes. The software included built-in rules that understood that certain workloads required a certain performance level. The software treated all the nodes as though they were simply one big pool of computing, storage, and networking assets, and moved processes to another node without interruption if a node failed, using the technology of virtualization. Chapter 5 covers virtualization and big data in more detail.

The changing economics of computing

Fast-forward and a lot has changed. Over the last several years, the cost to purchase computing and storage resources has decreased dramatically. Aided by virtualization, commodity servers that could be clustered and blades that could be networked in a rack changed the economics of computing. This change coincided with innovation in software automation solutions that dramatically improved the manageability of these systems. The capability to leverage distributed computing and parallel processing techniques dramatically transformed the landscape and dramatically reduce latency. There are special cases, such as High Frequency Trading (HFT), in which low latency can only be achieved by physically locating servers in a single location.

The problem with latency

One of the perennial problems with managing data — especially large quantities of data — has been the impact of latency. *Latency* is the delay within a system based on delays in execution of a task. Latency is an issue in every aspect of computing, including communications, data management, system performance, and more. If you have ever used a wireless phone, you have experienced latency firsthand. It is the delay in the transmissions between you and your caller. At times, latency has little impact on customer satisfaction, such as if companies need to analyze results behind the scenes to plan for a new product release. This probably doesn't require instant response or access. However, the closer that response is to a customer at the time of decision, the more that latency matters.

Distributed computing and parallel processing techniques can make a significant difference in the latency experienced by customers, suppliers, and partners. Many big data applications are dependent on low latency because of the big data requirements for speed and the volume and variety of the data. It may not be possible to construct a big data application in a high latency environment if high performance is needed. The need to verify the data in near real time can also be impacted by latency. In Chapter 16, we address the issue of real-time data streaming and complex event processing, which are critical to applications of big data. When you are dealing with real-time data, a high level of latency means the difference between success and failure.

Demand meets solutions

The growth of the Internet as a platform for everything from commerce to medicine transformed the demand for a new generation of data management. In the late 1990s, engine and Internet companies like Google, Yahoo!, and Amazon.com were able to expand their business models, leveraging inexpensive hardware for computing and storage. Next, these companies needed a new generation of software technologies that would allow them to monetize the huge amounts of data they were capturing from customers. These companies could not wait for results of analytic processing. They needed the capability to process and analyze this data in near real time.

Getting Performance Right

Just having a faster computer isn't enough to ensure the right level of performance to handle big data. You need to be able to distribute components of your big data service across a series of nodes. See Figure 3-3. In distributed computing, a *node* is an element contained within a cluster of systems or within a rack. A node typically includes CPU, memory, and some kind of disk. However, a node can also be a blade CPU and memory that rely on nearby storage within a rack.

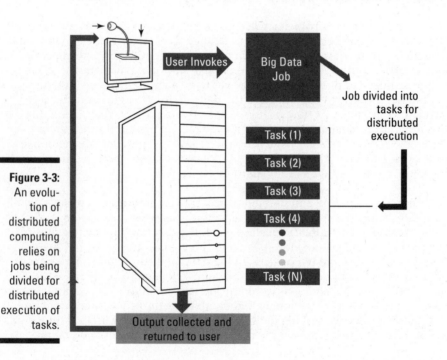

Figure 3-3: An evolution of distributed computing relies on jobs being divided for distributed execution of tasks.

Within a big data environment, these nodes are typically clustered together to provide scale. For example, you might start out with a big data analysis and continue to add more data sources. To accommodate the growth, an organization simply adds more nodes into a cluster so that it can scale out to accommodate growing requirements. However, it isn't enough to simply expand the number of nodes in the cluster. Rather, it is important to be able to send part of the big data analysis to different physical environments. Where you send these tasks and how you manage them makes the difference between success and failure.

In some complex situations, you may want to execute many different algorithms in parallel, even within the same cluster, to achieve the speed of analysis required. Why would you execute different big data algorithms in parallel within the same rack? The closer together the distributions of functions are, the faster they can execute. Although it is possible to distribute big data analysis across networks to take advantage of available capacity, you must do this type of distribution based on requirements for performance. In some situations, the speed of processing takes a back seat. However, in other situations, getting results fast is the requirement. In this situation, you want to make sure that the networking functions are in close proximity to each other. In general, the big data environment has to be optimized for the type of analytics task.

Therefore, scalability is the lynchpin of making big data operate successfully. Although it would be theoretically possible to operate a big data environment within a single large environment, it is not practical. To understand the needs for scalability in big data, one only has to look at cloud scalability and understand both the requirements and the approach. Like cloud computing, big data requires the inclusion of fast networks and inexpensive clusters of hardware that can be combined in racks to increase performance. These clusters are supported by software automation that enables dynamic scaling and load balancing.

The design and implementations of MapReduce are excellent examples of how distributed computing can make big data operationally visible and affordable. For more information on MapReduce, refer to Chapter 8. In essence, we are at one of the unique turning points in computing where technology concepts come together at the right time to solve the right problems. Combining distributed computing, improved hardware systems, and practical solutions such as MapReduce and Hadoop is changing data management in profound ways.

Part II
Technology Foundations for Big Data

Big Data Tech Stack

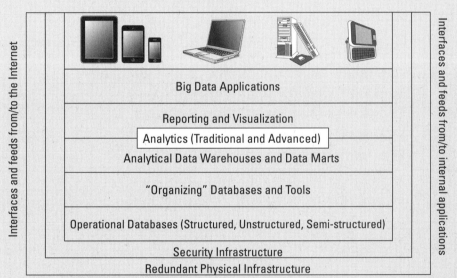

Explore the big data stack online at www.dummies.com/extras/bigdata.

In this part . . .

- ✔ Explain the various elements of the big data stack.
- ✔ Integrate analytics and applications with big data.
- ✔ Define virtualization.
- ✔ Explain how virtualization impacts big data.
- ✔ Add abstraction to the mix.
- ✔ Understand the cloud and its role in big data.

Chapter 4

Digging into Big Data Technology Components

As discussed in the first few chapters, big data is about high-volume and often high-velocity data streams with highly diverse data types. Many seasoned software architects and developers know how to address one or even two of these situations quite readily. For example, if you are faced with high-volume transactional data with fault tolerance requirements, you might choose to deploy redundant relational database clusters in a data center with a very fast network infrastructure. Similarly, if the requirements are to integrate different data types from many known and anonymous sources, the choice might be to construct an extensible meta-model driving a customized data warehouse.

However, you may not have had the luxury of creating specific deployments in a much more dynamic big data world. When you move out of the world where you own and tightly control your data, you need to create an architectural model for addressing this type of hybrid environment. This new environment requires an architecture that understands both the dynamic nature of big data and the requirement to apply the knowledge to a business solution. In this chapter, we examine the architectural considerations associated with big data. We also dig a bit deeper into the big data technology stack we introduce in Chapter 1.

Exploring the Big Data Stack

Like any important data architecture, you should design a model that takes a holistic look at how all the elements need to come together. Although this will take some time in the beginning, it will save many hours of development and lots of frustration during the subsequent implementations. You need to think about big data as a strategy, not a project.

Good design principles are critical when creating (or evolving) an environment to support big data — whether dealing with storage, analytics, reporting, or applications. The environment must include considerations for hardware, infrastructure software, operational software, management software, well-defined application programming interfaces (APIs), and even software developer tools. Your architecture will have to be able to address all the foundational requirements that we discuss in Chapter 1:

✔ Capture

✔ Integrate

✔ Organize

✔ Analyze

✔ Act

Figure 4-1 presents the layered reference architecture we introduce in Chapter 1. It can be used as a framework for how to think about big data technologies that can address functional requirements for your big data projects.

This is a comprehensive stack, and you may focus on certain aspects initially based on the specific problem you are addressing. However, it is important to understand the entire stack so that you are prepared for the future. You'll no doubt use different elements of the stack depending on the problem you're addressing.

Big Data Tech Stack

Figure 4-1:
The big data technology stack.

Layer 0: Redundant Physical Infrastructure

At the lowest level of the stack is the physical infrastructure — the hardware, network, and so on. Your company might already have a data center or made investments in physical infrastructures, so you're going to want to find a way to use the existing assets. Big data implementations have very specific requirements on all elements in the reference architecture, so you need to examine these requirements on a layer-by-layer basis to ensure that your implementation will perform and scale according to the demands of your business. As you start to think about your big data implementation, it is important to have some overarching principles that you can apply to the approach. A prioritized list of these principles should include statements about the following:

✔ **Performance:** How responsive do you need the system to be? Performance, also called *latency,* is often measured end to end, based on a single transaction or query request. Very fast (high-performance, low-latency) infrastructures tend to be very expensive.

✔ **Availability:** Do you need a 100 percent uptime guarantee of service? How long can your business wait in the case of a service interruption or failure? Highly available infrastructures are also very expensive.

- ✓ **Scalability:** How big does your infrastructure need to be? How much disk space is needed today and in the future? How much computing power do you need? Typically, you need to decide what you need and then add a little more scale for unexpected challenges.

- ✓ **Flexibility:** How quickly can you add more resources to the infrastructure? How quickly can your infrastructure recover from failures? The most flexible infrastructures can be costly, but you can control the costs with cloud services, where you only pay for what you actually use (see Chapter 6 for more on cloud computing).

- ✓ **Cost:** What can you afford? Because the infrastructure is a set of components, you might be able to buy the "best" networking and decide to save money on storage (or vice versa). You need to establish requirements for each of these areas in the context of an overall budget and then make trade-offs where necessary.

As big data is all about high-velocity, high-volume, and high-data variety, the physical infrastructure will literally "make or break" the implementation. Most big data implementations need to be highly available, so the networks, servers, and physical storage must be both resilient and redundant. Resiliency and redundancy are interrelated. An infrastructure, or a system, is resilient to failure or changes when sufficient redundant resources are in place, ready to jump into action. In essence, there are always reasons why even the most sophisticated and resilient network could fail, such as a hardware malfunction. Therefore, redundancy ensures that such a malfunction won't cause an outage.

Resiliency helps to eliminate single points of failure in your infrastructure. For example, if only one network connection exists between your business and the Internet, no network redundancy exists, and the infrastructure is not resilient with respect to a network outage. In large data centers with business continuity requirements, most of the redundancy is in place and can be leveraged to create a big data environment. In new implementations, the designers have the responsibility to map the deployment to the needs of the business based on costs and performance.

As more vendors provide cloud-based platform offerings, the design responsibility for the hardware infrastructure often falls to those service providers.

This means that the technical and operational complexity is masked behind a collection of services, each with specific terms for performance, availability, recovery, and so on. These terms are described in service-level agreements (SLAs) and are usually negotiated between the service provider and the customer, with penalties for noncompliance.

For example, if you contract with a managed service provider, you are theoretically absolved from the worry associated with the specifics of the physical environment and the core components of the data center. The networks, servers, operating systems, virtualization fabric, requisite management tools, and day-to-day operations are inclusive in your service agreements. In effect, this creates a virtual data center. Even with this approach, you should still know what is needed to build and run a big data deployment so that you can make the most appropriate selections from the available service offerings. Despite having an SLA, your organization still has the ultimate responsibility for performance.

Physical redundant networks

Networks should be redundant and must have enough capacity to accommodate the anticipated volume and velocity of the inbound and outbound data in addition to the "normal" network traffic experienced by the business. As you begin making big data an integral part of your computing strategy, it is reasonable to expect volume and velocity to increase.

Infrastructure designers should plan for these expected increases and try to create physical implementations that are "elastic." As network traffic ebbs and flows, so too does the set of physical assets associated with the implementation. Your infrastructure should offer monitoring capabilities so that operators can react when more resources are required to address changes in workloads.

Managing hardware: Storage and servers

Likewise, the hardware (storage and server) assets must have sufficient speed and capacity to handle all expected big data capabilities. It's of little use to have a high-speed network with slow servers because the servers will most likely become a bottleneck. However, a very fast set of storage and compute servers can overcome variable network performance. Of course, nothing will work properly if network performance is poor or unreliable.

Infrastructure operations

Another important design consideration is infrastructure operations management. The greatest levels of performance and flexibility will be present only in a well-managed environment. Data center managers need to be able to anticipate and prevent catastrophic failures so that the integrity of the data, and by extension the business processes, is maintained. IT organizations often overlook and therefore underinvest in this area. We talk more about what's involved with operationalizing big data in Chapter 17.

Layer 1: Security Infrastructure

Security and privacy requirements for big data are similar to the requirements for conventional data environments. The security requirements have to be closely aligned to specific business needs. Some unique challenges arise when big data becomes part of the strategy, which we briefly describe in this list:

- **Data access:** User access to raw or computed big data has about the same level of technical requirements as non-big data implementations. The data should be available only to those who have a legitimate business need for examining or interacting with it. Most core data storage platforms have rigorous security schemes and are often augmented with a federated identity capability, providing appropriate access across the many layers of the architecture.

- **Application access:** Application access to data is also relatively straightforward from a technical perspective. Most application programming interfaces (APIs) offer protection from unauthorized usage or access. This level of protection is probably adequate for most big data implementations.

- **Data encryption:** Data encryption is the most challenging aspect of security in a big data environment. In traditional environments, encrypting and decrypting data really stresses the systems' resources. With the volume, velocity, and varieties associated with big data, this problem is exacerbated. The simplest (brute-force) approach is to provide more and faster computational capability. However, this comes with a steep price tag — especially when you have to accommodate resiliency requirements. A more temperate approach is to identify the data elements requiring this level of security and to encrypt only the necessary items.

- **Threat detection:** The inclusion of mobile devices and social networks exponentially increases both the amount of data and the opportunities for security threats. It is therefore important that organizations take a multiperimeter approach to security.

We talk more about big data security and governance in Chapter 19. We also discuss how big data is being used to *help* detect threats and other security issues.

Interfaces and Feeds to and from Applications and the Internet

So, physical infrastructure enables everything and security infrastructure protects all the elements in your big data environment. The next level in the stack is the interfaces that provide bidirectional access to all the components of the stack — from corporate applications to data feeds from the Internet. An important part of the design of these interfaces is the creation of a consistent structure that is shareable both inside and perhaps outside the company as well as with technology partners and business partners.

For decades, programmers have used APIs to provide access to and from software implementations. Tool and technology providers will go to great lengths to ensure that it is a relatively straightforward task to create new applications using their products. Although very helpful, it is sometimes necessary for IT professionals to create custom or proprietary APIs exclusive to the company. You might need to do this for competitive advantage, a need unique to your organization, or some other business demand, and it is not a simple task. APIs need to be well documented and maintained to preserve the value to the business. For this reason, some companies choose to use API toolkits to get a jump-start on this important activity.

API toolkits have a couple of advantages over internally developed APIs. The first is that the API toolkits are products that are created, managed, and maintained by an independent third party. Second, they are designed to solve a specific technical requirement. If you need APIs for web applications or mobile applications, you have several alternatives to get you started.

Take a REST

No discussion of big data APIs would be complete without examining a technology called Representational State Transfer (REST). REST was designed specifically for the Internet and is the most commonly used mechanism for connecting one web resource (a server) to another web resource (a client). A RESTful API provides a standardized way to create a temporary relationship (also called *loose coupling*) between and among web resources. As the name implies, loosely coupled resources are not rigidly connected and are resilient to changes in the networks and other infrastructure components. For example, if your refrigerator breaks in the middle of the night, you need to buy a new one. You might have to wait until a retail store opens before you can do so. In addition, you may need to wait longer for delivery. This is very similar to web resources using RESTful APIs. Your request may not be answered until the service is available to address it. Many, if not all, big data technologies support REST, as you see in subsequent chapters.

Big data challenges require a slightly different approach to API development or adoption. Because much of the data is unstructured and is generated outside of the control of your business, a new technique, called Natural Language Processing (NLP), is emerging as the preferred method for interfacing between big data and your application programs. NLP allows you to formulate queries with natural language syntax instead of a formal query language like SQL. For most big data users, it will be much easier to ask "List all married male consumers between 30 and 40 years old who reside in the southeastern United States and are fans of NASCAR" than to write a 30-line SQL query for the answer.

One way to deal with interfaces is to implement a "connector" factory. This connector factory adds a layer of abstraction and predictability to the process, and it leverages many of the lessons and techniques used in Service Oriented Architecture (SOA). For more information on SOA, check out *Service Oriented Architecture (SOA) For Dummies,* 2nd Edition (written by our team and published by John Wiley & Sons, Inc.).

Because most data gathering and movement have very similar characteristics, you can design a set of services to gather, cleanse, transform, normalize, and store big data items in the storage system of your choice. To create as much flexibility as necessary, the factory could be driven with interface descriptions written in Extensible Markup Language (XML). This level of abstraction allows specific interfaces to be created easily and quickly without the need to build specific services for each data source.

In practice, you could create a description of SAP or Oracle application interfaces using something like XML. Each interface would use the same underlying software to migrate data between the big data environment and the production application environment independent of the specifics of SAP or Oracle. If you need to gather data from social sites on the Internet (such as Facebook, Google+, and so on), the practice would be identical. Describe the interfaces to the sites in XML, and then engage the services to move the data back and forth. Typically, these interfaces are documented for use by internal and external technologists.

Layer 2: Operational Databases

At the core of any big data environment are the database engines containing the collections of data elements relevant to your business. These engines need to be fast, scalable, and rock solid. They are not all created equal, and certain big data environments will fare better with one engine than another, or more likely with a mix of database engines. For example, although it is possible to use relational database management systems (RDBMSs) for all your big data implementations, it is not practical to do so because of performance, scale, or even cost. A number of different database technologies are available, and you must take care to choose wisely. We talk more about these choices in Chapter 7.

No single right choice exists regarding database languages. Although SQL is the most prevalent database query language in use today, other languages may provide a more effective or efficient way of solving your big data challenges. It is useful to think of the engines and languages as tools in an "implementer's toolbox." Your job is to choose the right tool.

For example, if you use a relational model, you will probably use SQL to query it. However, you can also use alternative languages like Python or Java. It is very important to understand what types of data can be manipulated by the database and whether it supports true transactional behavior. Database designers describe this behavior with the acronym *ACID*. It stands for

- ✓ **Atomicity:** A transaction is "all or nothing" when it is atomic. If any part of the transaction or the underlying system fails, the entire transaction fails.

- ✓ **Consistency:** Only transactions with valid data will be performed on the database. If the data is corrupt or improper, the transaction will not complete and the data will not be written to the database.

- ✓ **Isolation:** Multiple, simultaneous transactions will not interfere with each other. All valid transactions will execute until completed and in the order they were submitted for processing.

- ✓ **Durability:** After the data from the transaction is written to the database, it stays there "forever."

Table 4-1 offers a comparison of these characteristics of SQL and NoSQL databases.

Table 4-1   Important Characteristics of SQL and NoSQL Databases

Engine	Query Language	MapReduce	Data Types	Transactions	Examples
Relational	SQL, Python, C	No	Typed	ACID	PostgreSQL, Oracle, DB/2
Columnar	Ruby	Hadoop	Predefined and typed	Yes, if enabled	HBase
Graph	Walking, Search, Cypher	No	Untyped	ACID	Neo4J
Document	Commands	JavaScript	Typed	No	MongoDB, CouchDB
Key-value	Lucene, Commands	JavaScript	BLOB, semityped	No	Riak, Redis

After you understand your requirements and understand what data you're gathering, where to put it, and what to do with it, you need to organize it so that it can be consumed for analytics, reporting, or specific applications.

Layer 3: Organizing Data Services and Tools

Organizing data services and tools capture, validate, and assemble various big data elements into contextually relevant collections. Because big data is massive, techniques have evolved to process the data efficiently and seamlessly. MapReduce, covered in Chapter 8, is one heavily used technique. Suffice it to say here that many of these organizing data services are MapReduce engines, specifically designed to optimize the organization of big data streams.

Organizing data services are, in reality, an ecosystem of tools and technologies that can be used to gather and assemble data in preparation for further processing. As such, the tools need to provide integration, translation, normalization, and scale. Technologies in this layer include the following:

- **A distributed file system:** Necessary to accommodate the decomposition of data streams and to provide scale and storage capacity
- **Serialization services:** Necessary for persistent data storage and multilanguage remote procedure calls (RPCs)
- **Coordination services:** Necessary for building distributed applications (locking and so on)
- **Extract, transform, and load (ETL) tools:** Necessary for the loading and conversion of structured and unstructured data into Hadoop
- **Workflow services:** Necessary for scheduling jobs and providing a structure for synchronizing process elements across layers

In Chapters 9 and 10, we examine Hadoop, the most widely used set of products for organizing big data. It is an open source initiative maintained by the Apache Foundation.

Layer 4: Analytical Data Warehouses

The data warehouse , and its companion the data mart, have long been the primary techniques that organizations use to optimize data to help decision makers. Typically, data warehouses and marts contain normalized data gathered from a variety of sources and assembled to facilitate analysis of the business. Data warehouses and marts simplify the creation of reports and the visualization of disparate data items. They are generally created from relational databases, multidimensional databases, flat files, and object databases — essentially any storage architecture. In a traditional environment, where performance may not be the highest priority, the choice of the underlying technology is driven by the requirements for the analysis, reporting, and visualization of the company data.

As the organization of the data and its readiness for analysis are key, most data warehouse implementations are kept current via batch processing. The problem is that batch-loaded data warehouses and data marts may be insufficient for many big data applications. The stress imposed by high-velocity data streams will likely require a more real-time approach to big data warehouses. This doesn't mean that you won't be creating and feeding an analytical data warehouse or a data mart with batch processes. Rather, you may end up having multiple data warehouses or data marts, and the performance and scale will reflect the time requirements of the analysts and decision makers.

Because many data warehouses and data marts are comprised of data gathered from various sources within a company, the costs associated with the cleansing and normalizing of the data must also be addressed. With big data, you find some key differences:

- ✔ Traditional data streams (from transactions, applications, and so on) can produce a lot of disparate data.

- ✔ Dozens of new data sources also exist, each of them needing some degree of manipulation before it can be timely and useful to the business.

- ✔ Content sources will also need to be cleansed, and these may require different techniques than you might use with structured data.

Historically, the contents of data warehouses and data marts were organized and delivered to business leaders in charge of strategy and planning. With big data, we are seeing a new set of teams that are leveraging data for decision making. Many big data implementations provide real-time capabilities, so businesses should be able to deliver content to enable individuals with operational roles to address issues such as customer support, sales opportunities, and service outages in near real time. In this way, big data helps move action from the back office to the front office.

In Chapter 11, we examine several technology approaches for big data warehousing, with recommendations for using them effectively and efficiently.

Big Data Analytics

Existing analytics tools and techniques will be very helpful in making sense of big data. However, there is a catch. The algorithms that are part of these tools have to be able to work with large amounts of potentially real-time and disparate data. The infrastructure that we cover earlier in the chapter will need to be in place to support this. And, vendors providing analytics tools will also need to ensure that their algorithms work across distributed implementations. Because of these complexities, we also expect a new class of tools to help make sense of big data.

We list three classes of tools in this layer of our reference architecture. They can be used independently or collectively by decision makers to help steer the business. The three classes of tools are as follows:

- **Reporting and dashboards:** These tools provide a "user-friendly" representation of the information from various sources. Although a mainstay in the traditional data world, this area is still evolving for big data. Some of the tools that are being used are traditional ones that can now access the new kinds of databases collectively called NoSQL (Not Only SQL). We explore NoSQL databases in Chapter 7.

- **Visualization:** These tools are the next step in the evolution of reporting. The output tends to be highly interactive and dynamic in nature. Another important distinction between reports and visualized output is animation. Business users can watch the changes in the data utilizing a variety of different visualization techniques, including mind maps, heat maps, infographics, and connection diagrams. Often, reporting and visualization occur at the end of the business activity. Although the data may be imported into another tool for further computation or examination, this is the final step.

- **Analytics and advanced analytics:** These tools reach into the data warehouse and process the data for human consumption. Advanced analytics should explicate trends or events that are transformative, unique, or revolutionary to existing business practice. Predictive analytics and sentiment analytics are good examples of this science. Issues relating to analytics are covered in greater detail in Part IV, including Chapters 12, 13, and 14.

Big Data Applications

Custom and third-party applications offer an alternative method of sharing and examining big data sources. Although all the layers of the reference architecture are important in their own right, this layer is where most of the innovation and creativity is evident.

These applications are either horizontal, in that they address problems that are common across industries, or vertical, in that they are intended to help solve an industry-specific problem. Needless to say, you have many applications to choose from, and many more coming. We expect categories of commercially available big data applications to grow as fast or faster than the adoption rate of the underlying technology. The most prevalent categories as of this writing are log data applications (Splunk, Loggly), ad/media applications (Bluefin, DataXu), and marketing applications (Bloomreach, Myrrix). Solutions are also being developed for the healthcare industry, manufacturing, and transportation management, to name a few.

Like any other custom application development initiative, the creation of big data applications will require structure, standards, rigor, and well-defined APIs. Most business applications wanting to leverage big data will need to subscribe to APIs across the entire stack. It may be necessary to process raw data from the low-level data stores and combine the raw data with synthesized output from the warehouses. As you might expect, the operative term is *custom,* and it creates a different type of pressure on the big data implementation.

Big data moves fast and changes in the blink of an eye, so software development teams need to be able to rapidly create applications germane to solving the business challenge of the moment. Companies may need to think about creating development "tiger teams," which rapidly respond to changes in the business environment by creating and deploying applications on demand. In fact, it may be more appropriate to think of these applications as "semicustom" because they involve more assembly than actual low-level coding.

Over time, we expect certain types of applications will be created, in context, by the end user, who can assemble the solution from a palette of components. Needless to say, this is where the structure and standardization are most necessary. Software developers need to create consistent, standardized development environments and devise new development practices for rapid rollout of big data applications.

Chapter 5

Virtualization and How It Supports Distributed Computing

*V*irtualization is a foundational technology applicable to the implementation of both cloud computing and big data. It provides the basis for many of the platform attributes required to access, store, analyze, and manage the distributed computing components in big data environments. Virtualization — the process of using computer resources to imitate other resources — is valued for its capability to increase IT resource utilization, efficiency, and scalability. One primary application of virtualization is server consolidation, which helps organizations increase the utilization of physical servers and potentially save on infrastructure costs. However, you find many benefits to virtualization. Companies that initially focused solely on server virtualization are now recognizing that it can be applied across the entire IT infrastructure, including software, storage, and networks.

In this chapter, we define virtualization and provide insight into the benefits and challenges of virtualized environments. Our primary focus is on the role of virtualization in big data.

Understanding the Basics of Virtualization

Virtualization separates resources and services from the underlying physical delivery environment, enabling you to create many virtual systems within a single physical system. Figure 5-1 shows a typical virtualization environment.

One of the primary reasons that companies have implemented virtualization is to improve the performance and efficiency of processing of a diverse mix of workloads. Rather than assigning a dedicated set of physical resources to each set of tasks, a pooled set of virtual resources can be quickly allocated as needed across all workloads. Reliance on the pool of virtual resources allows companies to improve latency. This increase in service delivery speed and efficiency is a function of the distributed nature of virtualized environments and helps to improve overall time-to-value.

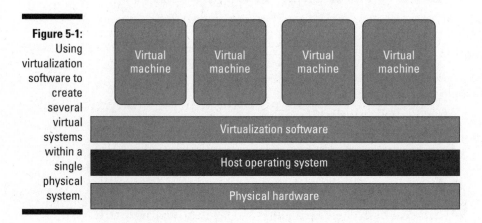

Figure 5-1:
Using virtualization software to create several virtual systems within a single physical system.

Using a distributed set of physical resources, such as servers, in a more flexible and efficient way delivers significant benefits in terms of cost savings and improvements in productivity. The practice has several benefits, including the following:

- ✔ Virtualization of physical resources (such as servers, storage, and networks) enables substantial improvement in the utilization of these resources.

- ✔ Virtualization enables improved control over the usage and performance of your IT resources.

- ✔ Virtualization can provide a level of automation and standardization to optimize your computing environment.

- ✔ Virtualization provides a foundation for cloud computing.

Although being able to virtualize resources adds a huge amount of efficiency, it doesn't come without a cost. Virtual resources have to be managed so that they are secure. An image can become a technique for an intruder to get direct access to critical systems. In addition, if companies do not have a process for deleting unused images, systems will no longer behave efficiently.

The importance of virtualization to big data

Solving big data challenges typically requires the management of large volumes of highly distributed data stores along with the use of compute- and data-intensive applications. Therefore, you need a highly efficient IT environment to support big data. Virtualization provides the added level of efficiency to make big data platforms a reality. Although virtualization is technically not a requirement for big data analysis, software frameworks such as MapReduce, which are used in big data environments, are more efficient in a virtualized environment. Chapter 8 covers MapReduce in more detail. If you need your big data environment to scale — almost without bounds — you should virtualize elements of your environment.

Virtualization has three characteristics that support the scalability and operating efficiency required for big data environments:

- **Partitioning:** In virtualization, many applications and operating systems are supported in a single physical system by partitioning (separating) the available resources.

- **Isolation:** Each virtual machine is isolated from its host physical system and other virtualized machines. Because of this isolation, if one virtual instance crashes, the other virtual machines and the host system aren't affected. In addition, data isn't shared between one virtual instance and another.

- **Encapsulation:** A virtual machine can be represented (and even stored) as a single file, so you can identify it easily based on the services it provides. For example, the file containing the encapsulated process could be a complete business service. This encapsulated virtual machine could be presented to an application as a complete entity. Thus, encapsulation could protect each application so that it doesn't interfere with another application.

One of the most important requirements for success with big data is having the right level of performance to support the analysis of large volumes and varied types of data. As you begin to leverage environments such as Hadoop and MapReduce, it is critical that you have a supporting infrastructure that can scale. Virtualization adds efficiency at every layer of the IT infrastructure. Applying virtualization across your environment will help to achieve the scalability required for big data analysis.

Implementing virtualization by following an end-to-end approach will deliver benefits for big data and other types of workloads in your environment. An end-to-end approach will mean that errors can be corrected more quickly — a requirement in a big data environment. When working with big data, your infrastructure needs to be prepared to manage data that is potentially very large (volume), very fast (velocity), and highly unstructured (variety).

As a result, your entire IT environment needs to be optimized at every layer, from the network to the databases, storage, and servers. If you only virtualize your servers, you may experience bottlenecks from other infrastructure elements such as storage and networks. If you only focus on virtualizing one element of your infrastructure, you are less likely to achieve the latency and efficiency you need and more likely to expose your company to higher costs and security risks.

The reality is that most organizations do not attempt to virtualize all elements of their infrastructures at one time. Many organizations begin with server virtualization and achieve a certain level of efficiency improvements. Realistically, other elements may be virtualized as needed to continue to improve overall system performance and efficiency. The following describes how virtualization of each element across the IT environment — servers, storage, applications, data, networks, processors, memory, and services — can have a positive impact on big data analysis.

Server virtualization

In server virtualization, one physical server is partitioned into multiple virtual servers. The hardware and resources of a machine — including the random access memory (RAM), CPU, hard drive, and network controller — can be virtualized (logically split) into a series of virtual machines that each runs its own applications and operating system. A virtual machine (VM) is a software representation of a physical machine that can execute or perform the same functions as the physical machine. A thin layer of software is actually inserted into the hardware that contains a virtual machine monitor, or *hypervisor*. The hypervisor can be thought of as the technology that manages traffic between the VMs and the physical machine.

Server virtualization uses the hypervisor to provide efficiency in the use of physical resources. Of course, installation, configuration, and administrative tasks are associated with setting up these virtual machines. This includes license management, network management, and workload administration, as well as capacity planning.

Server virtualization helps to ensure that your platform can scale as needed to handle the large volumes and varied types of data included in your big data analysis. You may not know the extent of the volume or variety of structured and unstructured data needed before you begin your analysis. This uncertainty makes the need for server virtualization even greater, providing your environment with the capability to meet the unanticipated demand for processing very large data sets.

In addition, server virtualization provides the foundation that enables many of the cloud services used as data sources in a big data analysis. Virtualization increases the efficiency of the cloud that makes many complex systems easier to optimize. As a result, organizations have the performance and optimization to be able to access data that was previously either unavailable or very hard to collect. Big data platforms are increasingly used as sources of enormous amounts of data about customer preferences, sentiment, and behaviors. Companies can integrate this information with internal sales and product data to gain insight into customer preferences to make more targeted and personalized offers.

Application virtualization

Application infrastructure virtualization provides an efficient way to manage applications in context with customer demand. The application is encapsulated in a way that removes its dependencies from the underlying physical computer system. This helps to improve the overall manageability and portability of the application. In addition, the application infrastructure virtualization software typically allows for codifying business and technical usage policies to make sure that each of your applications leverages virtual and physical resources in a predictable way. Efficiencies are gained because you can more easily distribute IT resources according to the relative business value of your applications. In other words, your most critical applications can receive top priority to draw from pools of available computing and storage capacity as needed.

Application infrastructure virtualization used in combination with server virtualization can help to ensure that business service-level agreements (SLAs) are met. Server virtualization monitors CPU and memory usage, but does not account for variations in business priority when allocating resources. For example, you might require that all applications are treated with the same business-level priority. By implementing application infrastructure virtualization in addition to server virtualization, you can ensure that the most high-priority applications have top-priority access to resources.

Your big data applications may have significant IT resource requirements, due to the large volumes of data or the speed at which that data is generated. Your big data environment needs to have the right level of predictability and repeatability to make sure that the applications have access to the required resources. Application infrastructure virtualization can ensure that each application deployed for a big data analysis has access to the compute power required at the right time based on its relative priority. In addition, application infrastructure virtualization makes it easier to run applications on different computers, and previously incompatible or legacy applications can be run together on the same physical machine. You will not need to create multiple versions such as Windows or Linux.

Big data platforms designed to support highly distributed, data-intensive applications will run better and faster in a virtual environment. This does not mean that you will want to virtualize all big data–related applications. For example, a text analytics application may run best in a self-contained environment and virtualization would not add any benefit.

Network virtualization

Network virtualization — software-defined networking — provides an efficient way to use networking as a pool of connection resources. Networks are virtualized in a similar fashion to other physical technologies. Instead of relying on the physical network for managing traffic between connections, you can create multiple virtual networks all utilizing the same physical implementation. This can be useful if you need to define a network for data gathering with a certain set of performance characteristics and capacity and another network for applications with different performance and capacity. Limitations in the network layer can lead to bottlenecks that lead to unacceptable latencies in big data environments. Virtualizing the network helps reduce these bottlenecks and improve the capability to manage the large distributed data required for big data analysis.

Processor and memory virtualization

Processor virtualization helps to optimize the processor and maximize performance. Memory virtualization decouples memory from the servers.

In big data analysis, you may have repeated queries of large data sets and the creation of advanced analytic algorithms, all designed to look for patterns and trends that are not yet understood. These advanced analytics can require lots of processing power (CPU) and memory (RAM). For some of these computations, it can take a long time without sufficient CPU and memory resources. Processor and memory virtualization can help speed the processing and get your analysis results sooner.

Data and storage virtualization

Data virtualization can be used to create a platform for dynamic linked data services. This allows data to be easily searched and linked through a unified reference source. As a result, data virtualization provides an abstract service that delivers data in a consistent form regardless of the underlying physical database. In addition, data virtualization exposes cached data to all applications to improve performance.

Storage virtualization combines physical storage resources so that they are more effectively shared. This reduces the cost of storage and makes it easier to manage data stores required for big data analysis.

Data and storage virtualization play a significant role in making it easier and less costly to store, retrieve, and analyze the large volumes of fast and varying types of data. Remember that some big data may be unstructured and not easily stored using traditional methods. Storage virtualization makes it easier to store large and unstructured data types. In a big data environment, it is advantageous to have access to a variety of operational data stores on demand. For example, you may only need access to a columnar database infrequently. With virtualization, the database can be stored as a virtual image and invoked whenever it is needed without consuming valuable data center resources or capacity.

Management and security challenges with virtualization

Virtualized environments need to be adequately managed and governed to realize cost savings and efficiency benefits. If you rely on big data services to solve your analytics challenges, you need to be assured that the virtual environment is as well managed and secure as the physical environment. Some of the benefits of virtualization, including ease of provisioning, can easily lead to management and security problems without proper oversight. Virtualization makes it easy for developers to create a virtual image, or a copy, of a resource. As a result, many companies have implemented virtualization only to find that the number of virtual images spirals out of control. Problems to watch out for include the following:

✔ Too many virtual images are created, leading to a sharp drop in server and memory performance.

✔ Lack of control over the life cycle of virtual images leads to the introduction of security vulnerabilities.

✔ An overabundance of virtual images increases storage costs and reduces cost savings.

✔ Administrators may increase security risks through either malicious or uninformed management of virtual images.

✔ Compliance requirements may be compromised if you are not able to accurately monitor virtual infrastructure logs.

Managing Virtualization with the Hypervisor

In an ideal world, you don't want to worry about the underlying operating system and the physical hardware. A *hypervisor* is the technology responsible for ensuring that resource sharing takes place in an orderly and repeatable way. It is the traffic cop that allows multiple operating systems to share a single host. It creates and runs virtual machines. The hypervisor sits at the lowest levels of the hardware environment and uses a thin layer of code (often called a *fabric*) to enable dynamic resource sharing. The hypervisor makes it seem like each operating system has the physical resources all to itself.

In the world of big data, you may need to support many different operating environments. The hypervisor becomes an ideal delivery mechanism for the technology components of the big data stack. The hypervisor lets you show the same application on lots of systems without having to physically copy that application onto each system. As an added benefit, because of the hypervisor architecture, it can load any (or many) different operating systems as though they were just another application. So, the hypervisor is a very practical way of getting things virtualized quickly and efficiently.

You need to understand the nature of the hypervisor. It's designed like a server OS rather than like the Windows OS. Each virtual machine running on a physical machine is called a guest machine. The hypervisor, therefore, schedules the access that guest operating systems have to everything, including the CPU, memory, disk I/O, and other I/O mechanisms. The guest operating systems are the operating systems running on the virtual machines. With virtualization technology, you can set up the hypervisor to split the physical computer's resources. Resources can be split 50/50 or 80/20 between two guest operating systems, for example.

The beauty of this arrangement is that the hypervisor does all the heavy lifting. The guest operating system doesn't care (or have any idea) that it's running in a virtual partition; it thinks it has a computer all to itself.

You find basically two types of hypervisors:

 ✔ **Type 1 hypervisors** run directly on the hardware platform. They achieve higher efficiency because they're running directly on the platform.

 ✔ **Type 2 hypervisors** run on the host operating system. They are often used when a need exists to support a broad range of I/O devices.

Abstraction and Virtualization

For IT resources and services to be virtualized, they are separated from the underlying physical delivery environment. The technical term for this act of separation is called *abstraction*. Abstraction is a key concept in big data. MapReduce and Hadoop are distributed computing environments where everything is abstracted. The detail is abstracted out so that the developer or analyst does not need to be concerned with where the data elements are actually located.

Abstraction minimizes the complexity of something by hiding the details and providing only the relevant information. For example, if you were going to pick up someone whom you've never met before, he might tell you the location to meet him, how tall he is, his hair color, and what he will be wearing. He doesn't need to tell you where he was born, how much money he has in the bank, his birth date, and so on. That's the idea with abstraction — it's about providing a high-level specification rather than going into lots of detail about how something works. In the cloud, for instance, in an Infrastructure as a Service (IaaS) delivery model, the details of the physical and virtual infrastructure are abstracted from the user.

Implementing Virtualization to Work with Big Data

Virtualization helps makes your IT environment smart enough to handle big data analysis. By optimizing all elements of your infrastructure, including hardware, software, and storage, you gain the efficiency needed to process and manage large volumes of structured and unstructured data. With big data, you need to access, manage, and analyze structured and unstructured data in a distributed environment.

Big data assumes distribution. In practice, any kind of MapReduce will work better in a virtualized environment. You need the capability to move workloads around based on requirements for compute power and storage.

Virtualization will enable you to tackle larger problems that have not yet been scoped. You may not know in advance how quickly you will need to scale.

Virtualization will enable you to support a variety of operational big data stores. For example, a graph database can be spun up as an image.

The most direct benefit from virtualization is to ensure that MapReduce engines work better. Virtualization will result in better scale and performance for MapReduce. Each one of the Map and Reduce tasks needs to be executed independently. If the MapReduce engine is parallelized and configured to run in a virtual environment, you can reduce management overhead and allow for expansions and contractions in the task workloads. MapReduce itself is inherently parallel and distributed. By encapsulating the MapReduce engine in a virtual container, you can run what you need whenever you need it. With virtualization, you increase your utilization of the assets you have already paid for by turning them into generic pools of resources.

Chapter 6

Examining the Cloud and Big Data

*T*he power of the cloud is that users can access needed computing and storage resources with little or no IT support or the need to purchase more hardware or software. One of the key characteristics of the cloud is elastic scalability: Users can add or subtract resources in almost real time based on changing requirements. The cloud plays an important role within the big data world. Dramatic changes happen when these infrastructure components are combined with the advances in data management. Horizontally expandable and optimized infrastructure supports the practical implementation of big data.

In this chapter, we review the fundamentals of the cloud in the context of what it means for big data. Then we discuss how and why the cloud is often so ideal for various use cases for big data.

Defining the Cloud in the Context of Big Data

Cloud computing is a method of providing a set of shared computing resources that include applications, computing, storage, networking, development, and deployment platforms, as well as business processes. Cloud computing turns traditional siloed computing assets into shared pools of resources based on an underlying Internet foundation. In cloud computing, everything, from compute power to computing infrastructure and from applications and business processes to data and analytics, can be delivered to you as a service. To be operational in the real world, the cloud must be implemented with common standardized processes and automation.

If you want to find out a lot more about the cloud, we recommend that you read another book we have written, *Hybrid Cloud For Dummies* (published by John Wiley & Sons, Inc.).

Many businesses leverage cloud services for everything from backup to Software as a Service (SaaS) options such as customer relationship management (CRM) services. With the growth of mobile computing, more consumers, professionals, and corporations are creating and accessing data with cloud-based services. The average consumer may be sent an online coupon for a favorite store; a quality control manager in a manufacturing plant might collect sensor data from a variety of machines to determine whether a quality problem exists. These scenarios are predicated on the cloud-based data services infrastructure.

A popular example of the benefits of cloud supporting big data can be noted at both Google and Amazon.com. Both companies depend on the capability to manage massive amounts of data to move their businesses forward. These providers needed to come up with infrastructures and technologies that could support applications at a massive scale. Consider Gmail and the millions upon millions of messages that Google processes per day as part of this service. Google has been able to optimize the Linux operating system and its software environment to support e-mail in the most efficient manner; therefore, it can easily support hundreds of millions of users. Even more importantly, Google is able to capture and leverage the massive amount of data about both its mail users and its search engine users to drive the business.

Likewise, Amazon.com, with its IaaS data centers, is optimized to support these workloads so that Amazon can continue to offer new services and support a growing number of customers without breaking the bank. To grow its retail business, Amazon must be able to manage data about its merchandise, its buyers, and its channel of partner merchants. Targeted advertising based on customer buying patterns is critical to the company's success. These companies now offer a range of cloud-based services for big data that we talk about later in this chapter.

Understanding Cloud Deployment and Delivery Models

Two key cloud models are important in the discussion of big data — public clouds and private clouds. For those organizations that adopt cloud deployment and delivery models, most will use a combination of private computing resources (data centers and private clouds) and public services (operated by an external company for the shared use of a variety of customers who pay a per-usage fee). How these companies balance public and private providers depends on a number of issues, including privacy, latency, and purpose. It is important to understand these environments and what they mean for a potential big data deployment. In that way, you can determine whether you might want to use a public cloud IaaS (described later) — for example, for your big data projects — or if you want to continue to keep all your data on premises. Or, you might want to use a combination of both. So, we outline these deployment and delivery models first and then talk more about what they mean to big data.

Cloud deployment models

The two types of deployment models for cloud computing are public and private. These are offered for general purpose computing needs as opposed to specific types of cloud delivery models. We examine the delivery models later in the chapter. In the meantime, take a look at the differences between public and private cloud models and how you might use them.

The public cloud

The public cloud is a set of hardware, networking, storage, services, applications, and interfaces owned and operated by a third party for use by other companies and individuals. These commercial providers create a highly scalable data center that hides the details of the underlying infrastructure from the consumer. Public clouds are viable because they typically manage relatively repetitive or straightforward workloads. For example, electronic mail is a very simple application. Therefore, a cloud provider can optimize the environment so that it is best suited to support a large number of customers, even if it saves many messages.

Likewise, public cloud providers offering storage or computing services optimize their computing hardware and software to support these specific types of workloads.

In contrast, the typical data center supports so many different applications and workloads that it cannot be easily optimized. A public cloud can be very effective when an organization is executing a complex data analysis project and needs extra computing cycles to handle the task. In addition, companies may choose to store data in a public cloud where the cost per gigabyte is relatively inexpensive when compared to purchased storage. The overriding issues with public clouds for big data are the security requirements and the amount of latency that is acceptable.

All public clouds are not the same. Some public clouds are scalable managed services with a high level of security and a high level of service management.

Other public clouds are less robust and less secure, but they are much less expensive to use. Your choice will depend on the nature of your big data projects and the amount of risk you can assume.

The private cloud

A private cloud is a set of hardware, networking, storage, services, application, and interfaces owned and operated by an organization for the use of its employees, partners, and customers. A private cloud can be created and managed by a third party for the exclusive use of one enterprise. The private cloud is a highly controlled environment not open for public consumption. Thus, the private cloud sits behind a firewall. The private cloud is highly automated with a focus on governance, security, and compliance. Automation replaces more manual processes of managing IT service to support customers. In this way, business rules and processes can be implemented inside software so that the environment becomes more predictable and manageable. If organizations are managing a big data project that demands processing massive amounts of data, the private cloud might be the best choice in terms of latency and security.

A *hybrid* cloud is a combination of a private cloud combined with the use of public cloud services with one or several touch points between the environments. The goal is to create a well-managed cloud environment that can combine services and data from a variety of cloud models to create a unified, automated, and well-managed computing environment.

Cloud delivery models

In addition to the cloud deployment models discussed previously, a number of cloud delivery models also exist. Four of the most popular are described in the following sections.

Infrastructure as a Service

Infrastructure as a Service (IaaS) is one of the most straightforward of the cloud computing services. IaaS is the delivery of computing services including hardware, networking, storage, and data center space based on a rental model. The consumer of the service acquires a resource and is charged for that resource based on amount used and the duration of that usage. You find both public and private versions of IaaS. In the public IaaS, the user utilizes a credit card to acquire these resources. When the user stops paying, the resource disappears. In a private IaaS service, it is usually the IT organization or an integrator who creates the infrastructure designed to provide resources on demand for internal users and sometimes business partners.

Platform as a Service

Platform as a Service (PaaS) is a mechanism for combining IaaS with an abstracted set of middleware services, software development, and deployment tools that allow the organization to have a consistent way to create and deploy applications on a cloud or on premises. A PaaS offers a consistent set of programming or middleware services that ensure that developers have a well-tested and well-integrated way to create applications in a cloud environment. A PaaS environment brings development and deployment together to create a more manageable way to build, deploy, and scale applications. A PaaS requires an IaaS.

Software as a Service

Software as a Service (SaaS) is a business application created and hosted by a provider in a multitenant model. *Multitenancy* refers to the situation where a single instance of an application runs in a cloud environment, but serves multiple client organizations (tenants), keeping all their data separate. Customers pay for the service per user either on a monthly or yearly contract model. The SaaS model sits on top of both the PaaS and the foundational IaaS.

Data as a Service

Because this is a book about big data, we also want you to know about another delivery model called Data as a Service (DaaS). DaaS is closely related to SaaS. DaaS is a platform-independent service that would let you connect to the cloud to store and retrieve your data. In addition, you find a number of specialized data services that are of great benefit in a big data environment. For example, Google offers a service that can process a query with 5 terabytes of data in only 15 seconds. This type of query would typically take ten times as long with a typical data center. Hundreds of specialized analytic services have been developed by companies like IBM and others.

The Cloud as an Imperative for Big Data

Clearly, numerous combinations of deployment and delivery models exist for big data in the cloud. For example, you can utilize a public cloud IaaS or a private cloud IaaS. So, what does this mean for big data and why is the cloud a good fit for it? Well, big data requires distributed clusters of compute power, which is how the cloud is architected. For more on distributed computing, see Chapter 3.

In fact, a number of cloud characteristics make it an important part of the big data ecosystem:

- **Scalability:** Scalability with regard to hardware refers to the capability to go from small to large amounts of processing power with the same architecture. With regard to software, it refers to the consistency of performance per unit of power as hardware resources increase. The cloud can scale to large data volumes. Distributed computing, an integral part of the cloud model, really works on a "divide and conquer" plan. So if you have huge volumes of data, they can be partitioned across cloud servers. An important characteristic of IaaS is that it can dynamically scale. This means that if you wind up needing more resources than expected, you can get them. This ties into the concept of elasticity.

- **Elasticity:** Elasticity refers to the capability to expand or shrink computing resource demand in real time, based on need. One of the benefits of the cloud is that customers have the potential to access as much of a service as they need when they need it. This can be helpful for big data projects where you might need to expand the amount of computing resources you need to deal with the volume and velocity of the data. Of course, this very feature of the cloud that makes it attractive to end users means that the service provider needs to design a platform architecture that is optimized for this kind of service.

- **Resource pooling:** Cloud architectures enable the efficient creation of groups of shared resources that make the cloud economically viable.

- **Self-service:** With self-service, the user of a cloud resource is able to use a browser or a portal interface to acquire the resources needed, say, to run a huge predictive model. This is dramatically different than how you might gain resources from a data center, where you would have to request the resources from IT operations.

- **Often low up-front costs:** If you use a cloud provider, up-front costs can often be reduced because you are not buying huge amounts of hardware or leasing out new space for dealing with your big data. By taking advantage of the economies of scale associated with cloud environments, the cloud can look attractive. Of course, you will need to do your own calculation to evaluate whether you are interested in a public cloud, private cloud, hybrid cloud, or no cloud. We cover this in the section "Where to be careful when using cloud services," later in this chapter.

- **Pay as you go:** A typical billing option for a cloud provider is Pay as You Go (PAYG), which means that you are billed for resources used based on instance pricing. This can be useful if you're not sure what resources you need for your big data project (as long as you don't underbudget).

- **Fault tolerance:** Cloud service providers should have fault tolerance built into their architecture, providing uninterrupted services despite the failure of one or more of the system's components.

In some situations, a service provider can't anticipate the needs of a customer. Therefore, it is common for a service provider to add additional capacity from a third-party service provider. Typically, the consumer is unaware that he is dealing with an additional cloud service provider.

Making Use of the Cloud for Big Data

Clearly, the very nature of the cloud makes it an ideal computing environment for big data. So how might you use big data together with the cloud? Here are some examples:

- **IaaS in a public cloud:** In this scenario, you would be using a public cloud provider's infrastructure for your big data services because you don't want to use your own physical infrastructure. IaaS can provide the creation of virtual machines with almost limitless storage and compute power. You can pick the operating system that you want, and you have the flexibility to dynamically scale the environment to meet your needs. An example might be using the Amazon Elastic Compute Cloud (Amazon EC2) service, detailed later in the chapter, to run a real-time predictive model that requires data to be processed using massively parallel processing. It might be a service that processes big-box retail data. You might want to process billions of pieces of click-stream data for targeting customers with the right ad in real time.

- **PaaS in a private cloud:** PaaS is an entire infrastructure packaged so that it can be used to design, implement, and deploy applications and services in a public or private cloud environment. PaaS enables an organization to leverage key middleware services without having to deal with the complexities of managing individual hardware and software elements. PaaS vendors are beginning to incorporate big data technologies such as Hadoop and MapReduce into their PaaS offerings. For example, you might want to build a specialized application to analyze vast amounts of medical data. The application would make use of real-time as well as non-real-time data. It's going to require Hadoop and MapReduce for storage and processing. What's great about PaaS in this scenario is how quickly the application can be deployed. You won't have to wait for internal IT teams to get up to speed on the new technologies and you can experiment more liberally. Once you have identified a solid solution, you can bring it in house when IT is ready to support it.

- **SaaS in a hybrid cloud:** Here you might want to analyze "voice of the customer" data from multiple channels. Many companies have come to realize that one of the most important data sources is what the customer thinks and says about their company, their products, and their services. Getting access to voice of the customer data can provide invaluable insights into behaviors and actions. Increasingly, customers are "vocalizing" on public sites across the Internet. The value of the customers' input can be greatly enhanced by incorporating this public data into your analysis. Your SaaS vendor provides the platform for the analysis as well as the social media data. In addition, you might utilize your enterprise CRM data in your private cloud environment for inclusion in the analysis.

 Some industry insiders are using the term *big data applications* when describing applications that run in the cloud that use big data. Examples of this include Amazon.com and LinkedIn. Now some people might argue (and have) that these are really SaaS applications that solve a particular business problem. It's often a matter of semantics in an emerging space.

Providers in the Big Data Cloud Market

Cloud players come in all shapes and sizes and offer many different products. Some are household names while others are recently emerging. Some of the cloud providers that offer IaaS services that can be used for big data include Amazon.com, AT&T, GoGrid, Joyent, Rackspace, IBM, and Verizon/Terremark.

However, cloud companies and cloud service providers are also offering software targeted specifically for big data. These are described in the following sections.

Amazon's Public Elastic Compute Cloud

Currently, one of the most high-profile IaaS service providers is Amazon Web Services with its Elastic Compute Cloud (Amazon EC2). Amazon didn't start out with a vision to build a big infrastructure services business. Instead, the company built a massive infrastructure to support its own retail business and discovered that its resources were underused. Instead of allowing this asset to sit idle, it decided to leverage this resource while adding to the bottom line. Amazon's EC2 service was launched in 2006 and continues to evolve.

Amazon EC2 offers scalability under the user's control, with the user paying for resources by the hour. The use of the term *elastic* in the naming of Amazon's EC2 is significant. Here, elasticity refers to the capability that the EC2 users have to increase or decrease the infrastructure resources assigned to meet their needs.

Amazon also offers other big data services to customers of its Amazon Web Services portfolio. These include the following:

- **Amazon Elastic MapReduce:** Targeted for processing huge volumes of data. Elastic MapReduce utilizes a hosted Hadoop framework (see Chapter 9 for more on Hadoop) running on EC2 and Amazon Simple Storage Service (Amazon S3). Users can now run HBase (a distributed, column-oriented data store).

- **Amazon DynamoDB:** A fully managed not only SQL (NoSQL) database service. DynamoDB is a fault tolerant, highly available data storage service offering self-provisioning, transparent scalability, and simple administration. It is implemented on SSDs (solid state disks) for greater reliability and high performance. We talk more about NoSQL in Chapter 7.

- **Amazon Simple Storage Service (S3):** A web-scale service designed to store any amount of data. The strength of its design center is performance and scalability, so it is not as feature laden as other data stores. Data is stored in "buckets" and you can select one or more global regions for physical storage to address latency or regulatory needs.

- **Amazon High Performance Computing:** Tuned for specialized tasks, this service provides low-latency tuned high performance computing clusters. Most often used by scientists and academics, HPC is entering the mainstream because of the offering of Amazon and other HPC providers. Amazon HPC clusters are purpose built for specific workloads and can be reconfigured easily for new tasks.

- **Amazon RedShift:** Available in limited preview, RedShift is a petabyte-scale data warehousing service built on a scalable MPP architecture. Managed by Amazon, it offers a secure, reliable alternative to in-house data warehouses and is compatible with several popular business intelligence tools.

Google big data services

Google, the Internet search giant, also offers a number of cloud services targeted for big data. These include the following:

- **Google Compute Engine:** A cloud-based capability for virtual machine computing, Google Compute Engine offers a secure, flexible computing environment from energy efficient data centers. Google also offers workload management solutions from several technology partners who have optimized their products for Google Compute Engine.

- ✔ **Google Big Query:** Allows you to run SQL-like queries at a high speed against large data sets of potentially billions of rows. Although it is good for querying data, data cannot be modified after it is in it. Consider Google Big Query a sort of Online Analytical Processing (OLAP) system for big data. It is good for ad hoc reporting or exploratory analysis.

- ✔ **Google Prediction API:** A cloud-based, machine learning tool for vast amounts of data, Prediction is capable of identifying patterns in data and then remembering them. It can learn more about a pattern each time it is used. The patterns can be analyzed for a variety of purposes, including fraud detection, churn analysis, and customer sentiment. Prediction is covered in more depth in Chapter 12.

Microsoft Azure

Based on Windows and SQL abstractions, Microsoft has productized a set of development tools, virtual machine support, management and media services, and mobile device services in a PaaS offering. For customers with deep expertise in .Net, SQLServer, and Windows, the adoption of the Azure-based PaaS is straightforward.

To address the emerging requirements to integrate big data into Windows Azure solutions, Microsoft has also added Windows Azure HDInsight. Built on Hortonworks Data Platform (HDP), which according to Microsoft, offers 100 percent compatibility with Apache Hadoop, HDInsight supports connection with Microsoft Excel and other business intelligence (BI) tools. In addition to Azure HDInsight can also be deployed on Windows Server.

OpenStack

Initiated by Rackspace and NASA, OpenStack (www.openstack.org) is implementing an open-cloud platform aimed at either public or private clouds. While the organization is tightly managed by Rackspace, it moved to a separate OpenStack foundation. Although companies can leverage OpenStack to create proprietary implementations, the OpenStack designation requires conformance to a standard implementation of services.

OpenStack's goal is to provide a massively scaled, multitenant cloud specification that can run on any hardware. OpenStack is building a large ecosystem of partners interested in adopting its cloud platform, including Dell, HP, Intel, Cisco, Red Hat, and IBM, along with at least 100 others that are using OpenStack as the foundation for their cloud offerings. In essence, OpenStack is an open source IaaS initiative built on Ubuntu, an operating system based on the Debian Linux distribution. It can also run on Red Hat's version of Linux.

OpenStack offers a range of services, including compute, object storage, catalog and repository, dashboarding, identity, and networking. In terms of big data, Rackspace and Hortonworks (a provider of an open source data management platform based on Apache Hadoop) announced that Rackspace will release an OpenStack public cloud-based Hadoop service, which will be validated and supported by Hortonworks and will enable customers to quickly create a big data environment.

Where to be careful when using cloud services

Cloud-based services can provide an economical solution to your big data needs, but the cloud has its issues. It's important to do your homework before moving your big data there. Here are some issues to consider:

- ✔ **Data integrity:** You need to make sure that your provider has the right controls in place to ensure that the integrity of your data is maintained.

- ✔ **Compliance:** Make sure that your provider can comply with any compliance issues particular to your company or industry.

- ✔ **Costs:** Little costs can add up. Be careful to read the fine print of any contract, and make sure that you know what you want to do in the cloud.

- ✔ **Data transport:** Be sure to figure out how you get your data into the cloud in the first place. For example, some providers will let you mail it to them on media. Others insist on uploading it over the network. This can get expensive, so be careful.

- ✔ **Performance:** Because you're interested in getting performance from your service provider, make sure that explicit definitions of service-level agreements exist for availability, support, and performance. For example, your provider may tell you that you will be able to access your data 99.999 percent of the time; however, read the contract. Does this uptime include scheduled maintenance?

- ✔ **Data access:** What controls are in place to make sure that you and only you can access your data? In other words, what forms of secure access control are in place? This might include identity management, where the primary goal is protecting personal identity information so that access to computer resources, applications, data, and services is controlled properly.

- ✔ **Location:** Where will your data be located? In some companies and countries, regulatory issues prevent data from being stored or processed on machines in a different country.

Part III
Big Data Management

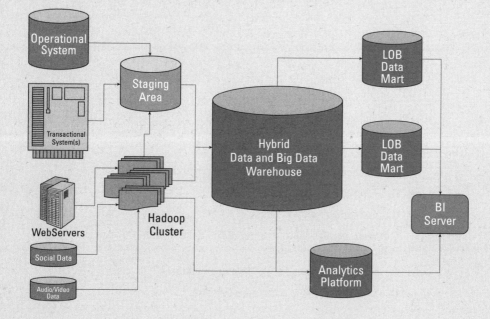

In this part . . .

- Differentiate databases in the big data world.
- Use MapReduce for data analysis.
- Understand Hadoop.
- Enhance your Hadoop Distributed File System with programming languages and tools.
- Develop applications for big data in analytics.
- Use appliances in big data management.

Chapter 7

Operational Databases

*B*ig data is becoming an important element in the way organizations are leveraging high-volume data at the right speed to solve specific data problems. However, big data does not live in isolation. To be effective, companies often need to be able to combine the results of big data analysis with the data that exists within the business. In other words, you can't think about big data in isolation from operational data sources. There are a variety of important operational data services. In this chapter, we provide an explanation of what these sources are so that you can understand how the data inevitably will be used in conjunction with big data solutions.

One of the most important services provided by operational databases (also called *data stores*) is persistence. Persistence guarantees that the data stored in a database won't be changed without permissions and that it will available as long as it is important to the business. What good is a database if it cannot be trusted to protect the data you put in it? Given this most important requirement, you must then think about what kind of data you want to persist, how can you access and update it, and how can you use it to make business decisions. At this most fundamental level, the choice of your database engines is critical to your overall success with your big data implementation.

The forefather of persistent data stores is the relational database management system, or RDBMS. In its infancy, the computing industry used what are now considered primitive techniques for data persistence. In essence, these are the systems of record and are foundational to how companies store data about everything from customer transactions to the details of the operating the business. Even though the underlying technology has been around for quite some time, many of these systems are in operation today because the businesses they support are highly dependent on the data. To replace them would be akin to changing the engines of an airplane on a transoceanic flight. You may recall the "flat files" or "network" data stores that were prevalent before 1980 or so. Although these mechanisms were useful, they were very difficult to master and always required system programmers to write custom programs to manipulate the data. The relational model is still in wide usage today and has an important role to play in the evolution of big data.

Relational databases are built on one or more relations and are represented by tables. These tables are defined by their columns, and the data is stored in the rows. The primary key is often the first column in the table. The consistency of the database and much of its value are achieved by "normalizing" the data. As the name implies, normalized data has been converted from native format into a shared, agreed upon format. For example in one database you might have "telephone" as XXX-XXX-XXXX while in another it might be XXXXXXXXX. To achieve a consistent view of the information, the field will need to be normalized to one form or the other. Five levels of standards exist for normalization. The choice of normal form is often relegated to the database designer and is mostly invisible to the end users. The collection of tables, keys, elements, and so on is referred to as the database *schema*.

Over the years, the structured query language (SQL) has evolved in lock step with RDBMS technology and is the most widely used mechanism for creating, querying, maintaining, and operating relational databases. These tasks are referred to as CRUD: Create, retrieve, update, and delete are common, related operations you can use directly on a database or through an application programming interface (API). Although originally devised for use with RDBMS, the popularity of SQL has also made it prevalent among nonrelational databases, as we cover later in this chapter.

How the relational database evolved

Throughout the history of the relational database, many specialty database technologies appeared specifically to address shortcomings in early RDBMS products. We witnessed the emergence of object databases, content databases, data warehouses, data marts, and others. For companies that needed these new capabilities, they created independent solutions and integrated these new solutions with the existing RDBMS applications. This was tedious, clumsy, and costly. Over time, RDBMSs embraced these new technologies and embedded them in their core product offerings, eliminating the necessity to include additional, now redundant, solutions. We suspect this will occur with big data as well. Given the fundamental differences between big data and traditional data solutions, the encapsulation of big data technologies into RDBMSs will take a few years. In contrast, we are already beginning to see the big data technologies embrace SQL and other traditional RDBMS features as peers to MapReduce.

RDBMSs Are Important in a Big Data Environment

In companies both small and large, most of their important operational information is probably stored in RDBMSs. Many companies have different RDBMSs for different areas of their business. Transactional data might be stored in one vendor's database, while customer information could be stored in another. Knowing what data is stored and where it is stored are critical building blocks in your big data implementation. It is not likely you will use RDBMSs for the core of the implementation, but you will need to rely on the data stored in RDBMSs to create the highest level of value to the business with big data. Although many different commercial relational databases are available from companies like Oracle, IBM, and Microsoft, you need to understand an open source relational database called PostgreSQL.

PostgreSQL relational database

PostgreSQL (www.postgresql.org) is the most widely used open source relational database. It was originally developed at the University of California at Berkeley and has been under active development as an open source project for more than 15 years. Several factors contribute to the popularity of PostgreSQL. As an RDBMS with support for the SQL standard, it does all the things expected in a database product, plus its longevity and wide usage have made it "battle tested." It is also available on just about every variety of operating system, from PCs to mainframes.

Providing the basics and doing so reliably are only part of the story. PostgreSQL also supports many features only found in expensive proprietary RDBMSs, including the following:

- Capability to directly handle "objects" within the relational schema
- Foreign keys (referencing keys from one table in another)
- Triggers (events used to automatically start a stored procedure)
- Complex queries (subqueries and joins across discrete tables)
- Transactional integrity
- Multiversion concurrency control

The real power of PostgreSQL is its extensibility. Users and database programmers can add new capabilities without affecting the fundamental operation or reliability of the database. Possible extensions include

- ✔ Data types
- ✔ Operators
- ✔ Functions
- ✔ Indexing methods
- ✔ Procedural languages

This high level of customization makes PostgreSQL desirable when rigid, proprietary products won't get the job done. It is infinitely extensible.

Finally, the PostgreSQL license permits modification and distribution in any form, open or closed source. Any modifications can be kept private or shared with the community as you wish.

Although relational databases (including PostgreSQL) play a key role in the big data "enterprise," you also have some alternative approaches.

Nonrelational Databases

Nonrelational databases do not rely on the table/key model endemic to RDBMSs. A number of nonrelational database technologies are covered throughout this chapter, each with its own set of unique capabilities focused on specific problems outside the scope of traditional RDBMSs. In short, specialty data in the big data world requires specialty persistence and data manipulation techniques. Although these new styles of databases offer some answers to your big data challenges, they are not an express ticket to the finish line.

One emerging, popular class of nonrelational database is called not only SQL (NoSQL). Originally the originators envisioned databases that did not require the relational model and SQL. As these products were introduced into the market, the definition softened a bit and now they are thought of as "not only SQL," again bowing to the ubiquity of SQL. The other class is databases that do not support the relational model, but rely on SQL as a primary means of manipulating the data within. Even though relational and nonrelational databases have similar fundamentals, how the fundamentals are accomplished creates the differentiation. Nonrelational database technologies have the following characteristics in common:

- ✔ **Scalability:** In this instance, we are referring to the capability to write data across multiple data stores simultaneously without regard to physical limitations of the underlying infrastructure. Another important dimension is seamlessness. The databases must be able to expand and contract in response to data flows and do so invisibly to the end users.

- ✔ **Data and Query model:** Instead of the row, column, key structure, non-relational databases use specialty frameworks to store data with a requisite set of specialty query APIs to intelligently access the data.

- ✔ **Persistence design:** Persistence is still a critical element in nonrelational databases. Due to the high velocity, variety, and volume of big data, these databases use difference mechanisms for persisting the data. The highest performance option is "in memory," where the entire database is kept in the very fast memory system of your servers.

- ✔ **Interface diversity:** Although most of these technologies support RESTful APIs as their "go to" interface, they also offer a wide variety of connection mechanisms for programmers and database managers, including analysis tools and reporting/visualization.

- ✔ **Eventual Consistency:** While RDBMS uses ACID (Atomicity, Consistency, Isolation, Durability) as a mechanism for ensuring the consistency of data, non-relational DBMS use BASE. BASE stands for Basically Available, Soft state, and Eventual Consistency. Of these, eventual consistency is most important because it is responsible for conflict resolution when data is in motion between nodes in a distributed implementation. The data state is maintained by the software and the access model relies on basic availability.

Next we examine some of the most popular styles and the open source implementations of nonrelational databases.

Key-Value Pair Databases

By far, the simplest of the NoSQL databases are those employing the key-value pair (KVP) model. KVP databases do not require a schema (like RDBMSs) and offer great flexibility and scalability. KVP databases do not offer ACID (Atomicity, Consistency, Isolation, Durability) capability, and require implementers to think about data placement, replication, and fault tolerance as they are not expressly controlled by the technology itself. KVP databases are not typed. As a result, most of the data is stored as strings. Table 7-1 lists some sample key-value pairs.

Table 7-1	Sample Key-Value Pairs
Key	*Value*
Color	Blue
Libation	Beer
Hero	Soldier

This is a very simplified set of keys and values. In a big data implementation, many individuals will have differing ideas about colors, libations, and heroes, as presented in Table 7-2.

Table 7-2	Big Data Key-Value Pairs
Key	*Value*
FacebookUser12345_Color	Red
TwitterUser67890_Color	Brownish
FoursquareUser45678_Libation	"White wine"
Google+User24356_Libation	"Dry martini with a twist"
LinkedInUser87654_Hero	"Top sales performer"

As the number of users increases, keeping track of precise keys and related values can be challenging. If you need to keep track of the opinions of millions of users, the number of key-value pairs associated with them can increase exponentially. If you do not want to constrain choices for the values, the generic string representation of KVP provides flexibility and readability.

You might need some additional help organizing data in a key-value database. Most offer the capability to aggregate keys (and their related values) into a collection. Collections can consist of any number of key-value pairs and do not require exclusive control of the individual KVP elements.

Riak key-value database

One widely used open source key-value pair database is called Riak (http://wiki.basho.com). It is developed and supported by a company called Basho Technologies (www.basho.com) and is made available under the Apache Software License v2.0.

Riak is a very fast and scalable implementation of a key-value database. It supports a high-volume environment with fast-changing data because it is lightweight. Riak is particularly effective at real-time analysis of trading in financial services. It uses "buckets" as an organizing mechanism for collections of keys and values. Riak implementations are clusters of physical or virtual nodes arranged in a peer-to-peer fashion. No master node exists, so the cluster is resilient and highly scalable. All data and operations are distributed across the cluster. Riak clusters have an interesting performance profile. Larger clusters (with more nodes) perform better and faster than clusters with fewer nodes. Communication in the cluster is implemented via a special protocol called Gossip. Gossip stores status information about the cluster and shares information about buckets.

Riak has many features and is part of an ecosystem consisting of the following:

- **Parallel processing:** Using MapReduce, Riak supports a capability to decompose and recompose queries across the cluster for real-time analysis and computation.

- **Links and link walking:** Riak can be constructed to mimic a graph database using links. A link can be thought of as a one-way connection between key-value pairs. Walking (following) the links will provide a map of relationships between key-value pairs.

- **Search:** Riak Search has a fault-tolerant, distributed full-text searching capability. Buckets can be indexed for rapid resolution of value to keys.

- **Secondary indexes:** Developers can tag values with one or more key field values. The application can then query the index and return a list of matching keys. This can be very useful in big data implementations because the operation is atomic and will support real-time behaviors.

Riak implementations are best suited for

- User data for social networks, communities, or gaming
- High-volume, media-rich data gathering and storage
- Caching layers for connecting RDBMS and NoSQL databases
- Mobile applications requiring flexibility and dependability

Document Databases

You find two kinds of document databases. One is often described as a repository for full document-style content (Word files, complete web pages, and so on). The other is a database for storing document components for permanent storage as a static entity or for dynamic assembly of the parts of a document. The structure of the documents and their parts is provided by JavaScript Object Notation (JSON) and/or Binary JSON (BSON). Document databases are most useful when you have to produce a lot of reports and they need to be dynamically assembled from elements that change frequently. A good example is document fulfillment in healthcare, where content composition will vary based on member profile (age, residency, income level), healthcare plan, and government program eligibility. For big data implementations, both styles are important, so you should understand the details of each.

At its core, JSON is a data-interchange format, based on a subset of the JavaScript programming language. Although part of a programming language, it is textual in nature and very easy to read and write. It also has the advantage of being easy for computers to handle. Two basic structures exist in JSON, and they are supported by many, if not all, modern programming languages. The first basic structure is a collection of name/value pairs, and they are represented programmatically as objects, records, keyed lists, and so on. The second basic structure is an ordered list of values, and they are represented programmatically as arrays, lists, or sequences. BSON is a binary serialization of JSON structures designed to increase performance and scalability.

Document databases are becoming a gold standard for big data adoption, so we examine two of the most popular implementations.

MongoDB

MongoDB (www.mongodb.com) is the project name for the "hu(mongo)us database" system. It is maintained by a company called 10gen as open source and is freely available under the GNU AGPL v3.0 license. Commercial licenses with full support are available from 10gen (www.10gen.com).

MongoDB is growing in popularity and may be a good choice for the data store supporting your big data implementation. MongoDB is composed of databases containing "collections." A collection is composed of "documents," and each document is composed of fields. Just as in relational databases, you can index a collection. Doing so increases the performance of data lookup. Unlike other databases, however, MongoDB returns something called a "cursor," which serves as a pointer to the data. This is a very useful capability because it offers the option of counting or classifying the data without extracting it. Natively, MongoDB supports BSON, the binary implementation of JSON documents.

MongoDB is also an ecosystem consisting of the following elements:

- High-availability and replication services for scaling across local and wide-area networks.

- A grid-based file system (GridFS), enabling the storage of large objects by dividing them among multiple documents.

- MapReduce to support analytics and aggregation of different collections/documents.

- A sharding service that distributes a single database across a cluster of servers in a single or in multiple data centers. The service is driven by a shard key. The shard key is used to distribute documents intelligently across multiple instances.

- A querying service that supports ad hoc queries, distributed queries, and full-text search.

Effective MongoDB implementations include

- High-volume content management

- Social networking

- Archiving

- Real-time analytics

CouchDB

Another very popular nonrelational database is CouchDB (http:// couchdb.apache.org). Like MongoDB, CouchDB is open source. It is maintained by the Apache Software Foundation (www.apache.org) and is made available under the Apache License v2.0. Unlike MongoDB, CouchDB was designed to mimic the web in all respects. For example, CouchDB is resilient to network dropouts and will continue to operate beautifully in areas where network connectivity is spotty. It is also at home on a smartphone or in a data center. This all comes with a few trade-offs. Because of the underlying web mimicry, CouchDB is high latency resulting in a preference for local data storage. Although capable of working in a non-distributed manner, CouchDB is not well suited to smaller implementations. You must determine whether these trade-offs can be ignored as you begin your big data implementation.

CouchDB databases are composed of documents consisting of fields and attachments as well as a "description" of the document in the form of metadata that is automatically maintained by the system. The underlying technology features all ACID capabilities that you are familiar with from the RDBMS world. The advantage in CouchDB over relational is that the data is packaged and ready for manipulation or storage rather than scattered across rows and tables.

CouchDB is also an ecosystem with the following capabilities:

- ✔ **Compaction:** The databases are compressed to eliminate wasted space when a certain level of emptiness is reached. This helps performance and efficiency for persistence.

- ✔ **View model:** A mechanism for filtering, organizing, and reporting on data utilizing a set of definitions that are stored as documents in the database. You find a one-to-many relationship of databases to views, so you can create many different ways of representing the data you have "sliced and diced."

- ✔ **Replication and distributed services:** Document storage is designed to provide bidirectional replication. Partial replicas can be maintained to support criteria-based distribution or migration to devices with limited connectivity. Native replication is peer based, but you can implement Master/Slave, Master/Master, and other types of replication modalities.

Effective CouchDB implementations include

- ✔ High-volume content management
- ✔ Scaling from smartphone to data center
- ✔ Applications with limited or slow network connectivity

Columnar Databases

Relational databases are *row oriented,* as the data in each row of a table is stored together. In a columnar, or column-oriented database, the data is stored *across* rows. Although this may seem like a trivial distinction, it is the most important underlying characteristic of columnar databases. It is very easy to add columns, and they may be added row by row, offering great flexibility, performance, and scalability. When you have volume and variety of data, you might want to use a columnar database. It is very adaptable; you simply continue to add columns.

HBase columnar database

One of the most popular columnar databases is HBase (`http://hbase.apache.org`). It, too, is a project in the Apache Software Foundation distributed under the Apache Software License v2.0. HBase uses the Hadoop file system and MapReduce engine for its core data storage needs. For more on MapReduce, refer to Chapter 8; for more on Hadoop, check out Chapter 9.

The design of HBase is modeled on Google's BigTable (an efficient form of storing nonrelational data). Therefore, implementations of HBase are highly scalable, sparse, distributed, persistent multidimensional sorted maps. The map is indexed by a row key, column key, and a timestamp; each value in the map is an uninterpreted array of bytes. When your big data implementation requires random, real-time read/write data access, HBase is a very good solution. It is often used to store results for later analytical processing.

Important characteristics of HBase include the following:

- **Consistency:** Although not an "ACID" implementation, HBase offers strongly consistent reads and writes and is not based on an eventually consistent model. This means you can use it for high-speed requirements as long as you do not need the "extra features" offered by RDBMS like full transaction support or typed columns.

- **Sharding:** Because the data is distributed by the supporting file system, HBase offers transparent, automatic splitting and redistribution of its content.

- **High availability:** Through the implementation of region servers, HBase supports LAN and WAN failover and recovery. At the core, there is a master server responsible for monitoring the region servers and all metadata for the cluster.

- **Client API:** HBase offers programmatic access through a Java API.

- **Support for IT operations:** Implementers can expose performance and other metrics through a set of built-in web pages.

HBase implementations are best suited for

- High-volume, incremental data gathering and processing

- Real-time information exchange (for example, messaging)

- Frequently changing content serving

Graph Databases

The fundamental structure for graph databases is called "node-relationship." This structure is most useful when you must deal with highly interconnected data. Nodes and relationships support *properties,* a key-value pair where the data is stored. These databases are navigated by following the relationships. This kind of storage and navigation is not possible in RDBMSs due to the rigid table structures and the inability to follow connections between the data wherever they might lead us. A graph database might be used to manage geographic data for oil exploration or to model and optimize a telecommunications provider's networks.

Neo4J graph database

One of the most widely used graph databases is Neo4J (www.neo4j.org). It is an open source project licensed under the GNU public license v3.0. A supported, commercial version is provided by Neo Technology under the GNU AGPL v3.0 and commercial licensing. Neo4J is an ACID transaction database offering high availability through clustering. It is a trustworthy and scalable database that is easy to model because of the node-relationship properties' fundamental structure and how naturally it maps to our own human relationships. It does not require a schema, nor does it require data typing, so it is inherently very flexible.

With this flexibility comes a few limitations. Nodes cannot reference themselves directly. For example, you (as a node) cannot also be *your own* father or mother (as relationships), but you can be *a* father or mother. There might be real world cases where self-reference is required. If so, a graph database is not the best solution since the rules about self-reference are strictly enforced. While the replication capability is very good, Neo4J can only replicate entire graphs, placing a limit on the overall size of the graph (approximately 34 billion of nodes and 34 billion relationships).

Important characteristics of Neo4J include the following:

- **Integration with other databases:** Neo4J supports transaction management with rollback to allow seamless interoperability with nongraphing data stores.

- **Synchronization services:** Neo4J supports event-driven behaviors via an event bus, periodic synchronization using itself, or an RDBMS as the master, and traditional batch synchronization.

- **Resiliency:** Neo4J supports cold (that is, when database is not running) and hot (when it is running) backups, as well as a high-availability clustering mode. Standard alerts are available for integration with existing operations management systems.

- **Query language:** Neo4J supports a declarative language called Cypher, designed specifically to query graphs and their components. Cypher commands are loosely based on SQL syntax and are targeted at ad hoc queries of the graph data.

Neo4J implementations are best suited for

- Social networking
- Classification of biological or medical domains
- Creating dynamic communities of practice or interest

Spatial Databases

Whether you know it or not, you may interact with spatial data every day. If you use a smartphone or Global Positioning System (GPS) for directions to a particular place, or if you ask a search engine for the locations of seafood restaurants near a physical address or landmark, you are using applications relying on spatial data. Spatial data itself is standardized through the efforts of the Open Geospatial Consortium (OGC; www.opengeospatial.org), which establishes OpenGIS (Geographic Information System) and a number of other standards for spatial data.

This is important because spatial databases are implementations of the OGC standards, and your company might have specific needs met (or not met) by the standards. A spatial database becomes important when organizations begin to leverage several different dimensions of data to help make a decision. For example, a meteorologist doing research might want to store and evaluate data related to a hurricane, including temperature, wind speed, and humidity, and model those results in three dimensions.

In their simplest form, spatial databases store data about 2-dimensional, 2.5-dimensional, and 3-dimensional objects. You are probably familiar with 2D and 3D objects as we interact with them all the time. A 2D object has length and width. A 3D object adds depth to the length and width. A page from this book is a 2D object, while the entire book is a 3D object. What about 2.5D? 2.5D objects are a special type of spatial data. They are 2D objects with elevation as the extra "half" dimension. Most 2.5D spatial databases contain mapping information and are often referred to as Geographic Information Systems (GISs).

The atomic elements of spatial databases are lines, points, and polygons. They can be combined in any fashion to represent any object constrained by 2, 2.5, or 3 dimensions. Due to the special nature of spatial data objects, designers created indexing mechanisms (spatial indices) designed to support ad hoc queries and visual representations of the contents of the database. For example, a spatial index would answer the query "What is the distance between one point and another point?" or "Does a specific line intersect with a particular set of polygons?" If this seems like a huge problem, that's because it is. Spatial data may well represent the biggest big data challenge of all.

PostGIS/OpenGEO Suite

PostGIS (www.postgis.org) is an open source project maintained by Refractions Research (www.refractions.net) and is licensed under the GNU General Public License (GPL). PostGIS is also supplied as part of the OpenGeo Suite community edition and is offered and supported by OpenGeo (www.opengeo.org) under an enterprise license.

PostGIS is a little different than some of the other databases discussed in this chapter. It is a specialized, layered implementation running on the workhorse RDBMS PostgreSQL. This approach offers the best of both worlds. You get all the benefits of an SQL RDBMS (such as transactional integrity and ACID) and support for the specialized operations needed for spatial applications (reprojection, geodetic support, geometry conversion, and so on).

Although the database itself is very important, you will also require other pieces of technology to address spatial application requirements. Fortunately, PostGIS is part of an ecosystem of components designed to work together to address these needs. In addition to PostGIS, the OpenGEO Suite consists of the following:

- ✓ **GeoServer:** Implemented in Java, the GeoServer can publish spatial information from several of the major sources of spatial data on the web. It can integrate with Google Earth and also has an excellent web-based administrative front end.

- ✓ **OpenLayers:** A library for JavaScript that is useful for displaying maps and other representations of spatial data in a web browser. It can manipulate images from most of the mapping sources on the web, including Bing Maps, Google Maps, Yahoo! Maps, OpenStreetMap, and so on.

- ✓ **GeoExt:** Designed to make the map information from OpenLayers readily available to the web application developer. GeoExt widgets can be used to create editing, viewing, styling, and other interactive web experiences.

- ✓ **GeoWebCache:** After you have the data in a server and can display it in a browser, you need to find a way to make it fast. GeoWebCache is the accelerator. It caches chunks of image data (called tiles) and makes them available for rapid delivery to the display device.

While many of the uses of spatial data involve maps and locations, spatial data has many other contemporary and future applications, including

- ✔ Precise 3D modeling of the human body, buildings, the atmosphere, and so on

- ✔ Gathering and analysis of data from sensor networks

- ✔ Integration with historical data to examine 3D space/objects over time

Polyglot Persistence

The official definition of *polyglot* is "someone who speaks or writes several languages." The term is borrowed in this context and redefined as a set of applications that use several core database technologies, and this is the most likely outcome of your big data implementation planning. It is going to be difficult to choose one persistence style no matter how narrow your approach to big data might be. A polyglot persistence database is used when it is necessary to solve a complex problem by breaking that problem into segments and applying different database models. It is then necessary to aggregate the results into a hybrid data storage and analysis solution. A number of factors affect this decision:

- ✔ You are already using polyglot persistence in your existing workplace. If your enterprise or organization is large, you are probably using multiple RDBMSs, data warehouses, data marts, flat files, content management servers, and so on. This hybrid environment is common, and you need to understand it so that you can make the right decisions about integration, analytics, timeliness of data, data visibility, and so on. You need to understand all of that because you need to figure out how it is going to fit into your big data implementation.

- ✔ The most ideal of environments, where you have only one persistence technology, is probably not suited to big data problem solving. At the very least, you will need to introduce another style of database and other supporting technologies for your new implementation.

- ✔ Depending on the variety and velocity of your big data gathering, you may need to consider different databases to support one implementation. You should also consider your requirements for transactional integrity. Do you need to support ACID compliance or will BASE compliance be sufficient?

As an example, suppose that you need to identify all the customers for your consumer hard goods product who have purchased in the last 12 months and have commented on social websites about their experience — AND whether they have had any support cases (when, how many, how resolved), where they acquired the product, how it was delivered (and was the delivery routing cost efficient with respect to energy consumption?), what they paid, how they paid, whether they have been to the company website, how many times, what they did on the site, and so on. Then suppose that you want to offer them a promotional discount to their smartphone when they are entering one of your (or one of your partners') retail stores.

This is a big data challenge at its best. Multiple sources of data with very different structures need to be collected and analyzed so that you can get the answers to these questions. Then you need determine whether the customers qualify for the promotion and, in real time, push them a coupon offering them something new and interesting.

This type of problem cannot be solved easily or cost-effectively with one type of database technology. Even though some of the basic information is transactional and probably in an RDBMS, the other information is nonrelational and will require at least two types of persistence engines (spatial and graph). You now have polyglot persistence.

Chapter 8

MapReduce Fundamentals

While big data has dominated the headlines over the past year, large computing problems have existed since the beginning of the computer era. Each time a newer, faster, higher-capacity computer system was introduced, people found problems that were too big for the system to handle. Along came local-area networks, and the industry turned to combining the compute and storage capacities of systems on the network toward solving bigger and bigger problems. The distribution of compute- and data-intensive applications is at the heart of a solution to big data challenges. To best achieve reliable distribution at scale, new technology approaches were needed. MapReduce is one of those new approaches. MapReduce is a software framework that enables developers to write programs that can process massive amounts of unstructured data in parallel across a distributed group of processors.

Tracing the Origins of MapReduce

In the early 2000s, some engineers at Google looked into the future and determined that while their current solutions for applications such as web crawling, query frequency, and so on were adequate for most existing requirements, they were inadequate for the complexity they anticipated as the web scaled to more and more users. These engineers determined that if work could be distributed across inexpensive computers and then connected on the network in the form of a "cluster," they could solve the problem.

Distribution alone was not a sufficient answer. This distribution of work must be performed in parallel for the following three reasons:

- ✔ The processing must be able to expand and contract automatically.

- ✔ The processing must be able to proceed regardless of failures in the network or the individual systems.

- ✔ Developers leveraging this approach must be able to create services that are easy to leverage by other developers. Therefore, this approach must be independent of where the data and computations have executed.

MapReduce was designed as a generic programming model. Some of the initial implementations provided all the key requirements of parallel execution, fault tolerance, load balancing, and data manipulation. The engineers in charge of the project named the initiative MapReduce because it combines two capabilities from existing functional computer languages: *map* and *reduce*.

Google engineers designed MapReduce to solve a specific practical problem. Therefore, it was designed as a programming model combined with the implementation of that model — in essence, a reference implementation. The reference implementation was used to demonstrate the practicality and effectiveness of the concept and to help ensure that this model would be widely adopted by the computer industry. Over the years, other implementations of MapReduce have been created and are available as both open source and commercial products.

Functional versus procedural programming models

When we talk of map and reduce, we do so as operations within a functional programming model. Functional programming is one of the two ways that software developers create programs to address business problems. The other model is procedural programming. We take a quick look to understand the differences and to see when it's best to use one or the other model.

Procedural programs are highly structured and provide step-by-step instructions on what to do with input data. The order of the execution is important, and the input data is changed as it progresses through each step of the program. Examples of procedural languages include FORTRAN, COBOL, C, and C++. The best uses for procedural programs are those where it is okay to change the values of the input data or where you need to compare computed values in one of the steps to determine whether you

need to continue processing or exit the program and deliver the result.

In contrast, functional programs do not change the input data. They look at all the data for specific patterns and then apply rules to identify the important elements and then assemble them into lists. The order of the processing is not important because each operation is independent of another. Examples of functional languages include LISP, Scheme, Prolog, and R. Functional programs do not change the input data and are most often used when it is necessary to look at the data again and again for different patterns. For example, you could look through a list of all the counties in the United States that voted Republican in the last election and then go through the list for all Democratic counties. This will produce two distinct output lists.

Understanding the map Function

The *map* function has been a part of many functional programming languages for years, first gaining popularity with an artificial intelligence language called LISP. Good software developers understand the value of reuse, so map has been reinvigorated as a core technology for processing lists of data elements (keys and values). To further your understanding of why the map function is a good choice for big data (and the *reduce* function is as well), it's important to understand a little bit about functional programming.

Operators in functional languages do not modify the structure of the data; they create new data structures as their output. More importantly, the original data itself is unmodified as well. So you can use the map function with impunity because it will not harm your precious stored data. Another advantage to functional programming is not having to expressly manage the movement or flow of the data. This is helpful because it absolves the programmer from explicitly managing the data output and placement. Because you are operating in a distributed environment, dealing with where the data is stored can be a nightmare. The map function takes care of that. Finally, in the world of functional programming, the order of the operations on the data is not prescribed. Again, this is a great advantage in a computing cluster where tasks are being performed in parallel.

So what exactly can you expect from the map function? It applies a function to each element (defined as a key-value pair) of a list and produces a new list. Suppose that you wanted to create a program that counts the number of characters in a series or list of words. The following is not official programming code; it's just a way to represent how to construct a solution to the problem.

One way to accomplish the solution is to identify the input data and create a list:

```
mylist = ("all counties in the US that participated in the
          most recent general election")
```

Create the function howManyPeople using the map function. This selects only the counties with more than 50,000 people:

```
map howManyPeople (mylist) = [ howManyPeople "county 1";
        howManyPeople "county 2"; howManyPeople "county
        3"; howManyPeople "county 4"; . . . ]
```

Now produce a new output list of all the counties with populations greater than 50,000:

```
(no, county 1; yes, county 2; no, county 3; yes, county 4;
        ?, county nnn)
```

The function executes without making any changes to the original list. In addition, you can see that each element of the output list maps to a corresponding element of the input list, with a yes or no attached. If the county has met the requirement of more than 50,000 people, the map function identifies it with a yes. If not, a no is indicated. This is an important feature, as you shall soon see when you look at the *reduce* function.

Adding the reduce Function

Like the map function, *reduce* has been a feature of functional programming languages for many years. In some languages, it is called *fold,* but the behavior is exactly the same. The reduce function takes the output of a map function and "reduces" the list in whatever fashion the programmer desires. The first step that the reduce function requires is to place a value in something called an *accumulator,* which holds an initial value. After storing a starting value in the accumulator, the reduce function then processes each element of the list and performs the operation you need across the list. At the end of the list, the reduce function returns a value based on what operation you wanted to perform on the output list. Revisit the map function example now to see what the reduce function is capable of doing.

Suppose that you need to identify the counties where the majority of the votes were for the Democratic candidate. Remember that your howMany-People map function looked at each element of the input list and created an output list of the counties with more than 50,000 people (yes) and the counties with less than 50,000 people (no).

After invoking the howManyPeople map function, you are left with the following output list:

```
(no, county 1; yes, county 2; no, county 3; yes, county 4;
      ?, county nnn)
```

This is now the input for your reduce function. Here is what it looks like:

```
countylist = (no, county 1; yes, county 2; no, county 3;
         yes, county 4; ?, county nnn)
reduce isDemocrat (countylist)
```

The reduce function processes each element of the list and returns a list of all the counties with a population greater than 50,000, where the majority voted Democratic.

Now imagine that you would like to know in which counties with a population greater than 50,000 the majority voted Republican. All you need to do is invoke the reduce function again, but you will change the operator from isDemocrat to isRepublican:

```
reduce isRepublican (countylist)
```

This returns a list of all the counties where the majority of voters supported Republican candidates. Because you did not change the elements of county list, you can continue to perform the reduce functions on the input until you get the results you require. For example, you could look for independent majorities or refine the results to specific geographic regions.

Putting map and reduce Together

Sometimes producing an output list is just enough. Likewise, sometimes performing operations on each element of a list is enough. Most often, you want to look through large amounts of input data, select certain elements from the data, and then compute something of value from the relevant pieces of data. You don't always control the input data, so you need to do this work nondestructively — you don't want to change that input list so you can use it in different ways with new assumptions and new data.

Software developers design applications based on algorithms. An *algorithm* is nothing more than a series of steps that need to occur in service to an overall goal. It is very much like a cooking recipe. You start with the individual elements (flour, sugar, eggs, and so on) and follow step-by-step instructions (combine, knead, and bake) to produce the desired result (a loaf of bread). Putting the map and reduce functions to work efficiently requires an algorithm too. It might look a little like this:

1. Start with a large number or data or records.

2. Iterate over the data.

3. Use the map function to extract something of interest and create an output list.

4. Organize the output list to optimize for further processing.

5. Use the reduce function to compute a set of results.

6. Produce the final output.

Programmers can implement all kinds of applications using this approach, but the examples to this point have been very simple, so the real value of

MapReduce may not be apparent. What happens when you have extremely large input data? Can you use the same algorithm on terabytes of data? The good news is yes.

As illustrated in Figure 8-1, all of the operations seem independent. That's because they are. The real power of MapReduce is the capability to divide and conquer. Take a very large problem and break it into smaller, more manageable chunks, operate on each chunk independently, and then pull it all together at the end. Furthermore, the map function is commutative — in other words, the order that a function is executed doesn't matter.

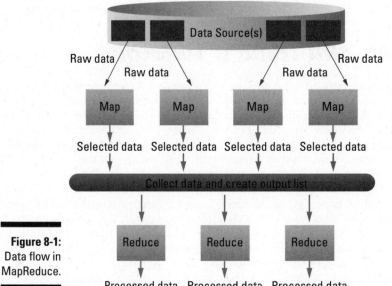

Figure 8-1:
Data flow in
MapReduce.

If you remember algebra at all, you may recall that when something is commutative, the result is the same, regardless of the order of the elements. For example:

```
5 + 7 = 7 + 5
```

or

```
3 * 4 = 4 * 3
```

So MapReduce can perform its work on different machines in a network and get the same result as if all the work was done on a single machine. It can also draw from multiple data sources, internal or external. MapReduce keeps track of its work by creating a unique key to ensure that all the processing is related to solving the same problem. This key is also used to pull all the output together at the end of all the distributed tasks.

When the map and reduce functions are used in this fashion, they work collectively to run as a single job within the cluster. All the dividing and conquering is done transparently by the execution framework of the MapReduce engine, and all the work is distributed to one or many nodes in the network.

You need to understand some characteristics of the execution framework so that you may get a better understanding of why things work the way they do. This can help you design better applications and also to optimize the execution for performance or efficiency. The following are the foundational behaviors of MapReduce:

✔ **Scheduling:** MapReduce jobs get broken down into individual tasks for the map and the reduce portions of the application. Because the mapping must be concluded before reducing can take place, those tasks are prioritized according to the number of nodes in the cluster. If you have more tasks than nodes, the execution framework will manage the map tasks until all are complete. Then the reduce tasks will run with the same behaviors. The entire process is complete only when all the reduce tasks have run successfully.

✔ **Synchronization:** When multiple processes execute concurrently in a cluster, you need a way to keep things running smoothly. Synchronization mechanisms do this automatically. Because the execution framework knows that the program is mapping and reducing, it keeps track of what has run and when. When all the mapping is complete, the reducing begins. Intermediate data is copied over the network as it is produced using a mechanism called "shuffle and sort." This gathers and prepares all the mapped data for reduction.

✔ **Code/data colocation:** The most effective processing occurs when the mapping functions (the code) is colocated on the same machine with the data it needs to process. The process scheduler is very clever and can place the code and its related data on the same node prior to execution (or vice versa).

✔ **Fault/error handling:** What happens when a failure occurs? Hopefully, nothing. Most MapReduce engines have very robust error handling and fault tolerance. With all the nodes in a MapReduce cluster and all the parts in each node, something is going to fail at some point. The engine must recognize that something is wrong and make the necessary correction. For example, if some of the mapping tasks do not return as complete, the engine could assign the tasks to a different node to finish the job. The engine is designed so that it recognizes when a job is incomplete and will automatically assign the task to a different node.

Optimizing MapReduce Tasks

Aside from optimizing the actual application code, you can use some optimization techniques to improve the reliability and performance of your MapReduce jobs. They fall into three categories: hardware/network topology, synchronization, and file system.

Hardware/network topology

Independent of application, the fastest hardware and networks will likely yield the fastest run times for your software. A distinct advantage of MapReduce is the capability to run on inexpensive clusters of commodity hardware and standard networks. If you don't pay attention to where your servers are physically organized, you won't get the best performance and high degree of fault tolerance necessary to support big data tasks.

Commodity hardware is often stored in racks in the data center. The proximity of the hardware within the rack offers a performance advantage as opposed to moving data and/or code from rack to rack. During implementation, you can configure your MapReduce engine to be aware of and take advantage of this proximity. Keeping the data and the code together is one of the best optimizations for MapReduce performance. In essence, the closer the hardware processing elements are to each other, the less latency you will have to deal with.

Synchronization

Because it is inefficient to hold all the results of your mapping within the node, the synchronization mechanisms copy the mapping results to the reducing nodes immediately after they have completed so that the processing can begin right away. All values from the same key are sent to the same reducer, again ensuring higher performance and better efficiency. The reduction outputs are written directly to the file system, so it must be designed and tuned for best results.

File system

Your MapReduce implementation is supported by a distributed file system. The major difference between local and distributed file systems is capacity. To handle the huge amounts of information in a big data world, file systems need to be spread across multiple machines or nodes in a network. MapReduce implementations rely on a master-slave style of distribution, where the master node stores all the metadata, access rights, mapping and location of files and blocks, and so on. The slaves are nodes where the actual data is stored. All the requests go to the master and then are handled by the appropriate slave node. As you contemplate the design of the file system you need to support a MapReduce implementation, you should consider the following:

- ✔ **Keep it warm:** As you might expect, the master node could get over-worked because everything begins there. Additionally, if the master node fails, the entire file system is inaccessible until the master is restored. A very important optimization is to create a "warm standby" master node that can jump into service if a problem occurs with the online master.

- ✔ **The bigger the better:** File size is also an important consideration. Lots of small files (less than 100MB) should be avoided. Distributed file systems supporting MapReduce engines work best when they are populated with a modest number of large files.

- ✔ **The long view:** Because workloads are managed in batches, highly sustained network bandwidth is more important than quick execution times of the mappers or reducers. The optimal approach is for the code to stream lots of data when it is reading and again when it is time to write to the file system.

- ✔ **Keep it secure:** But not overly so. Adding layers of security on the distributed file system will degrade its performance. The file permissions are there to guard against unintended consequences, not malicious behavior. The best approach is to ensure that only authorized users have access to the data center environment and to keep the distributed file system protected from the outside.

Now that you understand a bit about this powerful capability, we take a deep dive into the most widely used MapReduce engine and its ecosystem.

Chapter 9

Exploring the World of Hadoop

*W*hen you need to process big data sources, traditional approaches fall short. The volume, velocity, and variety of big data will bring most technologies to their knees, so new technologies had to be created to address this new challenge. MapReduce is one of those new technologies, but it is just an algorithm, a recipe for how to make sense of all the data. To get the most from MapReduce, you need more than just an algorithm. You need a collection of products and technologies designed to handle the challenges presented by big data.

Explaining Hadoop

Search engine innovators like Yahoo! and Google needed to find a way to make sense of the massive amounts of data that their engines were collecting. These companies needed to both understand what information they were gathering and how they could monetize that data to support their business model. Hadoop was developed because it represented the most pragmatic way to allow companies to manage huge volumes of data easily. Hadoop allowed big problems to be broken down into smaller elements so that analysis could be done quickly and cost-effectively.

By breaking the big data problem into small pieces that could be processed in parallel, you can process the information and regroup the small pieces to present results.

Hadoop (`http://hadoop.apache.org`) was originally built by a Yahoo! engineer named Doug Cutting and is now an open source project managed by the Apache Software Foundation. It is made available under the Apache License v2.0. Along with other projects that we examine in Chapter 10, Hadoop is a fundamental building block in our desire to capture and process big data. Hadoop is designed to parallelize data processing across computing nodes to speed computations and hide latency. At its core, Hadoop has two primary components:

> ✔ **Hadoop Distributed File System:** A reliable, high-bandwidth, low-cost, data storage cluster that facilitates the management of related files across machines.
>
> ✔ **MapReduce engine:** A high-performance parallel/distributed data-processing implementation of the MapReduce algorithm.

Hadoop is designed to process huge amounts of structured and unstructured data (terabytes to petabytes) and is implemented on racks of commodity servers as a Hadoop cluster. Servers can be added or removed from the cluster dynamically because Hadoop is designed to be "self-healing." In other words, Hadoop is able to detect changes, including failures, and adjust to those changes and continue to operate without interruption.

We now take a closer look at the Hadoop Distributed File System (HDFS) and MapReduce as implemented in Hadoop.

Understanding the Hadoop Distributed File System (HDFS)

The Hadoop Distributed File System is a versatile, resilient, clustered approach to managing files in a big data environment. HDFS is not the final destination for files. Rather, it is a data service that offers a unique set of capabilities needed when data volumes and velocity are high. Because the data is written once and then read many times thereafter, rather than the constant read-writes of other file systems, HDFS is an excellent choice for supporting big data analysis. The service includes a "NameNode" and multiple "data nodes" running on a commodity hardware cluster and provides the highest levels of performance when the entire cluster is in the same physical rack in the data center. In essence, the NameNode keeps track of where data is physically stored. Figure 9-1 depicts the basic architecture of HDFS.

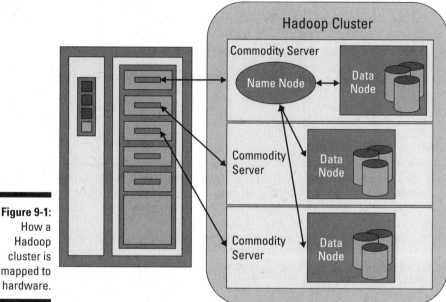

Figure 9-1:
How a
Hadoop
cluster is
mapped to
hardware.

NameNodes

HDFS works by breaking large files into smaller pieces called *blocks*. The blocks are stored on data nodes, and it is the responsibility of the NameNode to know what blocks on which data nodes make up the complete file. The NameNode also acts as a "traffic cop," managing all access to the files, including reads, writes, creates, deletes, and replication of data blocks on the data nodes. The complete collection of all the files in the cluster is sometimes referred to as the file system *namespace*. It is the NameNode's job to manage this namespace.

Even though a strong relationship exists between the NameNode and the data nodes, they operate in a "loosely coupled" fashion. This allows the cluster elements to behave dynamically, adding (or subtracting) servers as the demand increases (or decreases). In a typical configuration, you find one NameNode and possibly a data node running on one physical server in the rack. Other servers run data nodes only.

Data nodes are not very smart, but the NameNode is. The data nodes constantly ask the NameNode whether there is anything for them to do. This continuous behavior also tells the NameNode what data nodes are out there and how busy they are. The data nodes also communicate among themselves so that they can cooperate during normal file system operations. This is necessary because blocks for one file are likely to be stored on multiple data nodes. Since the NameNode is so critical for correct operation of the cluster, it can and should be replicated to guard against a single point failure.

Data nodes

Data nodes are not smart, but they are resilient. Within the HDFS cluster, data blocks are replicated across multiple data nodes and access is managed by the NameNode. The replication mechanism is designed for optimal efficiency when all the nodes of the cluster are collected into a rack. In fact, the NameNode uses a "rack ID" to keep track of the data nodes in the cluster. HDFS clusters are sometimes referred to as being "rack-aware." Data nodes also provide "heartbeat" messages to detect and ensure connectivity between the NameNode and the data nodes. When a heartbeat is no longer present, the NameNode unmaps the data node from the cluster and keeps on operating as though nothing happened. When the heartbeat returns (or a new heartbeat appears), it is added to the cluster transparently with respect to the user or application.

As with all file systems, data integrity is a key feature. HDFS supports a number of capabilities designed to provide data integrity. As you might expect, when files are broken into blocks and then distributed across different servers in the cluster, any variation in the operation of any element could affect data integrity. HDFS uses transaction logs and checksum validation to ensure integrity across the cluster.

Transaction logs are a very common practice in file system and database design. They keep track of every operation and are effective in auditing or rebuilding of the file system should something untoward occur.

Checksum validations are used to guarantee the contents of files in HDFS. When a client requests a file, it can verify the contents by examining its checksum. If the checksum matches, the file operation can continue. If not, an error is reported. Checksum files are hidden to help avoid tampering.

Data nodes use local disks in the commodity server for persistence. All the data blocks are stored locally, primarily for performance reasons. Data blocks are replicated across several data nodes, so the failure of one server may not necessarily corrupt a file. The degree of replication, the number of data nodes, and the HDFS namespace are established when the cluster is implemented. Because HDFS is dynamic, all parameters can be adjusted during the operation of the cluster.

Under the covers of HDFS

Big data brings the big challenges of volume, velocity, and variety. As covered in the previous sections, HDFS addresses these challenges by breaking files into a related collection of smaller blocks. These blocks are distributed among the data nodes in the HDFS cluster and are managed by the NameNode. Block sizes are configurable and are usually 128 megabytes (MB) or 256MB, meaning that a 1GB file consumes eight 128MB blocks for its basic storage needs. HDFS is resilient, so these blocks are replicated throughout the cluster in case of a server failure. How does HDFS keep track of all these pieces? The short answer is file system *metadata*.

Metadata is defined as "data about data." Software designers have been using metadata for decades under several names like data dictionary, metadata directory, and more recently, tags. Think of HDFS metadata as a template for providing a detailed description of the following:

✔ When the file was created, accessed, modified, deleted, and so on

✔ Where the blocks of the file are stored in the cluster

✔ Who has the rights to view or modify the file

✔ How many files are stored on the cluster

✔ How many data nodes exist in the cluster

✔ The location of the transaction log for the cluster

HDFS metadata is stored in the NameNode, and while the cluster is operating, all the metadata is loaded into the physical memory of the NameNode server. As you might expect, the larger the cluster, the larger the metadata footprint. For best performance, the NameNode server should have lots of physical memory and, ideally, lots of solid-state disks. The more the merrier, from a performance point of view.

As we cover earlier in the chapter, the data nodes are very simplistic. They are servers that contain the blocks for a given set of files. It is reasonable to think of data nodes as "block servers" because that is their primary function. What exactly does a block server do? Check out the following list:

✔ Stores (and retrieves) the data blocks in the local file system of the server. HDFS is available on many different operating systems and behaves the same whether on Windows, Mac OS, or Linux.

✔ Stores the metadata of a block in the local file system based on the metadata template in the NameNode.

✔ Performs periodic validations of file checksums.

✔ Sends regular reports to the NameNode about what blocks are available for file operations.

✔ Provides metadata and data to clients on demand. HDFS supports direct access to the data nodes from client application programs.

✔ Forwards data to other data nodes based on a "pipelining" model.

Block placement on the data nodes is critical to data replication and support for data pipelining. HDFS keeps one replica of every block locally. It then places a second replica on a different rack to guard against a complete rack failure. It also sends a third replica to the same remote rack, but to a different server in the rack. Finally, it can send additional replicas to random locations in local or remote clusters. HDFS is serious about data replication and resiliency. Fortunately, client applications do not need to worry about where all the blocks are located. In fact, clients are directed to the nearest replica to ensure highest performance.

HDFS supports the capability to create data pipelines. A *pipeline* is a connection between multiple data nodes that exists to support the movement of data across the servers. A client application writes a block to the first data node in the pipeline. The data node takes over and forwards the data to the next node in the pipeline; this continues until all the data, and all the data replicas, are written to disk. At this point, the client repeats the process by writing the next block in the file. As you see later in this chapter, this is an important feature for Hadoop MapReduce.

With all these files and blocks and servers, you might wonder how things are kept in balance. Without any intervention, it is possible for one data node to become congested while another might be nearly empty. HDFS has a "rebalancer" service that's designed to address these possibilities. The goal is to balance the data nodes based on how full each set of local disks might be. The rebalancer runs while the cluster is active and can be throttled to avoid congestion of network traffic. After all, HDFS needs to manage the files and blocks first and then worry about how balanced the cluster needs to be.

The rebalancer is effective, but it does not have a great deal of built-in intelligence. For example, you can't create access or load patterns and have the rebalancer optimize for those conditions. Nor will it identify data "hot spots" and correct for them. Perhaps these features will be offered in future versions of HDFS.

Hadoop MapReduce

To fully understand the capabilities of Hadoop MapReduce, we need to differentiate between MapReduce (the algorithm) and an implementation of MapReduce. Hadoop MapReduce is an implementation of the algorithm developed and maintained by the Apache Hadoop project. It is helpful to think about this implementation as a MapReduce engine, because that is exactly how it works. You provide input (fuel), the engine converts the input into output quickly and efficiently, and you get the answers you need. You are using Hadoop to solve business problems, so it is necessary for you to understand how and why it works. So, we take a look at the Hadoop implementation of MapReduce in more detail.

Hadoop MapReduce includes several stages, each with an important set of operations helping to get to your goal of getting the answers you need from big data. The process starts with a user request to run a MapReduce program and continues until the results are written back to the HDFS. Figure 9-2 illustrates how MapReduce performs its tasks.

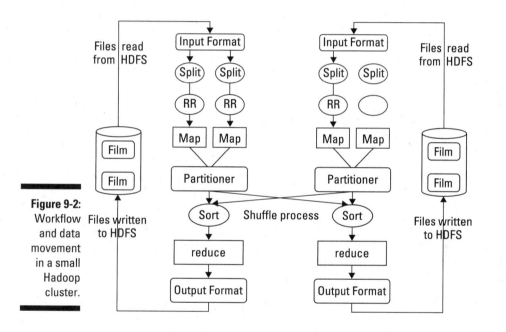

Figure 9-2: Workflow and data movement in a small Hadoop cluster.

HDFS and MapReduce perform their work on nodes in a cluster hosted on racks of commodity servers. To simplify the discussion, the diagram shows only two nodes.

Getting the data ready

When a client requests a MapReduce program to run, the first step is to locate and read the input file containing the raw data. The file format is completely arbitrary, but the data must be converted to something the program can process. This is the function of InputFormat and RecordReader (RR).

InputFormat decides how the file is going to be broken into smaller pieces for processing using a function called InputSplit. It then assigns a RecordReader to transform the raw data for processing by the map. If you read the discussion of map in Chapter 8, you know it requires two inputs: a key and a value. Several types of RecordReaders are supplied with Hadoop, offering a wide variety of conversion options. This feature is one of the ways that Hadoop manages the huge variety of data types found in big data problems.

Let the mapping begin

Your data is now in a form acceptable to map. For each input pair, a distinct instance of map is called to process the data. But what does it do with the processed output, and how can you keep track of them? Map has two additional capabilities to address the questions. Because map and reduce need to work together to process your data, the program needs to collect the output from the independent mappers and pass it to the reducers. This task is performed by an OutputCollector. A Reporter function also provides information gathered from map tasks so that you know when or if the map tasks are complete.

All this work is being performed on multiple nodes in the Hadoop cluster simultaneously. You may have cases where the output from certain mapping processes needs to be accumulated before the reducers can begin. Or, some of the intermediate results may need to be processed before reduction. In addition, some of this output may be on a node different from the node where the reducers for that specific output will run. The gathering and shuffling of intermediate results are performed by a partitioner and a sort. The map tasks will deliver the results to a specific partition as inputs to the reduce tasks. After all the map tasks are complete, the intermediate results are gathered in the partition and a shuffling occurs, sorting the output for optimal processing by reduce.

Reduce and combine

For each output pair, reduce is called to perform its task. In similar fashion to map, reduce gathers its output while all the tasks are processing. Reduce can't begin until all the mapping is done, and it isn't finished until all instances are complete. The output of reduce is also a key and a value. While this is necessary for reduce to do its work, it may not be the most effective output format for your application. Hadoop provides an OutputFormat feature, and it works very much like InputFormat. OutputFormat takes the key-value pair and organizes the output for writing to HDFS. The last task is to actually write the data to HDFS. This is performed by RecordWriter, and it performs similarly to RecordReader except in reverse. It takes the OutputFormat data and writes it to HDFS in the form necessary for the requirements of the application program.

The coordination of all these activities was managed in earlier versions of Hadoop by a job scheduler. This scheduler was rudimentary, and as the mix of jobs changed and grew, it was clear that a different approach was necessary. The primary deficiency in the old scheduler was the lack of resource management. The latest version of Hadoop has this new capability, and we look at it more closely in Chapter 10.

Hadoop MapReduce is the heart of the Hadoop system. It provides all the capabilities you need to break big data into manageable chunks, process the data in parallel on your distributed cluster, and then make the data available for user consumption or additional processing. And it does all this work in a highly resilient, fault-tolerant manner. This is just the beginning. The Hadoop ecosystem is a large, growing set of tools and technologies designed specifically for cutting your big data problems down to size.

Chapter 10

The Hadoop Foundation and Ecosystem

· ·

In This Chapter

▶ Why the Hadoop ecosystem is foundational for big data

▶ Managing resources and applications with Hadoop YARN

▶ Storing big data with HBase

▶ Mining big data with Hive

▶ Interacting with the Hadoop ecosystem

· ·

As Chapter 9 explains, Hadoop MapReduce and Hadoop Distributed File System (HDFS) are powerful technologies designed to address big data challenges. That's the good news. The bad news is that you really need to be a programmer or data scientist to be able to get the most out of these elemental components. Enter the Hadoop ecosystem. For several years and for the foreseeable future, open source as well as commercial developers all over the world have been building and testing tools to increase the adoption and usability of Hadoop. Many are working on bits of the ecosystem and offering their enhancements back to the Apache project. This constant flow of fixes and improvements helps to drive the entire ecosystem forward in a controlled and secure manner.

In this chapter, you take a look at the various technologies that make up the Hadoop ecosystem.

Building a Big Data Foundation with the Hadoop Ecosystem

Trying to tackle big data challenges without a toolbox filled with technology and services is like trying to empty the ocean with a spoon. As core components, Hadoop MapReduce and HDFS are constantly being improved and provide great starting points, but you need something more. The Hadoop ecosystem provides an ever-expanding collection of tools and technologies specifically created to smooth the development, deployment, and support of big data solutions. Before we look at the key components of the ecosystem, let's take a moment to discuss the Hadoop ecosystem and the role it plays on the big data stage.

No building is stable without a foundation. While important, stability is not the only important criterion in a building. Each part of the building must support its overall purpose. The walls, floors, stairs, electrical, plumbing, and roof need to complement each other while relying on the foundation for support and integration. It is the same with the Hadoop ecosystem. The foundation is MapReduce and HDFS. They provide the basic structure and integration services needed to support the core requirements of big data solutions. The remainder of the ecosystem provides the components you need to build and manage purpose-driven big data applications for the real world.

In the absence of the ecosystem it would be incumbent on developers, database administrators, system and network managers, and others to identify and agree on a set of technologies to build and deploy big data solutions. This is often the case when businesses want to adapt new and emerging technology trends. The chore of cobbling together technologies in a new market is daunting. That is why the Hadoop ecosystem is so fundamental to the success of big data. It is the most comprehensive collection of tools and technologies available today to target big data challenges. The ecosystem facilitate the creation of new opportunities for the widespread adoption of big data by businesses and organizations.

Managing Resources and Applications with Hadoop YARN

Job scheduling and tracking are integral parts of Hadoop MapReduce. The early versions of Hadoop supported a rudimentary job and task tracking system, but as the mix of work supported by Hadoop changed, the scheduler could not keep up. In particular, the old scheduler could not manage non-MapReduce jobs, and it was incapable of optimizing cluster utilization. So a new capability was designed to address these shortcomings and offer more flexibility, efficiency, and performance.

Yet Another Resource Negotiator (YARN) is a core Hadoop service providing two major services:

- Global resource management (ResourceManager)
- Per-application management (ApplicationMaster)

The ResourceManager is a master service and control NodeManager in each of the nodes of a Hadoop cluster. Included in the ResourceManager is Scheduler, whose sole task is to allocate system resources to specific running applications (tasks), but it does not monitor or track the application's status. All the required system information is stored in a Resource Container. It contains detailed CPU, disk, network, and other important resource attributes necessary for running applications on the node and in the cluster.

Each node has a NodeManager slaved to the global ResourceManager in the cluster. The NodeManager monitors the application's usage of CPU, disk, network, and memory and reports back to the ResourceManager. For each application running on the node there is a corresponding ApplicationMaster. If more resources are necessary to support the running application, the ApplicationMaster notifies the NodeManager and the NodeManager negotiates with the ResourceManager (Scheduler) for the additional capacity on behalf of the application. The NodeManager is also responsible for tracking job status and progress within its node.

Storing Big Data with HBase

HBase is a distributed, nonrelational (columnar) database that utilizes HDFS as its persistence store. It is modeled after Google BigTable and is capable of hosting very large tables (billions of columns/rows) because it is layered on Hadoop clusters of commodity hardware. HBase provides random, real-time read/write access to big data. HBase is highly configurable, providing a great deal of flexibility to address huge amounts of data efficiently. Now take a look at how HBase can help address your big data challenges.

HBase is a columnar database, so all data is stored into tables with rows and columns similar to relational database management systems (RDBMSs). The intersection of a row and a column is called a cell. One important difference between HBase tables and RDBMS tables is versioning. Each cell value includes a "version" attribute, which is nothing more than a timestamp uniquely identifying the cell. Versioning tracks changes in the cell and makes it possible to retrieve any version of the contents should it become necessary. HBase stores the data in cells in decreasing order (using the timestamp), so a read will always find the most recent values first.

Columns in HBase belong to a column family. The column family name is used as a prefix to identify members of its family. For example, *fruits:apple* and *fruits:banana* are members of the *fruits* column family. HBase implementations are tuned at the column family level, so it is important to be mindful of how you are going to access the data and how big you expect the columns to be.

The rows in HBase tables also have a key associated with them. The structure of the key is very flexible. It can be a computed value, a string, or even another data structure. The key is used to control access to the cells in the row, and they are stored in order from low value to high value.

All of these features together make up the schema. The schema is defined and created before any data can be stored. Even so, tables can be altered and new column families can be added after the database is up and running. This extensibility is extremely useful when dealing with big data because you don't always know about the variety of your data streams.

Mining Big Data with Hive

Hive is a batch-oriented, data-warehousing layer built on the core elements of Hadoop (HDFS and MapReduce). It provides users who know SQL with a simple SQL-lite implementation called HiveQL without sacrificing access via mappers and reducers. With Hive, you can get the best of both worlds: SQL-like access to structured data and sophisticated big data analysis with MapReduce.

Unlike most data warehouses, Hive is not designed for quick responses to queries. In fact, queries can take several minutes or even hours depending on the complexity. As a result, Hive is best used for data mining and deeper analytics that do not require real-time behaviors. Because it relies on the Hadoop foundation, it is very extensible, scalable, and resilient, something that the average data warehouse is not.

Hive uses three mechanisms for data organization:

- ✔ **Tables:** Hive tables are the same as RDBMS tables consisting of rows and columns. Because Hive is layered on the Hadoop HDFS, tables are mapped to directories in the file system. In addition, Hive supports tables stored in other native file systems.

- ✔ **Partitions:** A Hive table can support one or more partitions. These partitions are mapped to subdirectories in the underlying file system and represent the distribution of data throughout the table. For example, if a table is called *autos,* with a key value of *12345* and a maker value *Ford,* the path to the partition would be /hivewh/autos/kv=12345/Ford.

- ✔ **Buckets:** In turn, data may be divided into buckets. Buckets are stored as files in the partition directory in the underlying file system. The buckets are based on the hash of a column in the table. In the preceding example, you might have a bucket called *Focus,* containing all the attributes of a Ford Focus auto.

Hive metadata is stored externally in the "metastore." The metastore is a relational database containing the detailed descriptions of the Hive schema, including column types, owners, key and value data, table statistics, and so on. The metastore is capable of syncing catalog data with other metadata services in the Hadoop ecosystem.

Hive supports an SQL-like language called HiveQL. HiveQL supports many of the SQL primitives, such as select, join, aggregate, union all, and so on. It also supports multitable queries and inserts by sharing the input data within a single HiveQL statement. HiveQL can be extended to support user-defined aggregation, column transformation, and embedded MapReduce scripts.

Interacting with the Hadoop Ecosystem

Writing programs or using specialty query languages are not the only ways you interact with the Hadoop ecosystem. IT teams that manage infrastructures need to control Hadoop and the big data applications created for it. As big data becomes mainstream, non-technical professionals will want to try to solve business problems with big data. Look at some examples from the Hadoop ecosystem that help these constituencies.

Pig and Pig Latin

The power and flexibility of Hadoop are immediately visible to software developers primarily because the Hadoop ecosystem was built by developers, for developers. However, not everyone is a software developer. Pig was designed to make Hadoop more approachable and usable by nondevelopers. Pig is an interactive, or script-based, execution environment supporting Pig Latin, a language used to express data flows. The Pig Latin language supports the loading and processing of input data with a series of operators that transform the input data and produce the desired output.

The Pig execution environment has two modes:

- **Local mode:** All scripts are run on a single machine. Hadoop MapReduce and HDFS are not required.

- **Hadoop:** Also called MapReduce mode, all scripts are run on a given Hadoop cluster.

Under the covers, Pig creates a set of *map* and *reduce* jobs. The user is absolved from the concerns of writing code, compiling, packaging, submitting, and retrieving the results. In many respects, Pig is analogous to SQL in the RDBMS world. The Pig Latin language provides an abstract way to get answers from big data by focusing on the data and not the structure of a custom software program. Pig makes prototyping very simple. For example, you can run a Pig script on a small representation of your big data environment to ensure that you are getting the desired results before you commit to processing all the data.

Pig programs can be run in three different ways, all of them compatible with local and Hadoop mode:

- ✔ **Script:** Simply a file containing Pig Latin commands, identified by the `.pig` suffix (for example, `file.pig` or `myscript.pig`). The commands are interpreted by Pig and executed in sequential order.

- ✔ **Grunt:** Grunt is a command interpreter. You can type Pig Latin on the grunt command line and Grunt will execute the command on your behalf. This is very useful for prototyping and "what if" scenarios.

- ✔ **Embedded:** Pig programs can be executed as part of a Java program.

Pig Latin has a very rich syntax. It supports operators for the following operations:

- ✔ Loading and storing of data
- ✔ Streaming data
- ✔ Filtering data
- ✔ Grouping and joining data
- ✔ Sorting data
- ✔ Combining and splitting data

Pig Latin also supports a wide variety of types, expressions, functions, diagnostic operators, macros, and file system commands.

To get more examples, visit the Pig website within Apache.com. It is a rich resource that will provide you with all the details: `http://pig.apache.org`.

Sqoop

Many businesses store information in RDBMSs and other data stores, so they need a way to move data back and forth from these data stores to Hadoop. While it is sometimes necessary to move the data in real time, it is most often necessary to load or unload data in bulk. Sqoop (SQL-to-Hadoop) is a tool that offers the capability to extract data from non-Hadoop data stores, transform the data into a form usable by Hadoop, and then load the data into HDFS. This process is called ETL, for Extract, Transform, and Load. While getting data into Hadoop is critical for processing using MapReduce, it is also critical to get data out of Hadoop and into an external data source for use in other kinds of application. Sqoop is able to do this as well.

Like Pig, Sqoop is a command-line interpreter. You type Sqoop commands into the interpreter and they are executed one at a time. Four key features are found in Sqoop:

- ✔ **Bulk import:** Sqoop can import individual tables or entire databases into HDFS. The data is stored in the native directories and files in the HDFS file system.

- ✔ **Direct input:** Sqoop can import and map SQL (relational) databases directly into Hive and HBase.

- ✔ **Data interaction:** Sqoop can generate Java classes so that you can interact with the data programmatically.

- ✔ **Data export:** Sqoop can export data directly from HDFS into a relational database using a target table definition based on the specifics of the target database.

Sqoop works by looking at the database you want to import and selecting an appropriate import function for the source data. After it recognizes the input, it then reads the metadata for the table (or database) and creates a class definition of your input requirements. You can force Sqoop to be very selective so that you get just the columns you are looking for before input rather than doing an entire input and then looking for your data. This can save considerable time. The actual import from the external database to HDFS is performed by a MapReduce job created behind the scenes by Sqoop.

Sqoop is another effective tool for nonprogrammers. The other important item to note is the reliance on underlying technologies like HDFS and MapReduce. You see this repeatedly throughout the element of the Hadoop ecosystem.

Zookeeper

Hadoop's greatest technique for addressing big data challenges is its capability to divide and conquer. After the problem has been divided, the conquering relies on the capability to employ distributed and parallel processing techniques across the Hadoop cluster. For some big data problems, the interactive tools are unable to provide the insights or timeliness required to make business decisions. In those cases, you need to create distributed applications to solve those big data problems. Zookeeper is Hadoop's way of coordinating all the elements of these distributed applications.

Zookeeper as a technology is actually simple, but its features are powerful. Arguably, it would be difficult, if not impossible, to create resilient, fault-tolerant distributed Hadoop applications without it. Some of the capabilities of Zookeeper are as follows:

- ✔ **Process synchronization:** Zookeeper coordinates the starting and stopping of multiple nodes in the cluster. This ensures that all processing occurs in the intended order. When an entire process group is complete, then and only then can subsequent processing occur.

- ✔ **Configuration management:** Zookeeper can be used to send configuration attributes to any or all nodes in the cluster. When processing is dependent on particular resources being available on all the nodes, Zookeeper ensures the consistency of the configurations.

- ✔ **Self-election:** Zookeeper understands the makeup of the cluster and can assign a "leader" role to one of the nodes. This leader/master handles all client requests on behalf of the cluster. Should the leader node fail, another leader will be elected from the remaining nodes.

- ✔ **Reliable messaging:** Even though workloads in Zookeeper are loosely coupled, you still have a need for communication between and among the nodes in the cluster specific to the distributed application. Zookeeper offers a publish/subscribe capability that allows the creation of a queue. This queue guarantees message delivery even in the case of a node failure.

Because Zookeeper is managing groups of nodes in service to a single distributed application, it is best implemented *across* racks. This is very different than the requirements for the cluster itself (within racks). The underlying reason is simple: Zookeeper needs to perform, be resilient, and be fault tolerant at a level above the cluster itself. Remember that a Hadoop cluster is already fault tolerant, so it will heal itself. Zookeeper just needs to worry about its own fault tolerance.

The Hadoop ecosystem and the supported commercial distributions are ever-changing. New tools and technologies are introduced, existing technologies are improved, and some technologies are retired by a (hopefully better) replacement. This one of the greatest advantages of open source. Another is the adoption of open source technologies by commercial companies. These companies enhance the products, making them better for everyone by offering support and services at a modest cost. This is how the Hadoop ecosystem has evolved and why it is a good choice for helping to solve your big data challenges.

Chapter 11

Appliances and Big Data Warehouses

The concept of the data warehouse originated almost 30 years ago. The data warehouse was intended to solve a big problem for customers that had many operational systems that were siloed. Increasingly, management wanted to replace inefficient decision-support systems with a more stream-lined model. Companies wanted to be able to have a single architectural model that would make it much easier to make business decisions. This approach, whether in the form of a full data warehouse or a more limited data mart, has been the norm. However, with the advent of big data, the data warehouse concept is now changing so that it can be applied to new use cases. The traditional data warehouse will continue to survive and thrive because it is very useful in analyzing historical operational data for decision making. However, new types of data warehouses will be optimized for the big data world. In this chapter, we give you a perspective on how the data ware-house has evolved to support the characteristics of big data.

Integrating Big Data with the Traditional Data Warehouse

Unlike traditional operational database systems and applications, the data warehouse was used by business line and financial analysts to help make decisions about the direction of a business strategy. Data had to be gathered from a variety of relational database sources and then ensured that the metadata was consistent, and that the data itself was clean and then well integrated. Bill Inmon, considered the father of the modern data warehouse, established a set of principles of the data warehouse, which included the following characteristics:

✔ It should be subject oriented.

✔ It should be organized so that related events are linked together.

✔ The information should be nonvolatile so that it cannot be inadvertently changed.

✔ Information in the warehouse should include all the applicable operational sources. The information should be stored in a way that has consistent definitions and the most up-to-date values.

Optimizing the data warehouse

Data warehouses have traditionally supported structured data and have been closely tied to the operational and transactional systems of the enterprise. These carefully constructed systems are now in the midst of significant changes as organizations try to expand and modify the data warehouse so that it can remain relevant in the new world of big data. While the worlds of big data and the data warehouse will intersect, they are unlikely to merge anytime soon. You can think of the traditional data warehouse as a system of record for business intelligence, much like a customer relationship management (CRM) system or an accounting system. These systems are highly structured and optimized for specific purposes. In addition, these systems of record tend to be highly centralized. Figure 11-1 shows a typical approach to data flows with warehouses and marts.

Differentiating big data structures from data warehouse data

Organizations will inevitably continue to use data warehouses to manage the type of structured and operational data that characterizes systems of record. These data warehouses will still provide business analysts with the capability to analyze key data, trends, and so on. However, the advent of big data is both challenging the role of the data warehouse and providing a complementary approach. You might want to think about the relationship between the data warehouse and big data as merging to become a hybrid structure. In this hybrid model, the highly structured optimized operational data remains in the tightly controlled data warehouse, while the data that is highly distributed and subject to change in real time is controlled by a Hadoop-based (or similar NoSQL) infrastructure.

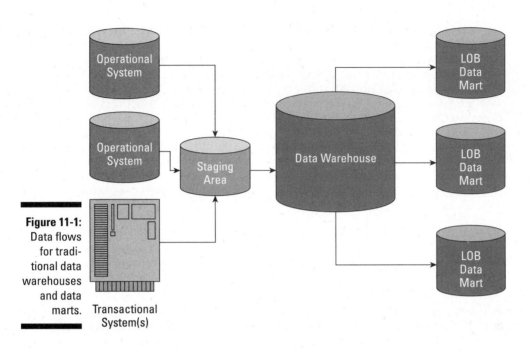

Figure 11-1:
Data flows
for tradi-
tional data
warehouses
and data
marts.

It is inevitable that operational and structured data will have to interact in the world of big data, where the information sources have not (necessarily) been cleansed or profiled. Increasingly, organizations are understanding that they have a business requirement to be able to combine traditional data warehouses with their historical business data sources with less structured and vetted big data sources. A hybrid approach supporting traditional and big data sources can help to accomplish these business goals.

Examining a hybrid process case study

Imagine that you are in charge of data management for an online travel site. Your company offers a wide range of services, including air travel, cruises, hotels, resorts, and more. The company offers these services in many different ways. For example, a public website is available that includes reviews of various trips, hotels, and so on. This website has relationships with various related companies that offer services such as trip insurance and local tour services. Specialized sites exist for different countries. In addition, a corporate travel service is customized for large companies. Needless to say, this travel company has to manage a huge volume of data and be able to present it differently depending on who is interacting with it. A data warehouse is used by the company to track its transactions and operational data. However, the data warehouse does not keep track of web traffic. Therefore, the company used web analytics solutions to capture customer interactions.

For example, what did the customer click on? What offers were made available to different customers, and which ones did they select? Was price the most important factor? Did customers like to be able to design their own travel packages, or were they more likely to purchase predesigned tours? Were some locations attracting more customers while other geographies were less popular? Which partners were attracting the most revenue?

While much of this data could be incredibly valuable for those planning for the future, it was not practical for the company to store all or most of this data in the data warehouse. As a result, most of this data was thrown away after it was examined. Soon the company realized that it would be valuable to keep as much of this data as possible to understand the changes and nuances of the business.

The information management team decided that rather than building a customized data warehouse to store this data, it would leverage a Hadoop distributed computing approach based on commodity servers. Now the company is able to keep all the data from the web interactions. This data is now stored across a vast array of servers running Hadoop and MapReduce. Leveraging tools such as Flume and Sqoop, the team is able to move data into and out of Hadoop and push it into a relational model so that it can be queried with familiar SQL tools.

Now the company is able to change its business offerings quickly when it is apparent that a demographic group of customers wants certain new services. The company can also predict changes in airfare that will impact how packages are priced. Some of this data remains in the Hadoop framework environment and is updated in near real time. Other data elements are cleansed and then are moved into the data warehouse so that the data is used to compare the historical information about customers and partners to the new data. The existing warehouse provides the context for the business while the Hadoop environment tracks what is happening on a minute-to-minute basis. The combination of the system-of-record approach with the data warehouse with the dynamic big data system provides a tremendous opportunity for the company to continue to evolve its business based on analyzing the massive amount of data generated by its web environments. Figure 11-2 depicts an example approach to hybridizing traditional and big data warehousing.

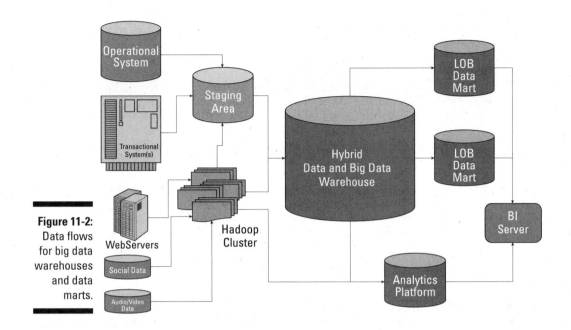

Figure 11-2:
Data flows
for big data
warehouses
and data
marts.

Big Data Analysis and the Data Warehouse

From the preceding examples, you find value in bringing the capabilities of the data warehouse and the big data environment together. You need to create a hybrid environment where big data can work hand in hand with the data warehouse. First it is important to recognize that the data warehouse as it is designed today will not change in the short term. Therefore, it is more pragmatic to use the data warehouse for what it has been designed to do — provide a well-vetted version of the truth about a topic that the business wants to analyze. The warehouse might include information about a particular company's product line, its customers, its suppliers, and the details of a year's worth of transactions. The information managed in the data warehouse or a departmental data mart has been carefully constructed so that metadata is accurate. With the growth of new web-based information, it is practical and often necessary to analyze this massive amount of data in context with historical data. This is where the hybrid model comes in.

Certain aspects of marrying the data warehouse with big data can be relatively easy. For example, many of the big data sources come from sources that include their own well-designed metadata. Complex e-commerce sites include well-defined data elements (customer, price, and so on). Therefore, when conducting analysis between the warehouse and the big data source, the information management organization is working with two data sets with carefully designed metadata models that have to be rationalized.

Of course, in some situations, the information sources lack explicit metadata. Before an analyst can combine the historical transactional data with the less structured big data, work has to be done. Typically, initial analysis of petabytes of data will reveal interesting patterns that can help predict subtle changes in business or potential solutions to a patient's diagnosis. The initial analysis can be completed leveraging tools like MapReduce with the Hadoop distributed file system framework. At this point, you can begin to understand whether it is able to help evaluate the problem being addressed. In the process of analysis, it is just as important to eliminate unnecessary data as it is to identify data relevant to the business context. When this phase is complete, the remaining data needs to be transformed so that metadata definitions are precise. In this way, when the big data is combined with traditional, historical data from the warehouse, the results will be accurate and meaningful.

The integration lynchpin

To make the process we describe practical requires a well-defined data integration strategy. We cover the issue of data integration in detail in Chapter 15. While data integration is a critical element of managing big data, it is equally important when creating a hybrid analysis with the data warehouse. In fact, the process of extracting data and transforming it in a hybrid environment is very similar to how this process is executed within a traditional data warehouse. In the data warehouse, data is extracted from traditional source systems such as CRM or ERP systems. It is critical that elements from these various systems be correctly matched.

Rethinking extraction, transformation, and loading

In the data warehouse, you often find a combination of relational database tables, flat files, and nonrelational sources. A well-constructed data warehouse will be architected so that the data is converted into a common format, allowing queries to be processed accurately and consistently. The extracted files must be transformed to match the business rules and processes of the subject area that the data warehouse is designed to analyze. For example, it is common to have the concept of a purchase price as a calculated field in a data warehouse because it will be used in many of the queries used by management. Processes may exist within the warehouse to validate that the calculations are accurate based on business rules. While these ideas are foundational to the data warehouse, it is also a key principle of marrying the warehouse to big data. In other words, the data has to be extracted from the big data sources so that these sources can safely work together and produce meaningful results. In addition, the sources have to be transformed so that they are helpful in analyzing the relationship between the historical data and the more dynamic and real-time data that comes from big data sources.

Loading information in the big data model will be different than what you would expect in a traditional data warehousing model. In the data warehouse, after data has been codified, it is never changed. A typical data warehouse will provide the business with a snapshot of data based on the need to analyze a particular business issue that requires monitoring, such as inventory or sales quotas. Loading information can be dramatically different with big data. The distributed structure of big data will often lead organizations to first load data into a series of nodes and then perform the extraction and transformation. When creating a hybrid of the traditional data warehouse and the big data environment, the distributed nature of the big data environment can dramatically change the capability of organizations to analyze huge volumes of data in context with the business.

Changing the Role of the Data Warehouse

It is useful to think about the similarities and differences between the way data is managed in the traditional data warehouse and when the warehouse is combined with big data.

Similarities between the two data management methods include

- ✔ Requirements for common data definitions
- ✔ Requirements to extract and transform key data sources
- ✔ The need to conform to required business processes and rules

Differences between the traditional data warehouse and big data include

✔ The distributed computing model of big data will be essential to allowing the hybrid model to be operational.

✔ The big data analysis will be the primary focus of the efforts, while the traditional data warehouse will be used to add historical and transactional business context.

Changing Deployment Models in the Big Data Era

With the advent of big data, the deployment models for managing data are changing. The traditional data warehouse is typically implemented on a single, large system within the data center. The costs of this model have led organizations to optimize these warehouses and limit the scope and size of the data being managed. However, when organizations want to leverage the massive amount of information generated by big data sources, the limitations of the traditional models no longer work. Therefore, the data warehouse appliance has become a practical method of creating an optimized environment to support the transition to new information management.

The appliance model

When companies need to combine their data warehouse structure with big data, the appliance model can be one answer to the problem of scaling. Typically, the appliance is an integrated system that incorporates hardware (typically in a rack) that is optimized for data storage and management. Because they are self-contained, appliances can be relatively easy and quick to implement, as well as offer lower costs to operation and maintain, Therefore, the system will be preloaded with a relational database, the Hadoop framework, MapReduce, and many of the tools that help ingest and organize data from a variety of sources. It also incorporates analytical engines and tools to simplify the process of analyzing data from multiple sources. The appliance is therefore a single-purpose system that typically includes interfaces to make it easier to connect to an existing data warehouse.

The cloud model

The cloud is becoming a compelling platform to manage big data and can be used in a hybrid environment with on-premises environments. Some of the new innovations in loading and transferring data are already changing the potential viability of the cloud as a big data warehousing platform. For example, Aspera, a company that specializes in fast data transferring between networks, is partnering with Amazon.com to offer cloud data management services. Other vendors such as FileCatalyst and Data Expedition are also focused on this market. In essence, this technology category leverages the network and optimizes it for the purpose of moving files with reduced latency. As this problem of latency in data transfer continues to evolve, it will be the norm to store big data systems in the cloud that can interact with a data warehouse that is also cloud based or a warehouse that sits in the data center.

Examining the Future of Data Warehouses

The data warehouse market has indeed begun to change and evolve with the advent of big data. In the past, it was simply not economical for companies to store the massive amount of data from a large number of systems of record. The lack of cost-effective and practical distributed computing architectures meant that a data warehouse had to be designed so that it could be optimized to operate on a single unified system. Therefore, data warehouses were purpose-built to address a single topic. In addition, the warehouse had to be carefully vetted so that data was precisely defined and managed. This approach has made data warehouses accurate and useful for the business to query these data sources. However, this same level of control and precision has made it difficult to provide the business with an environment that can leverage much more dynamic big data sources. The data warehouse will evolve slowly.

Data warehouses and data marts will continue to be optimized for business analysis. However, a new generation of offerings will combine historical and highly structured data stores with different stages of big data stores. First, big data stores will provide the capability to analyze huge volumes of data in near real time. Second, a big data store will take the results of an analysis and provide a mechanism to match the metadata of the big data analysis to the requirements of the data warehouse.

Part IV
Analytics and Big Data

Big Data Analysis

Analysis Type	Description
Basic analytics for insight	Slicing and dicing of data, reporting, simple visualizations, basic monitoring.
Advanced analytics for insight	More complex analysis such as predictive modeling and other pattern-matching techniques.
Operationalized analytics	Analytics become part of the business process.
Monetized analytics	Analytics are utilized to directly drive revenue.

Read how to get results with big data at www.dummies.com/extras/bigdata.

In this part . . .

- Use big data in reporting, visualization, and predictive analysis.
- Study structured analytics case studies.
- Explore unstructured data.
- Define and demonstrate text analytics.
- Integrate unstructured and structured data.
- Understand models for leveraging big data.

Chapter 12

Defining Big Data Analytics

- -

- -

*U*p until this point, we've been spending a lot of time describing the infrastructure you need to support your big data initiatives. However, because big data is most useful if you can do something with it, the question becomes, how do you analyze it?

Companies like Amazon and Google are masters at analyzing big data. And they use the resulting knowledge to gain a competitive advantage. Just think about Amazon's recommendation engine. The company takes all your buying history together with what it knows about you, your buying patterns, and the buying patterns of people like you to come up with some pretty good suggestions. It is a marketing machine, and its big data analytics capabilities have made it extremely successful.

The capability to analyze big data provides unique opportunities for your organization as well. You'll be able to expand the kind of analysis you can do. Instead of being limited to sampling large data sets, you can now utilize much more detailed and complete data to do your analysis. However, analyzing big data can also be challenging. Changing algorithms and technology, even for basic data analysis, often has to be addressed with big data.

So, in this chapter, we introduce big data analytics. We focus on the kinds of analysis you can do with big data. We also discuss some of the differences you need to think about between big data analytics and traditional analytics. In this chapter, we focus primarily on structured data analysis, although unstructured data is a very important part of the big data picture. We describe that in the next chapter.

Using Big Data to Get Results

The first question that you need to ask yourself before you dive into big data analysis is what problem are you trying to solve? You may not even be sure of what you are looking for. You know you have lots of data that you think you can get valuable insight from. And certainly, patterns can emerge from that data before you understand why they are there.

If you think about it though, you're sure to have an idea of what you're interested in. For instance, are you interested in predicting customer behavior to prevent churn? Do you want to analyze the driving patterns of your customers for insurance premium purposes? Are you interested in looking at your system log data to ultimately predict when problems might occur? The kind of high-level problem is going to drive the analytics you decide to use. Alternately, if you're not exactly sure of the business problem you're trying to solve, maybe you need to look at areas in your business that need improvement. Even an analytics-driven strategy — targeted at the right area — can provide useful results with big data.

When it comes to analytics, you might consider a range of possible kinds, which are outlined in Table 12-1.

Table 12-1	Big Data Analysis
Analysis Type	*Description*
Basic analytics for insight	Slicing and dicing of data, reporting, simple visualizations, basic monitoring.
Advanced analytics for insight	More complex analysis such as predictive modeling and other pattern-matching techniques.
Operationalized analytics	Analytics become part of the business process.
Monetized analytics	Analytics are utilized to directly drive revenue.

Before you start analyzing your data, make sure that you've dealt with all pre-processing issues. These are covered in detail in Chapter 15.

Basic analytics

Basic analytics can be used to explore your data, if you're not sure what you have, but you think something is of value. This might include simple visualizations or simple statistics. Basic analysis is often used when you have large amounts of disparate data. Here are some examples:

- ✔ **Slicing and dicing:** *Slicing and dicing* refers to breaking down your data into smaller sets of data that are easier to explore. For example, you might have a scientific data set of water column data from many different locations that contains numerous variables captured from multiple sensors. Attributes might include temperature, pressure, transparency, dissolved oxygen, pH, salinity, and so on, collected over time. You might want some simple graphs or plots that let you explore your data across different dimensions, such as temperature versus pH or transparency versus salinity. You might want some basic statistics such as average or range for each attribute, from each height, for the time period. The point is that you might use this basic type of exploration of the variables to ask specific questions in your problem space. The difference between this kind of analysis and what happens in a basic business intelligence system is that you're dealing with huge volumes of data where you might not know how much query space you'll need to examine it and you're probably going to want to run computations in real time.

- ✔ **Basic monitoring:** You might also want to monitor large volumes of data in real time. For example, you might want to monitor the water column attributes in the preceding example every second for an extended period of time from hundreds of locations and at varying heights in the water column. This would produce a huge data set. Or, you might be interested in monitoring the buzz associated with your product every minute when you launch an ad campaign. Whereas the water column data set might produce a large amount of relatively structured time-sensitive data, the social media campaign is going to produce large amounts of disparate kinds of data from multiple sources across the Internet.

- ✔ **Anomaly identification:** You might want to identify anomalies, such as an event where the actual observation differs from what you expected, in your data because that may clue you in that something is going wrong with your organization, manufacturing process, and so on. For example, you might want to analyze the records for your manufacturing operation to determine whether one kind of machine, or one operator, has a higher incidence of a certain kind of problem. This might involve some simple statistics like moving averages triggered by an alert from the problematic machine.

Advanced analytics

Advanced analytics provides algorithms for complex analysis of either structured or unstructured data. It includes sophisticated statistical models, machine learning, neural networks, text analytics (described in detail in Chapter 13), and other advanced data-mining techniques. (See the sidebar

"What is data mining?" later in this chapter, for more detail on data mining.) Among its many use cases, advanced analytics can be deployed to find patterns in data, prediction, forecasting, and complex event processing.

While advanced analytics has been used by statisticians and mathematicians for decades, it was not as big a part of the analytics landscape as it is today. Consider that 20 years ago, statisticians at companies were able to predict who might drop a service using advanced survival analysis or machine learning techniques. However, it was difficult to persuade other people in the organization to understand exactly what this meant and how it could be used to provide a competitive advantage. For one thing, it was difficult to obtain the computational power needed to interpret data that kept changing through time.

Today, advanced analytics is becoming more mainstream. With increases in computational power, improved data infrastructure, new algorithm development, and the need to obtain better insight from increasingly vast amounts of data, companies are pushing toward utilizing advanced analytics as part of their decision-making process. Businesses realize that better insights can provide a superior competitive position.

Here are a few examples of advanced analytics for big data:

- **Predictive modeling:** Predictive modeling is one of the most popular big data advanced analytics use cases. A predictive model is a statistical or data-mining solution consisting of algorithms and techniques that can be used on both structured and unstructured data (together or individually) to determine future outcomes. For example, a telecommunications company might use a predictive model to predict customers who might drop its service. In the big data world, you might have large numbers of predictive attributes across huge amounts of observations. Whereas in the past, it might have taken hours (or longer) to run a predictive model, with a large amount of data on your desktop, you might be able to now run it iteratively hundreds of times if you have a big data infrastructure in place.

- **Text analytics:** Unstructured data is such a big part of big data, so text analytics — the process of analyzing unstructured text, extracting relevant information, and transforming it into structured information that can then be leveraged in various ways — has become an important component of the big data ecosystem. The analysis and extraction processes used in text analytics take advantage of techniques that originated in computational linguistics, statistics, and other computer science disciplines. Text analytics is being used in all sorts of analysis, from predicting churn, to fraud, and to social media analytics. It is so important that we devote a considerable part of Chapter 13 to this issue of text analytics.

- **Other statistical and data-mining algorithms:** This may include advanced forecasting, optimization, cluster analysis for segmentation or even microsegmentation, or affinity analysis.

What is data mining?

Data mining involves exploring and analyzing large amounts of data to find patterns in that data. The techniques came out of the fields of statistics and artificial intelligence (AI), with a bit of database management thrown into the mix. Generally, the goal of the data mining is either classification or prediction. In classification, the idea is to sort data into groups. For example, a marketer might be interested in the characteristics of those who responded versus who didn't respond to a promotion. These are two classes. In prediction, the idea is to predict the value of a continuous (that is, nondiscrete) variable. For example, a marketer might be interested in predicting those who *will* respond to a promotion.

Typical algorithms used in data mining include the following:

- **Classification trees:** A popular data-mining technique that is used to classify a dependent categorical variable based on measurements of one or more predictor variables. The result is a tree with nodes and links between the nodes that can be read to form if-then rules.

- **Logistic regression:** A statistical technique that is a variant of standard regression but extends the concept to deal with classification. It produces a formula that predicts the probability of the occurrence as a function of the independent variables.

- **Neural networks:** A software algorithm that is modeled after the parallel architecture of animal brains. The network consists of input nodes, hidden layers, and output nodes. Each of the units is assigned a weight. Data is given to the input node, and by a system of trial and error, the algorithm adjusts the weights until it meets a certain stopping criteria. Some people have likened this to a black–box (you don't necessarily know what is going on inside) approach.

- **Clustering techniques like K-nearest neighbors:** A technique that identifies groups of similar records. The K-nearest neighbor technique calculates the distances between the record and points in the historical (training) data. It then assigns this record to the class of its nearest neighbor in a data set.

Here's a classification tree example. Consider the situation where a telephone company wants to determine which residential customers are likely to disconnect their service. The telephone company has information consisting of the following attributes: how long the person has had the service, how much he spends on the service, whether he has had problems with the service, whether he has the best calling plan for his needs, where he lives, how old he is, whether he has other services bundled together with his calling plan, competitive information concerning other carriers plans, and whether he still has the service or has disconnected the service. Of course, you can find many more attributes than this. The last attribute is the outcome variable; this is what the software will use to classify the customers into one of the two groups — perhaps called stayers and flight risks.

The data set is broken into training data and a test data set. The training data consists of observations (called attributes) and an outcome variable (binary in the case of a classification model) — in this case, the stayers or the flight risks. The algorithm is run over the training data and comes up with a tree that can be read like a series of rules. For example, if the customers have been with the company for more than ten years and they are over 55 years old, they are likely to remain as loyal customers.

(continued)

(continued)

> These rules are then run over the test data set to determine how good this model is on "new data." Accuracy measures are provided for the model. For example, a popular technique is the confusion matrix. This matrix is a table that provides information about how many cases were correctly versus incorrectly classified. If the model looks good, it can be deployed on other data, as it is available (that is, using it to predict new cases of flight risk). Based on the model, the company might decide, for example, to send out special offers to those customers whom it thinks are flight risks.

Advanced analytics doesn't require big data. However, being able to apply advanced analytics with big data can provide some important results.

Operationalized analytics

When you operationalize analytics, you make them part of a business process. For example, statisticians at an insurance company might build a model that predicts the likelihood of a claim being fraudulent. The model, along with some decision rules, could be included in the company's claims-processing system to flag claims with a high probability of fraud. These claims would be sent to an investigation unit for further review. In other cases, the model itself might not be as apparent to the end user. For example, a model could be built to predict customers who are good targets for upselling when they call into a call center. The call center agent, while on the phone with the customer, would receive a message on specific additional products to sell to this customer. The agent might not even know that a predictive model was working behind the scenes to make this recommendation.

Monetizing analytics

Analytics can be used to optimize your business to create better decisions and drive bottom- and top-line revenue. However, big data analytics can also be used to derive revenue above and beyond the insights it provides just for your own department or company. You might be able to assemble a unique data set that is valuable to other companies, as well. For example, credit card providers take the data they assemble to offer value-added analytics products. Likewise, with financial institutions. Telecommunications companies are beginning to sell location-based insights to retailers. The idea is that various sources of data, such as billing data, location data, text-messaging data, or web-browsing data can be used together or separately to make inferences about customer behavior patterns that retailers would find useful. As a regulated industry, they must do so in compliance with legislation and privacy policies.

Modifying Business Intelligence Products to Handle Big Data

Traditional business intelligence products weren't really designed to handle big data. They were designed to work with highly structured, well-understood data, often stored in a relational data repository and displayed on your desktop or laptop computer. This traditional business intelligence analysis is typically applied to snapshots of data rather than the entire amount of data available. So what's different when you start to analyze big data?

Data

As we discuss in Chapter 2, big data consists of structured, semi-structured, and unstructured data. You often have a lot of it, and it can be quite complex. When you think about analyzing it, you need to be aware of the potential characteristics of your data:

- ✔ **It can come from untrusted sources.** Big data analysis often involves aggregating data from various sources. These may include both internal and external data sources. How trustworthy are these external sources of information? For example, how trustworthy is social media data like a tweet? The information may be coming from an unverified source. The integrity of this data needs to be considered in the analysis. We talk more about big data security and governance in Chapter 19.

- ✔ **It can be dirty.** Dirty data refers to inaccurate, incomplete, or erroneous data. This may include the misspelling of words; a sensor that is broken, not properly calibrated, or corrupted in some way; or even duplicated data. Data scientists debate about where to clean the data — either close to the source or in real time. Of course, one school of thought says that the dirty data should not be cleaned at all because it may contain interesting outliers. The cleansing strategy will probably depend on the source and type of data and the goal of your analysis. For example, if you're developing a spam filter, the goal is to detect the bad elements in the data, so you would not want to clean it.

- ✔ **The signal-to-noise ratio can be low.** In other words, the signal (usable information) may only be a tiny percent of the data; the noise is the rest. Being able to extract a tiny signal from noisy data is part of the benefit of big data analytics, but you need to be aware that the signal may indeed be small.

- ✔ **It can be real-time.** In many cases, you'll be trying to analyze real-time data streams. We cover a whole set of complexities about how to analyze this data in Chapter 16.

Big data governance is going to be an important part of the analytics equation. Underneath business analytics, enhancements will need to be made to governance solutions to ensure the veracity coming from the new data sources, especially as it is being combined with existing trusted data stored in a warehouse. Data security and privacy solutions also need to be enhanced to support managing/governing big data stored within new technologies. Governance and security and so important that we devote Chapter 19 to it.

Analytical algorithms

When you're considering big data analytics, you need to be aware that when you expand beyond the desktop, the algorithms you use often need to be *refactored,* changing the internal code without affecting its external functioning. The beauty of a big data infrastructure is that you can run a model that used to take hours or days in minutes. This lets you iterate on the model hundreds of times over. However, if you're running a regression on a billion rows of data across a distributed environment, you need to consider the resource requirements relating to the volume of data and its location in the cluster. Your algorithms need to be data aware.

Additionally, vendors are starting to offer a new breed of analytics designed to be placed close to the big data sources to analyze data in place rather than first having to store it and then analyze it. This approach of running analytics closer to the data sources minimizes the amount of stored data by retaining only the high-value data. It is also enables you to analyze the data sooner, looking for key events, which is critical for real-time decision making. We discuss these kinds of techniques in more detail in Chapter 14.

Of course, analytics will continue to evolve. For example, you may need real-time visualization capabilities to display real-time data that is continuously changing. How do you practically plot a billion points on a graph plot? Or, how do you work with the predictive algorithms so that they perform fast enough and deep enough analysis to utilize an ever-expanding, complex data set? This is an area of active research.

Infrastructure support

We spend a good deal of this book talking about the infrastructure needed to support big data, so we don't go into detail about that here. You might want to turn to Chapter 4 for more details on infrastructure issues. Suffice it to say that if you're looking for a platform, it needs to achieve the following:

- **Integrate technologies:** The infrastructure needs to integrate new big data technologies with traditional technologies to be able to process all kinds of big data and make it consumable by traditional analytics.

- **Store large amounts of disparate data:** An enterprise-hardened Hadoop system may be needed that can process/store/manage large amounts of data at rest, whether it is structured, semi-structured, or unstructured.

- **Process data in motion:** A stream-computing capability may be needed to process data in motion that is continuously generated by sensors, smart devices, video, audio, and logs to support real-time decision making.

- **Warehouse data:** You may need a solution optimized for operational or deep analytical workloads to store and manage the growing amounts of trusted data.

And of course, you need the capability to integrate the data you already have in place along with the results of the big data analysis.

Studying Big Data Analytics Examples

Big data analytics has many different use cases. We mention examples throughout this book, but we now look at a few others from Internet companies and others.

Orbitz

If you've ever looked for deals on travel, you've probably been to sites like Orbitz (www.orbitz.com). The company was established in 1999, and its website went live in 2001. Users of Orbitz perform over a million searches a day, and the company collects hundreds of gigabytes of raw data each day from these searches. Orbitz realized that it might have useful information in the web log files that it was collecting from its web analytics software that contained information about consumer interaction with its site.

In particular, it was interested to see whether it could identify consumer preferences to determine the best-performing hotels to display to users so that it could increase conversions (bookings). It had not been utilizing this data in the past because it was too expensive to store all of it. It implemented

Hadoop and Hive running on commodity hardware to help. Hadoop provided the distributed file system and Hive provided an SQL-type interface. It took a series of steps to put the data into Hive. After the data was in Hive, the company used *machine learning* — a data-driven (and data-mining; see the sidebar earlier in this chapter) approach to unearthing patterns in data and helping to analyze the data. For more details about Hadoop and Hive, turn to Chapters 9 and 10.

Nokia

Nokia provides wireless communication devices and services. The company believes that its data is a strategic asset. Its big data analytics service includes a multipetabyte platform that executes over tens of thousands of jobs each day. This includes utilizing advanced analytics over terabytes of streaming data. For example, the company wants to understand how people interact with its different applications on its phones. Nokia wants to understand what features customers use, how they use a feature, and how they move from feature to feature and whether they get lost in the application as they are using it. This level of detail helps the company lay out new features for its applications and improve customer retention.

NASA

NASA is using predictive models to analyze safety data on aircrafts. It wants to understand whether the introduction of a new technology into an aircraft will make a dramatic impact in safety. Needless to say, NASA is dealing with a massive amount of data. Each airplane each day is recording a *thousand* parameters every second for every flight. Some of this data is streaming. The company also receives text data from reports written by pilots and other crew members. NASA also throws weather data (that changes in time and space) into the mix. The data scientists there are looking to predict outcomes — for example, what pattern indicates a possible accident or incident.

Big Data Analytics Solutions

A number of vendors on the market today support big data solutions. Here is a listing of a few solutions that you may find interesting:

- ✔ IBM (www.ibm.com) is taking an enterprise approach to big data and integrating across the platform including embedding/bundling its analytics. Its products include a warehouse (InfoSphere warehouse) that has its own built-in data-mining and cubing capability. Its new PureData Systems (a packaging of advanced analytics technology into an integrated systems platform) includes many packaged analytical integrations. Its InfoSphere Streams product is tightly integrated with its Statistical Package for the Social Sciences (SPSS) statistical software to support real-time predictive analytics, including the capability to dynamically update models based on real-time data. It is bundling a limited-use license of Cognos Business Intelligence with its key big data platform capabilities (enterprise-class Hadoop, stream computing, and warehouse solutions).

- ✔ SAS (www.sas.com) provides multiple approaches to analyze big data via its high-performance analytics infrastructure and its statistical software. SAS provides several distributed processing options. These include in-database analytics, in-memory analytics, and grid computing. Deployments can be on-site or in the cloud.

- ✔ Tableau (www.tableausoftware.com), a business analytics and data visualization software company, offers its visualization capabilities to run on top appliances and other infrastructure offered by a range of big data partners, including Cirro, EMC Greenplum, Karmasphere, Teradata/ Aster, HP Vertica, Hortonworks, ParAccel, IBM Netezza, and a host of others.

- ✔ Oracle (www.oracle.com) offers a range of tools to complement its big data platform called Oracle Exadata. These include advanced analytics via the R programming language, as well as an in-memory database option with Oracle's Exalytics in-memory machine and Oracle's data warehouse. Exadata is integrated with its hardware platform.

- ✔ Pentaho (www.pentaho.com) provides open source business analytics via a community and enterprise edition. Pentaho supports the leading Hadoop-based distributions and supports native capabilities, such as MapR's NFS high-performance mountable file system.

Chapter 13

Understanding Text Analytics and Big Data

In This Chapter

▶ Exploring the different types of unstructured data

▶ Defining text analytics

▶ Unstructured analytics use cases

▶ Putting unstructured data together with structured data

▶ Text analytics tools for big data

*M*ost data is unstructured. Unstructured data includes information stored internally, such as documents, e-mails, and customer correspondence, as well as external information sources that are important to your organization, such as tweets, blogs, YouTube videos, and satellite imagery. The amount and variety of this data are growing rapidly. Increasingly, companies want to take advantage of this wealth of data to understand the implications for their business today and in the future.

While image and audio analysis are still in the early adopter stage, text analytics is evolving into a mainstream technology. Here's an example of how one company was able to leverage its text data to support business decision making. A large automobile manufacturer needed to improve quality problems with its cars. It discovered that by analyzing the text from its repair partners, it could identify quality problems with its cars as they enter the marketplace. The company views this analysis as an early warning system. The earlier it can identify problems, the more changes it can make on the factory floor and the fewer customers will be dissatisfied. Prior to using text analytics, the company mined information from its line of business systems, including part numbers and defect codes. This worked well enough for many years, but only for problems the company already knew existed. The traditional system could not reveal hidden issues that were well known to the people who were interacting with customers.

Sounds exciting, right? In fact, text analytics is being used in a wide variety of big data use cases from social media analysis to warranty analysis to fraud analysis. In addition, businesses are increasingly beginning to analyze a merge view of structured and unstructured data together to get a full picture. In this chapter, we delve into this technology and provide an in-depth example of how it works. We also provide you with some other use cases of text analytics in action, including the capability to merge unstructured data with structured data. We end the chapter with the names of some vendors that are providing text analytics tools for big data.

Exploring Unstructured Data

What sets unstructured data apart from structured data is that its structure is unpredictable. As we mention in Chapter 2, some people believe that the term *unstructured data* is misleading because each text source may contain its own specific structure or formatting based on the software that created it. In fact, it is the content of the document that is really unstructured.

Just think about the kinds of text that are out there and the structure that might be associated with each:

✔ **Documents:**

In return for a loan that I have received, I promise to pay $2,000 (this amount is called *principal*), plus interest, to the order of the lender. The lender is First Bank. I will make all payments under this note in the form of cash, check, or money order. I understand that the lender may transfer this note. The lender or anyone who takes this note by transfer and who is entitled . . .

✔ **E-mails:**

Hi Sam. How are you coming with the chapter on big data for the *For Dummies* book? It is due on Friday.

Joanne

✔ **Log files:**

222.222.222.222- - [08/Oct/2012:11:11:54 -0400] "GET / HTTP/1.1" 200 10801 "http://www.google.com/search?q=log+analyzer&ie=..... .

✔ **Tweets:**

#Big data is the future of data!

✔ **Facebook posts:**

LOL. What are you doing later? BFF

Clearly, some of these examples have more structure than others. For instance, a bank loan note has some structure in terms of sentences and the template it might follow. An e-mail might have little structure. A tweet or a Facebook message might have strange abbreviations or characters. A log file might have its own structure.

So, the question is, how do you analyze this disparate kind of unstructured text data?

Understanding Text Analytics

Numerous methods exist for analyzing unstructured data. Historically, these techniques came out of technical areas such as Natural Language Processing (NLP), knowledge discovery, data mining, information retrieval, and statistics. *Text analytics* is the process of analyzing unstructured text, extracting relevant information, and transforming it into structured information that can then be leveraged in various ways. The analysis and extraction processes take advantage of techniques that originated in computational linguistics, statistics, and other computer science disciplines.

Sometimes an example can help to explain a complex topic. Suppose that you work for the marketing department in a wireless phone company. You've just launched two new calling plans — Plan A and Plan B — and you are not getting the uptake you wanted on Plan A. The unstructured text from the call center notes might give you some insight as to why this happened. Figure 13-1 illustrates some of the call center notes.

Customer XYZ called about Plan A promotion. Explained plan. Customer thinks roll-over minutes should be included.

Customer ABC called about Plan A promotion. Customer thought it was ridiculous that roll-over minutes were not in plan.

Potential called about Plan A promotion. Said that plan was expensive.

Potential called about Plan A promotion. Said that 4GB data not enough.

Customer XYT called about Plan A promotion. Said that data plan was insufficient and stupid.

Figure 13-1: Sample call center records.

The underlined words provide the information you might need to understand why Plan A isn't gaining rapid adoption. For example, the entity Plan A appears throughout the call center notes, indicating that the reports mention the plan. The terms *roll-over minutes, 4GB data, data plan,* and *expensive* are evidence that an issue exists with roll-over minutes, the data plan, and the price. Words like *ridiculous* and *stupid* provide insight into the caller sentiment, which in this case is negative.

The text analytics process uses various algorithms, such as understanding sentence structure, to analyze the unstructured text and then extract information, and transform that information into structured data. The structured data extracted from the unstructured text is illustrated in Table 13-1.

Table 13-1	Making Structured Data from Unstructured Text		
Identifier	*Entity*	*Issue*	*Sentiment*
Cust XYZ	Plan A	Roll-over minutes	Neutral
Cust ABC	Plan A	Roll-over minutes	Negative
XXXX	Plan A	Expensive	Neutral
XXXX	Plan A	Data plan	Neutral
Cust XYT	Plan A	Data plan	Negative

You may look at this and say, "But I could have figured that out by looking at the call center records." However, these are just a small subset of the information being recorded by thousands of call center agents. Each individual agent cannot possibly sense a broad trend regarding the problem with each plan being offered by the company. Agents do not have the time or requirement to share this information across all the other call center agents who may be getting similar numbers of calls about Plan A. However, after this information is aggregated and processed using text analytics algorithms, a trend may emerge from this unstructured data. That's what makes text analytics so powerful.

The difference between text analytics and search

Notice that we are focusing on extracting text, not on keyword search. Search is about retrieving a document based on what end users already know they are looking for. Text analytics is about discovering information. While text analytics differs from search, it can augment search techniques. For example, text analytics combined with search can be used to provide better categorization or classification of documents and to produce abstracts or summaries of documents.

Table 13-2 illustrates four technologies: query, data mining, search, and text analytics. On the left side of the table are query and search, which are both about retrieval. For example, an end user could query a database to find out how many customers stopped using the company's services in the past month. The query would return a single number. Only by asking more and different queries will the end user get the information required to determine why customers are leaving. Likewise, keyword search allows the end user to find the documents that contain the names of a company's competitors. The search would return a group of documents. Only by reading the documents would the end user come up with any relevant answers to his or her questions.

Table 13-2	Query, Data Mining, Search, and Text Analytics	
	Retrieval	*Insight*
Structured	Query: Returns data	Data mining: Insight from structured data
Unstructured	Search: Returns documents	Text analytics: Insight from text

The technologies on the left return pieces of information and require human interaction to synthesize and analyze that information. The technologies on the right — data mining (discussed in Chapter 12) and text analytics — deliver insight much more quickly. Hopefully, the value of text analytics to your organization is becoming clear.

Analysis and Extraction Techniques

Okay, now it's time to get a little bit more technical. In general, text analytics solutions use a combination of statistical and Natural Language Processing (NLP) techniques to extract information from unstructured data. NLP is a broad and complex field that has developed over the last 20 years. A primary goal of NLP is to derive meaning from text. Natural Language Processing generally makes use of linguistic concepts such as grammatical structures and parts of speech. Often, the idea behind this type of analytics is to determine who did what to whom, when, where, how, and why.

NLP performs analysis on text at different levels:

- **Lexical/morphological analysis** examines the characteristics of an individual word — including prefixes, suffixes, roots, and parts of speech (noun, verb, adjective, and so on) — information that will contribute to understanding what the word means in the context of the text provided. Lexical analysis depends on a dictionary, thesaurus, or any list of words that provides information about those words. In the case of a wireless communication company's sales promotion, a dictionary might provide the information that *promotion* is a noun that can mean an advancement in position, an advertising or publicity effort, or an effort to encourage someone's growth. Lexical analysis would also enable an application to recognize that *promotion, promotions,* and *promoting* are all versions of the same word and idea.

- **Syntactic analysis** uses grammatical structure to dissect the text and put individual words into context. Here you are widening your gaze from a single word to the phrase or the full sentence. This step might diagram the relationship between words (the grammar) or look for sequences of words that form correct sentences or for sequences of numbers that represent dates or monetary values. For example, the wireless communication company's call center records included this complaint: "The customer thought it was ridiculous that roll-over minutes were not in the plan." Syntactic analysis would tag the noun phrases in addition to providing the part-of-speech tags.

- **Semantic analysis** determines the possible meanings of a sentence. This can include examining word order and sentence structure and disambiguating words by relating the syntax found in the phrases, sentences, and paragraphs.

- **Discourse-level analysis** attempts to determine the meaning of text beyond the sentence level.

In practice, to extract information from various document sources, organizations sometimes need to develop rules. These rules can be simple:

The name of a person must start with a capital letter.

Every course on the college website must follow a three-digit course number and a semicolon.

A logo must appear in a certain location on every page.

Of course, the rules can be much more complex. Organizations can generate rules manually, automatically, or by a combination of both approaches:

✔ In the manual approach, someone uses a proprietary language to build a series of rules for extraction. This person may also build dictionaries and/or synonym lists. While the manual approach can be time-consuming, it can provide very accurate results.

✔ Automated approaches may use machine learning or other statistical techniques. The software generates rules based on a set of training and text data. First, the system processes a set of similar documents (for example, newspaper articles) to develop — that is, learn — the rules. Then the user runs a set of test data to test the accuracy of the rules.

Understanding the extracted information

The techniques described earlier in the chapter are generally combined with other statistical or linguistic techniques to automate the tagging and markup of text documents to extract the following kinds of information:

✔ **Terms:** Another name for keywords.

✔ **Entities:** Often called *named entities,* these are specific examples of abstractions (tangible or intangible). Examples are names of persons, names of companies, geographical locations, contact information, dates, times, currencies, titles and positions, and so on. For example, text analytic software can extract the entity *Jane Doe* as a person referred to in the text being analyzed. The entity *March 3, 2007* can be extracted as a date, and so on. Many vendors provide entity extraction out of the box.

✔ **Facts:** Also called *relationships,* facts indicate the who/what/where relationships between two entities. John Smith is the *CEO of Company Y* and *Aspirin reduces fever* are examples of facts.

✔ **Events:** While some experts use the terms *fact, relationship,* and *event* interchangeably, others distinguish between events and facts, stating that events usually contain a time dimension and often cause facts to change. Examples include a change in management within a company or the status of a sales process.

✔ **Concepts:** These are sets of words and phrases that indicate a particular idea or topic with which the user is concerned. This can be done manually or by using statistical, rule-based, or hybrid approaches to categorization. For example, the concept *unhappy customer* may include the words *angry, disappointed,* and *confused* and the phrases *disconnect* *service, didn't call back,* and *waste of money* — among many others. Thus the concept *unhappy customer* can be extracted even without the words *unhappy* or *customer* appearing in the text. Concepts can be defined by users to suit their particular needs.

✔ **Sentiments:** Sentiment analysis is used to identify viewpoints or emotions in the underlying text. Some techniques do this by classifying text as, for example, subjective (opinion) or objective (fact), using machine-learning or NLP techniques. Sentiment analysis has become very popular in "voice of the customer" kinds of applications.

Taxonomies

Taxonomies are often critical to text analytics. A *taxonomy* is a method for organizing information into hierarchical relationships. It is sometimes referred to as a way of organizing categories. Because a taxonomy defines the relationships between the terms a company uses, it makes it easier to find and then analyze text.

For example, a telecommunications service provider offers both wired and wireless service. Within the wireless service, the company may support cellular phones and Internet access. The company may then have two or more ways of categorizing cellular phone service, such as plans and phone types. The taxonomy could reach all the way down to the parts of a phone itself.

Taxonomies can also use synonyms and alternate expressions, recognizing that cellphone, cellular phone, and mobile phone are all the same. These taxonomies can be quite complex and can take a long while to develop.

 Some vendors will state that a taxonomy is not necessary when using their product and that business users can categorize already extracted information. This will actually depend on the subjects you're interested in. Often, the topics can be very complex, nuanced, or specific to a certain industry. That's going to require a focused taxonomy.

Putting Your Results Together with Structured Data

After your unstructured data is structured, you can combine it with other structured information that might exist in your data warehouse, and then apply business intelligence or data-mining tools to gather further insight.

For example, in Table 13-3, text analytics results are merged with structured billing information. You can see that the contents of Table 13-3 are the same as Table 13-1, except we've added a Segment column on the right. Essentially, you can match information from your customers that live in the billing system with the information from the call center notes. Of course, when prospects call in, no information is available to match; this is why "XXXX" appear in these rows.

Table 13-3		Marrying Structured and Unstructured Data		
Identifier	*Entity*	*Issue*	*Sentiment*	*Segment*
Cust XYZ	Plan A	Roll-over minutes	Neutral	Gold
Cust ABC	Plan A	Roll-over minutes	Negative	Silver
XXXX	Plan A	Expensive	Neutral	XXX
XXXX	Plan A	Data plan	Neutral	XXX
Cust XYT	Plan A	Data plan	Negative	Bronze

In this example, the structured data together with the unstructured data indicate that at least one of your customers is a gold customer, so it would be worthwhile for the company to make an extra effort to retain him or her. Of course, in reality, you will have a lot more data than this to work with.

Putting Big Data to Use

The wireless promotion use case is just one example of how text analytics can be used to help gain insight into data. So, what if the data is big data? A big data use case would mean that the unstructured data being analyzed is either high volume, high velocity, or both. The following sections describe a few examples.

Voice of the customer

Optimizing the customer experience and improving customer retention are dominant drivers for many service industries. Organizations concerned with these issues might ask questions such as

- What are major areas of complaints by customers and how are these changing over time?
- What is the level of satisfaction of customers with specific services?

✔ What are the most frequent issues that lead to customer churn?

✔ What are some key customer segments that provide higher potential upsell opportunities?

Information, such as e-mails to the company, customer satisfaction surveys, call center notes, and other internal documents, hold a lot of information about customer concerns and sentiment. Text analytics can help to identify and address causes of customer dissatisfaction in a timely manner. It can help improve brand image by proactively solving problems before they become a big sticking point with customers.

Is this a big data problem? It can be. It depends on the volume of the information. You may have a large volume of information that is delivered in batch mode. Companies may want to merge this data with structured data, as we discuss earlier in this chapter.

Social media analytics

Another form of voice of the customer or customer experience management, social media analytics, has gotten a lot of visibility recently and, in fact, is helping to drive the text analytics market. In social media analytics, data across the Internet is gathered together. This includes unstructured text from blogs, microblogs, news articles, text from online forums, and so on. This huge stream of data is then analyzed — often using text analytics — to get answers to questions such as

✔ What are people saying about my brand?

✔ What do they like about my brand?

✔ What do they dislike about my brand?

✔ How does my brand compare to my competitors'?

✔ How loyal are my customers?

And, social media isn't just being used by marketers concerned about their brand. The government is using it to look for terrorist conversations. Health agencies are using it to identify public health threats worldwide. The list goes on.

This is a big data use case, especially when you can work with a service provider that can assemble all the tweets from Twitter, together with all the other data.

IBM Watson

You may have seen a machine playing and winning *Jeopardy!* a few years ago. That machine is called Watson. IBM Watson is a set of technologies that processes and analyzes massive amounts of both structured and unstructured data in a unique way. Watson can process and analyze information from 200 million books in three seconds. While Watson is very advanced, it uses technologies that are commercially available with some "secret sauce" technologies that IBM Research has either enhanced or developed. It combines software technologies from big data, content and predictive analytics, and industry-specific software to make it work. IBM is working together with the medical industry to develop a Watson for that industry. It is only the first in a series of Watsons that IBM will develop with its partners.

So what is this secret sauce? Watson understands natural language, generates and evaluates hypotheses, and adapts and learns.

First, Watson uses Natural Language Processing. IBM is using a set of annotators to extract information like symptoms, age, location, and so on. Watson is processing vast amounts of this unstructured data quickly, using an architecture designed for this.

Second, Watson works by generating *hypotheses* that are potential answers to a question. It is trained by feeding question-and-answer (Q/A) data into the system. In other words, it is shown representative questions and it learns from the supplied answers. This is called *evidence-based learning*. The goal is to generate a model that can produce a confidence score (think logistic regression with a bunch of attributes). Watson starts with a generic statistical model, then look at the first Q/A, and use that to tweak coefficients. As it gains more evidence, it continues

to tweak the coefficients until it can "say" that confidence is high. Training Watson is key because what is really happening is that the trainers are building statistical models that are scored. At the end of the training, Watson has a system that has feature vectors and models so that eventually it can use the model to probabilistically score the answers. The key here is something that *Jeopardy!* did not showcase, which is that it is not deterministic (that is, using rules). Watson is probabilistic and that makes it dynamic.

When Watson generates a hypothesis, it then scores the hypothesis based on the evidence. Its goal is to get the right answer for the right reason. (So, theoretically, if five symptoms must be positive for a certain disease and four must be negative and Watson only has four of the nine pieces of information, it could ask for more.) The hypothesis with the highest score is presented. By the end of the analysis, Watson is confident when it knows the answer and when it doesn't know the answer.

Here's an example. Suppose that you see your doctor because you are not feeling well. Specifically, you might have heart palpitations, fatigue, hair loss, and muscle weakness. You decide to go see a doctor to determine whether something is wrong with your thyroid or whether it is something else. If your doctor has access to a Watson system, he could use it to help advise him regarding your diagnosis. In this case, Watson would already have ingested and curated all the information in books and journals associated with thyroid disease. It also has the diagnosis and related information from other patients from this hospital and other doctors in the practice from the electronic medical records of prior cases that it has in its data banks.

(continued)

(continued)

Based on the first set of symptoms you might report, it would generate a hypothesis along with probabilities associated with the hypothesis (for example, 60 percent hyperthyroidism, 40 percent anxiety, and so on). It might then ask for more information. As it is fed this information, such as patient history, Watson would continue to refine its hypothesis along with the probability of the hypothesis being correct. After it is given all the information and it iterates through it and presents the diagnosis with the highest confidence level, the physician would use this information to help assist him in making the diagnosis and developing a treatment plan. If Watson doesn't know the answer, it will state that it does not have an answer or doesn't have enough information to provide an answer.

IBM likens the process of training a Watson to teaching a child how to learn. A child can read a book to learn. However, he can also learn by a teacher asking questions and reinforcing the answers about that text.

Text Analytics Tools for Big Data

In the following sections, we provide an overview of some of the players in this market. Some are small while others are household names. Some call what they do *big data text analytics,* while some just refer to it as *text analytics.*

Attensity

Attensity (www.attensity.com) is one of the original text analytics companies that began developing and selling products more than ten years ago. At this time, it has over 150 enterprise customers and one of the world's largest NLP development groups. Attensity offers several engines for text analytics. These include Auto-Classification, Entity Extraction, and Exhaustive Extraction. Exhaustive Extraction is Attensity's flagship technology that automatically extracts facts from parsed text (who did what to whom, when, where, under what conditions) and organizes this information.

The company is focused on social and multichannel analytics and engagement by analyzing text for reporting from internal and external sources and then routing it to business users for engagement. It recently purchased Biz360, a social media company that aggregates huge streams of social media. It has developed a grid computing system that provides high-performance capabilities for processing massive amounts of real-time text. Attensity uses a Hadoop framework (MapReduce, HDFS, and HBase) to store data. It also has a data-queuing system that creates an orchestration process that recognizes spikes in inbound data and adjusts processing across more/less servers as needed.

Clarabridge

Another pure-play text analytics vendor, Clarabridge (`www.clarabridge.com`) is actually a spin-off of a business intelligence (BI) consulting firm (called Claraview) that realized the need to deal with unstructured data. Its goal is to help companies drive measurable business value by looking at the customer holistically, pinpointing key experiences and issues, and helping everyone in an organization take actions and collaborate in real time. This includes real-time determination of sentiment and classification of customer feedback data / text and staging the verbatim for future processing into the Clarabridge system.

At this time, Clarabridge is offering its customers some sophisticated and interesting features, including single-click root cause analysis to identify what is causing a change in the volume of text feeds, sentiment, or satisfaction associated with emerging issues. It also offers its solution as a Software as a Service (SaaS).

IBM

Software giant IBM (`www.ibm.com`) offers several solutions in the text analytics space under its Smarter Planet strategy umbrella. Aside from Watson and IBM SPSS (see Chapter 12 for more on SPSS), IBM also offers IBM Content Analytics with Enterprise Search (ICAES). IBM Content Analytics was developed based on work done at IBM Research.

IBM Content Analytics is used to transform content into analyzed information, and this is available for detailed analyses similar to the way structured data would be analyzed in a BI toolset. IBM Content Analytics and Enterprise Search were once two separate products. The converged solution targets both enhanced enterprise search that uses text analytics, as well as stand-alone content analytics needs. ICAES has tight integration with the IBM InfoSphere BigInsights platform, enabling very large search and content analytics collections.

OpenText

OpenText (`www.opentext.com`), a Canadian-based company, is probably best known for its leadership in enterprise information management (EIM) solutions. Its vision revolves around managing, securing, and extracting value from the unstructured data of enterprises. It provides what it terms "semantic middleware." According to the company, its semantic technology evolution is rooted in its capability "to enable real-time analytics with high accuracy on large data sets (that is, content) across languages, formats, and industry domains." The idea behind semantic middleware is that semantics can be exposed at different levels and work with different technologies (for example, document management, predictive analytics, and so on) to address business issues. In other words, the text analytics can be enabled and utilized where needed. OpenText provides this middleware as a stand-alone product to be used in a variety of solutions as well as embedded in its products.

The idea of pluggable semantic enablers is starting to gain more steam, and smaller players are also looking at ways that these enablers can provide value to big data applications.

SAS

SAS (www.sas.com) has been solving complex big data problems for a long time. Several years ago, it purchased text analytics vendor Teragram to enhance its strategy to use both structured and unstructured data in analysis and to integrate this data for descriptive and predictive modeling. Now, its text analytics capabilities are part of its overall analytics platform and text data is viewed as simply another source of data.

SAS continues to innovate in the area of high-performance analytics to ensure that performance meets customer expectations. The goal is to take problems that used to take weeks to solve and solve them in days, or problems that used to take days to solve and solve them in minutes instead. For example, the SAS High Performance Analytics Server is an in-memory solution that allows you to develop analytical models using complete data, not just a subset of aggregate data. SAS says that you can use thousands of variables and millions of documents as part of this analysis. The solution runs on EMC Greenplum or Teradata appliances as well as on commodity hardware using Hadoop Distributed File System (HDFS).

Chapter 14

Customized Approaches for Analysis of Big Data

··

In This Chapter

▶ New models and approaches evolving to support big data analysis

▶ Full custom versus semi-custom analysis approaches

▶ Optimal environment for big data analysis

▶ Big to small is the goal

··

*T*he beauty of big data is that, theoretically, all the data you need, both inside and outside of your company, can be used to drive your analysis. Ideally, this means that if you increase the amount or type of data you analyze, you can derive new insights from it.

As we discuss in Chapters 12 and 13, many tools used to analyze big data are an evolution of what's already out there in the market in terms of business intelligence and advanced analysis. These include data-mining software, predictive modeling, advanced statistics, and text analytics. As we also mention in the previous two chapters, often, vendors have had to rewrite their algorithms to run this software across new big data infrastructures.

Figure 14-1 shows the focus of this chapter.

According to some experts in the field, the mind-set around analyzing big data is different than traditional analysis and is one of exploration and experimentation — going where the data takes you. While others disagree, the reality is that the big data analytics ecosystem will require some new technology platforms, algorithms, and skill sets to support this kind of analysis — especially when it comes to pushing the envelope in terms of what can be done. Because we are in the early stages of big data usage and adoption, a large percentage of the analysis will need to be delivered in the form of "customized" or "special-purpose" applications. This chapter examines some of these changes and describes how to address them.

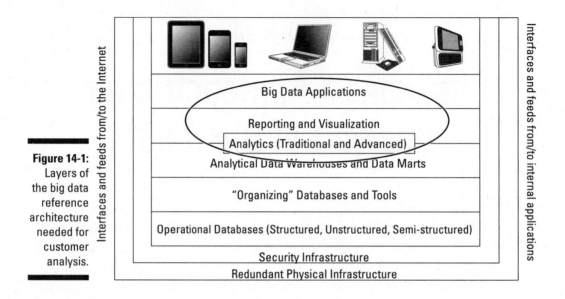

Figure 14-1:
Layers of the big data reference architecture needed for customer analysis.

Building New Models and Approaches to Support Big Data

Big data analysis has gotten a lot of hype recently, and for good reason. Companies are excited to be able to access and analyze data that they've been collecting or want to gain insight from, but have not been able to manage or analyze effectively. These companies know that something is out there, but until recently, have not been able to mine it. This pushing the envelope on analysis is an exciting aspect of the big data analysis movement. It might involve visualizing huge amounts of disparate data, or it might involve advanced analyzed streaming at you in real time. It is evolutionary in some respects and revolutionary in others.

Characteristics of big data analysis

So, what's different when your company is pushing the envelope with big data analysis? We talk a little bit about this in Chapter 12. We describe that the infrastructure supporting big data analysis is different and algorithms have been changed to be infrastructure aware.

Big data analysis should be viewed from two perspectives:

- ✔ Decision-oriented
- ✔ Action-oriented

Decision-oriented analysis is more akin to traditional business intelligence. We look at selective subsets and representations of larger data sources and try to apply the results to the process of making business decisions. Certainly these decisions might result in some kind of action or process change, but the purpose of the analysis is to augment decision making.

Action-oriented analysis is used for rapid response, when a pattern emerges or specific kinds of data are detected and action is required. We discuss these kinds of use cases throughout the book, but here is where the "rubber meets the road." Taking advantage of big data through analysis and causing proactive or reactive behavior changes offer great potential for early adopters.

Finding and utilizing big data by creating analysis applications can hold the key to extracting value sooner rather than later. To accomplish this task, it is more effective to build these custom applications from scratch or by leveraging platforms and/or components. We cover this topic later in this chapter.

First, we look at some of the additional characteristics of big data analysis that make it different from traditional kinds of analysis aside from the three Vs of volume, velocity, and variety:

- ✔ **It can be *programmatic*.** One of the biggest changes in terms of analysis is that in the past you were dealing with data sets you could manually load into an application and visualize and explore. With big data analysis, you may be faced with a situation where you might start with the raw data that often needs to be handled *programmatically* (using code) to manipulate it or to do any kind of exploration because of the scale of the data.

- ✔ **It can be *data driven*.** While many data scientists use a hypothesis-driven approach to data analysis (develop a premise and collect data to see whether that premise is correct), you can also use the data to drive the analysis — especially if you've collected huge amounts of it. For example, you can use a machine-learning algorithm (for more on machine learning, see Chapter 12) to do this kind of hypothesis-free analysis.

- ✔ **It can use a lot of *attributes*.** In the past, you might have been dealing with hundreds of attributes or characteristics of that data source. Now you might be dealing with hundreds of gigabytes of data that consist of thousands of attributes and millions of observations. Everything is now happening on a larger scale.

- ✔ **It can be *iterative*.** More compute power means that you can iterate on your models until you get them the way you want them. Here's an example. Assume that you're building a model that is trying to find the predictors for certain customer behaviors associated with certain products. You might start off extracting a reasonable sample of data or connecting to where the data resides. You might build a model to test a hypothesis.

Whereas in the past you might not have had that much memory to make your model work effectively, you will need a tremendous amount of physical memory to go through the necessary iterations required to train the algorithm. It may also be necessary to use advanced computing techniques like natural language processing or neural networks that automatically evolve the model based on learning as more data is added.

✔ **It can be *quick* to get the compute cycles you need by leveraging a cloud-based Infrastructure as a Service.** With Infrastructure as a Service (IaaS) platforms like Amazon Cloud Services (ACS), you can rapidly provision a cluster of machines to ingest large data sets and analyze them quickly.

Now that you have a better understanding of some of the characteristics, look at some of the means at your disposal for analyzing big data.

Understanding Different Approaches to Big Data Analysis

In many cases, big data analysis will be represented to the end user through reports and visualizations. Because the raw data can be incomprehensively varied, you will have to rely on analysis tools and techniques to help present the data in meaningful ways. Traditionally generated reports are familiar, but they may not be able to provide new insights or create the unanticipated findings decision makers are searching for. Data visualization techniques will help, but they too will need to be enhanced or supported by more sophisticated tools to address big data.

While traditional reporting and visualization are familiar, they are insufficient, so it will become necessary to create new applications and approaches for analysis of big data. Otherwise, you will be in a holding pattern until vendors begin to catch up with the demand. Even when they catch up, the resulting solution may not do what you need. Early adoption of big data requires the creation of new applications designed to address analysis requirements and time frames. Why is this so important? It is important because a well-used representation from traditional data analysis will be inadequate.

These new applications will fall broadly into two categories: custom (coded from scratch) or semi-custom (based on frameworks or components). We examine some examples to help understand why and how we can use these approaches to make big data more useful in our daily work lives sooner rather than later.

Custom applications for big data analysis

In general, a custom application is created for a specific purpose or a related set of purposes. Certain areas of a business or organization will always require a custom set of technologies to support unique activities or to provide a competitive advantage. For example, if you are involved in financial services, you want your trading applications to be faster and more accurate than your competitors'. In contrast, the applications that do your client billing probably do not need very much specialization, so a packaged system can do the trick.

For big data analysis, the purpose of custom application development is to speed the time to decision or the time to action. As big data evolves as a science and a market, software vendors of traditional solutions will be slow to bring new technologies to market. Little value exists in a big data infrastructure if very few opportunities are available to decide or act upon because of the lack of analysis capabilities germane to the business area. As we discuss in Chapters 12 and 13, some packages support a wide variety of analysis techniques for big data. The vendors discussed in these chapters can utilize their technology components to help build solutions for their customers. However, the reality is that there is no such thing as a completely packaged application that will work out of the box for a sophisticated big data solution. We now examine some additional options that are available for those of us who may need custom analysis applications for big data.

R environment

The "R" environment is based on the "S" statistics and analysis language developed in the 1990s by Bell Laboratories. It is maintained by the GNU project and is available under the GNU license. Over the years, many users of S and R have contributed greatly to the base system, enhancing and expanding its capabilities. While challenging to fully comprehend, its depth and flexibility make it a compelling choice for analytics application developers and "power users." In addition, the CRAN (Comprehensive R Archive Network) R project maintains a worldwide set of File Transfer Protocol (FTP) and web servers with the most up-to-date versions of the R environment. A commercially supported, enterprise version of R is also available from Revolution Analytics in Palo Alto, California (www.revolution-computing.com).

More specifically, R is an integrated suite of software tools and technologies designed to create custom applications used to facilitate data manipulation, calculation, analysis, and visual display. Among other advanced capabilities, it supports

✔ Effective data-handling and manipulation components.

✔ Operators for calculations on arrays and other types of ordered data.

✔ Tools specific to a wide variety of data analyses.

> ✔ Advanced visualization capabilities.
>
> ✔ S programming language designed by programmers, for programmers with many familiar constructs, including conditionals, loops, user-defined recursive functions, and a broad range of input and output facilities. Most of the system-supplied functions are written in the S language.

R is a vehicle for developing new methods of interactive big data analysis. It has developed rapidly and has been extended by a large collection of *packages*. It is well suited to single-use, custom applications for analysis of big data sources.

Google Prediction API

The Google Prediction API is an example of an emerging class of big data analysis application tools. It is available on the Google developers website and is well documented and provided with several mechanisms for access using different programming languages. To help you get started, it is freely available (with some restrictions) for six months. Subsequent licensing is very modest and project based.

The Prediction API is fairly simple. It looks for patterns and matches them to proscriptive, prescriptive, or other existing patterns. While performing its pattern matching, it also "learns." In other words, the more you use it, the smarter it gets. What kinds of things could you "learn" from using the Prediction API? Suppose that you wanted to understand consumer behavior. You might want to source postings from Facebook, Twitter, Amazon, and/or foursquare social sites looking for specific patterns of behavior. If you are a consumer products company, you might want to suggest new or existing products based on the information on the social sites. If you are a Hollywood production company, you might want to notify people of a new movie with one of their favorite stars. The Prediction API gives you the opportunity to predict (or even encourage) future behaviors by analyzing habits and prior actions.

Prediction is implemented as a RESTful API with language support for .NET, Java, PHP, JavaScript, Python, Ruby, and many others. Google also provides scripts for accessing the API as well as a client library for R.

Predictive analysis is one of the most powerful potential capabilities of big data, and the Google Prediction API is a very useful tool for creating custom applications.

As big data evolves, many new types of custom application tools will be introduced to the market. Some may resemble R, and others (like Google Prediction API) will be introduced as APIs or libraries that programmers can use to create new ways to compute and analyze big data. In the real world, many people do not have software developers available to code custom applications. Fortunately, some other means are available and emerging that you can use to address the needs of analysis users.

Semi-custom applications for big data analysis

In truth, what many people perceive as custom applications are actually created using "packaged" or third-party components like libraries. It is not always necessary to completely code a new application. (When it is necessary, no substitute exists.) Using packaged applications or components requires developers or analysts to write code to "knit together" these components into a working custom application. The following are reasons why this is a sound approach:

✔ **Speed to deployment:** Because you don't have to write every part of the application, the development time can be greatly reduced.

✔ **Stability:** Using well-constructed, reliable, third-party components can help to make the custom application more resilient.

✔ **Better quality:** Packaged components are often subject to higher quality standards because they are deployed into a wide variety of environments and domains.

✔ **More flexibility:** If a better component comes along, it can be swapped into the application, extending the lifetime, adaptability, and usefulness of the custom application.

Another type of semi-custom application is one where the source code is available and is modified for a particular purpose. This can be an efficient approach because there are quite a few examples of application building blocks available to incorporate into your semi-custom application. Some of these include:

✔ **TA-Lib:** The Technical Analysis library is used extensively by software developers who need to perform technical analysis of financial market data. It is available as open source under the BSD license, allowing it to be integrated into semi-custom applications.

✔ **JUNG:** The Java Universal Network Graph framework is a library that provides a common framework for analysis and visualization of data that can be represented by a graph or network. It is useful for social network analysis, importance measures (PageRank, hits), and data mining. It is available as open source under the BSD license.

✔ **GeoTools:** An open source geospatial toolkit for manipulating GIS data in many forms, analyzing spatial and non-spatial attributes or GIS data, and creating graphs and networks of the data. It is available under the GPL2 license, allowing for integration into semi-custom applications.

Going mobile

It is true that many (if not all) mobile applications are custom. Some third-party package providers offer mobile access, often through a mobile application, but they are generally not useful outside the providers' interests. As a result, many of the emerging custom component developers are delivering technology that can help create mobile applications for big data more easily.

The velocity of big data, coupled with its variety, will cause a move toward real-time observations, allowing better decision making or quick action. As the market evolves, it is likely that most of these observations will be the result of custom applications designed to augment the ability to react to changes in the environment. Analysis frameworks and components will help to create, modify, share, and maintain these applications with greater ease and efficiency.

Characteristics of a Big Data Analysis Framework

Even though new sets of tools continue to be available to help you manage and analyze big data more effectively, you may not be able to get what you need from what's already out there. In addition, a range of technologies that we talk about earlier in this book can support big data analysis and also support requirements such as availability, scalability, and high performance. Some of these technologies include big data appliances, columnar databases, in-memory databases, nonrelational databases, and massively parallel processing engines. Chapters 1, 4, and 7 cover these topics in more detail.

So, what are business users looking for when it comes to big data analysis? The answer to that question depends on the type of business problem they are trying to solve. Earlier in the chapter, we discuss decision orientation and action orientation as two broad types of business challenges. Many of the characteristics are common to both, and because decisions often lead to actions, the commonality is required. Some important considerations you need to take in as you select a big data application analysis framework include the following:

✔ **Support for multiple data types:** Many organizations are incorporating, or expect to incorporate, all types of data as part of their big data deployments, including structured, semi-structured, and unstructured data.

- ✔ **Handle batch processing and/or real time data streams:** Action orientation is a product of analysis on real-time data streams, while decision orientation can be adequately served by batch processing. Some users will require both, as they evolve to include varying forms of analysis.

- ✔ **Utilize what already exists in your environment:** To get the right context, it may be important to leverage existing data and algorithms in the big data analysis framework.

- ✔ **Support NoSQL and other newer forms of accessing data:** While organizations will continue to use SQL, many are also looking at newer forms of data access to support faster response times or faster times to decision.

- ✔ **Overcome low latency:** If you're going to be dealing with high data velocity, you're going to need a framework that can support the requirements for speed and performance.

- ✔ **Provide cheap storage:** Big data means potentially lots of storage — depending on how much data you want to process and/or keep. This means that storage management and the resultant storage costs are important considerations.

- ✔ **Integrate with cloud deployments:** The cloud can provide storage and compute capacity on demand. More and more companies are using the cloud as an analysis "sandbox." Increasingly, the cloud is becoming an important deployment model to integrate existing systems with cloud deployments (either public or private) in a hybrid model. In addition, big data cloud services are beginning to emerge that will benefit customers. For more on this issue, check out Chapter 11.

While all these characteristics are important, the perceived and actual value of creating applications from a framework is quicker time to deployment. With all these capabilities in mind, we look at an example of a big data analysis application framework from a company called Continuity.

The Continuity AppFabric (www.continuity.com) is a framework supporting the development and deployment of big data applications. Deployment can be as a single instance, private cloud, or public cloud, without any recoding required for the target environment. The AppFabric itself is a set of technologies specifically designed to abstract away the vagaries of low-level big data technologies. The application builder is an Eclipse plug-in permitting the developer to build, test, and debug locally and in familiar surroundings.

AppFabric capabilities include the following:

- ✔ Stream support for real-time analysis and reaction

- ✔ Unified API, eliminating the need to write to big data infrastructures

- ✔ Query interfaces for simple results and support for pluggable query processors

✔ Data sets representing queryable data and tables accessible from the Unified API

✔ Reading and writing of data independent of input or output formats or underlying component specifics (such as Hadoop data operations)

✔ Transaction-based event processing

✔ Multimodal deployment to a single node or the cloud

This approach is going to gain traction for big data application development primarily because of the plethora of tools and technologies required to create a big data environment. If a developer can write to a higher-level API, requiring that the "fabric" or abstraction layer manage the specifics of the underlying components, you should expect high-quality, reliable applications that can be easily modified and deployed.

It is a rare company that can afford to build a big data analysis capability from scratch. Therefore, it is best to think about your big data deployment as an ecosystem of people, processes, and technologies. Big data analysis is not an island. It is connected to many other data environments and business process environments throughout your enterprise. Even though these are the early days in the big data movement and many projects are experimenting with big data analysis in isolation from their overall computing environment, you need to think about integration as a requirement. As big data analysis becomes more mainstream, it should remain isolated from the rest of the data management environment.

Software developers seldom work in isolation. Likewise, data scientists and analysis experts like to share discoveries and leverage existing assets. The need to collaborate and share is even more pronounced in an emerging technology area. In fact, the lack of collaboration can be costly in many ways. Large organizations can benefit from tools that drive collaborations. Very often people doing similar work are unaware of each other's efforts leading to duplicate work (or worse!). This is costly in terms of money and productivity. Jump-starting a project with existing solutions can make a difference in quality and time-to-market.

Another good example of an application framework is OpenChorus (www. openchorus.org). In addition to rapid development of big data analysis applications, it also supports collaboration and provides many other features important to software developers, like tool integration, version control, and configuration management.

Open Chorus is a project maintained by EMC Corporation and is available under the Apache 2.0 license. EMC also produces and supports a commercial version of Chorus. Both Open Chorus and Chorus have vibrant partner networks as well as a large set of individual and corporate contributors.

Open Chorus is a generic framework. Its leading feature is the capability to create a communal "hub" for sharing big data sources, insights, analysis techniques, and visualizations. Open Chorus provides the following:

- Repository of analysis tools, artifacts, and techniques with complete versioning, change tracking, and archiving

- Workspaces and sandboxes that are self-provisioned and easily maintained by community members

- Visualizations, including heat maps, time series, histograms, and so on

- Federated search of any and all data assets, including Hadoop, metadata, SQL repositories, and comments

- Collaboration through social networking–like features encouraging discovery, sharing, and brainstorming

- Extensibility for integration of third-party components and technologies

As big data evolves, you will see the introduction of new kinds of application frameworks. Many of these will support mobile application development, while others will address vertical application areas. In any case, they are an important tool for early adopters of big data.

Big to Small: A Big Data Paradox

You'll find a nuance about big data analysis. It's really about small data. While this may seem confusing and counter to the whole premise of this book, small data is the product of big data analysis. This is not a new concept, nor is it unfamiliar to people who have been doing data analysis for any length of time. The overall working space is larger, but the answers lie somewhere in the "small."

Traditional data analysis began with databases filled with customer information, product information, transactions, telemetry data, and so on. Even then, too much data was available to efficiently analyze. Systems, networks, and software didn't have the performance or capacity to address the scale. As an industry, we addressed the shortcomings by creating smaller data sets.

These smaller data sets were still fairly substantive, and we quickly discovered other shortcomings; the most glaring was the mismatch between the data and the working context. If you worked in Accounts Payable, you had to look at a large amount of unrelated data to do your job. Again, the industry responded by creating smaller, contextually relevant data sets — big to small to smaller still.

You may recognize this as the migration from databases to data warehouses to data marts. More often than not, the data for the warehouses and the marts was chosen on arbitrary or experimental parameters resulting in a great deal of trial and error. We weren't getting the perspectives we needed or were possible because the capacity reductions weren't based on computational fact.

Enter big data, with all its volumes, velocities, and varieties, and the problem remains or perhaps worsens. We have addressed the shortcomings of the infrastructure and can store and process huge amounts of additional data, but we also had to introduce new technologies specifically to help us manage big data.

Despite the outward appearances, this is a wonderful thing. Today and in the future, we will have more data than we can imagine and we'll have the means to capture and manage it. What is more necessary than ever is the capability to analyze the *right* data in a timely enough fashion to make decisions and take actions. We will still shrink the data sets into "fighting trim," but we can do so computationally. We process the big data and turn it into small data so that it's easier to comprehend. It's more precise and, because it was derived from a much larger starting point, it's more contextually relevant.

Part V
Big Data Implementation

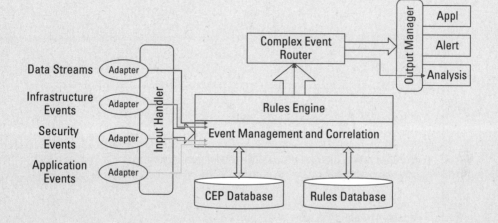

In this part . . .

- ✔ Identify and integrate the right data for your big data implementation.
- ✔ Determine the accuracy of your results.
- ✔ Use streaming data.
- ✔ Understand complex event processing.
- ✔ Operationalize big data.
- ✔ Design an implementation road map for big data.

Chapter 15

Integrating Data Sources

To get the most business value from big data, it needs to be integrated into your business processes. How can you take action based on your analysis of big data unless you can understand the results in context with your operational data? Differentiating your company as a result of making good business decisions depends on many factors. One factor that is becoming increasingly important is your capability to integrate internal and external data sources comprised of both traditional relational data and newer forms of unstructured data. While this may seem like a daunting task, the reality is that you probably already have a lot of experience with data integration. Don't toss aside everything you have learned about delivering data as a trusted source to your organization. You will want to place a high priority on data quality as you move to make big data analytics actionable. However, to bring your big data environments and enterprise data environments together, you will need to incorporate new methods of integration that support Hadoop and other nontraditional big data environments.

Two major categories of big data integration are covered in this chapter: the integration of multiple big data sources in big data environments and the integration of unstructured big data sources with structured enterprise data. We cover the traditional forms of integration such as extract, transform, and load (ETL) and new solutions designed for big data platforms.

Identifying the Data You Need

Before you can begin to plan for integration of your big data, you need to take stock of the type of data you are dealing with. Many organizations are recognizing that a lot of internally generated data has not been used to its full potential in the past. By leveraging new tools, organizations are gaining new insight from previously untapped sources of unstructured data in e-mails, customer service records, sensor data, and security logs. In addition, much interest exists in looking for new insight based on analysis of data that is primarily external to the organization, such as social media, mobile phone location, traffic, and weather.

Your analysis may require that you bring several of these big data sources together. To complete your analysis, you need to move large amounts of data from log files, Twitter feeds, RFID tags, and weather data feeds and integrate all these elements across highly distributed data systems. After you complete your analysis, you may need to integrate your big data with your operational data. For example, healthcare researchers explore unstructured information from patient records in combination with traditional medical record patient data such as test results to begin improving patient care and improving quality of care. Big data sources like information from medical devices and clinical trials may be incorporated into the analysis as well.

As you begin your big data analysis, you probably do not know exactly what you will find. Your analysis will go through several stages. You may begin with petabytes of data, and as you look for patterns, you may narrow your results. The following three stages are described in more detail:

- ✔ Exploratory stage
- ✔ Codifying stage
- ✔ Integration and incorporation stage

Exploratory stage

In the early stages of your analysis, you will want to search for patterns in the data. It is only by examining very large volumes (terabytes and petabytes) of data that new and unexpected relationships and correlations among elements may become apparent. These patterns can provide insight into customer preferences for a new product, for example. You will need a platform such as Hadoop for organizing your big data to look for these patterns.

As described in Chapters 9 and 10, Hadoop is widely used as an underlying building block for capturing and processing big data. Hadoop is designed with capabilities that speed the processing of big data and make it possible to identify patterns in huge amounts of data in a relatively short time. The two primary components of Hadoop — Hadoop Distributed File System (HDFS) and MapReduce — are used to manage and process your big data.

In the exploratory stage, you are not so concerned about integration with operational data. That will come later.

Using FlumeNG for big data integration

However, one type of integration is critical during the exploratory stage. It is often necessary to collect, aggregate, and move extremely large amounts of streaming data to search for hidden patterns in big data. Traditional integration tools such as ETL would not be fast enough to move the large streams of data in time to deliver results for analysis such as real-time fraud detection. FlumeNG (a more advanced version of the original Flume) loads data in real time by streaming your data into Hadoop.

Typically, Flume is used to collect large amounts of log data from distributed servers. It keeps track of all the physical and logical nodes in a Flume installation. Agent nodes are installed on the servers and are responsible for managing the way a single stream of data is transferred and processed from its beginning point to its destination point. In addition, collectors are used to group the streams of data into larger streams that can be written to a Hadoop file system or other big data storage container. Flume is designed for scalability and can continually add more resources to a system to handle extremely large amounts of data in an efficient way. Flume's output can be integrated with Hadoop and Hive for analysis of the data. Flume also has transformation elements to use on the data and can turn your Hadoop infrastructure into a streaming source of unstructured data.

Looking for patterns in big data

You find many examples of companies beginning to realize competitive advantages from big data analytics. For many companies, social media data streams are increasingly becoming an integral component of a digital marketing strategy. For example, Wal-Mart analyzes customer location-based data, tweets, and other social media streams to make more targeted product recommendations for customers and to tailor in-store product selection to customer demand. Wal-Mart acquired social media company Kosmix in 2011 to gain access to its technology platform for searching and analyzing real-time data streams. In the exploratory stage, this technology can be used to rapidly search through huge amounts of streaming data and pull out the trending patterns that relate to specific products or customers. The results can be used to optimize inventory based on the likes and dislikes of shoppers near a specific geographic location.

As companies search for patterns in big data, the huge data volumes are narrowed down as if they are passed through a funnel. You may start with petabytes of data and then, as you look for data with similar characteristics or data that forms a particular pattern, you eliminate data that does not match up.

Codifying stage

To make the leap from identifying a pattern to incorporating this trend into your business process needs some sort of process to follow. For example, if a large retailer monitors social media and identifies lots of chatter about an upcoming college football event near one of its stores, how will the company make use of this information? With hundreds of stores and many thousands of customers, you need a repeatable process to make the leap from pattern identification to implementation of new product selection and more targeted marketing. With a process in place, the retailer can quickly take action and stock the local store with clothing and accessories with the team logo. After you find something interesting in your big data analysis, you need to codify it and make it a part of your business process. You need to make the connection between your big data analytics and your inventory and product systems.

To codify the relationship between your big data analytics and your operational data, you need to integrate the data.

Integration and incorporation stage

Big data is having a major impact on many aspects of data management, including data integration. Traditionally, data integration has focused on the movement of data through middleware, including specifications on message passing and requirements for application programming interfaces (APIs). These concepts of data integration are more appropriate for managing data at rest rather than data in motion. The move into the new world of unstructured data and streaming data changes the conventional notion of data integration. If you want to incorporate your analysis of streaming data into your business process, you need advanced technology that is fast enough to enable you to make decisions in real time. One important goal with big data analytics is to look for patterns that apply to your business and narrow down the data set based on business context. Therefore, the analysis of big data is only one step in your implementation. After your big data analysis is complete, you need an approach that will allow you to integrate or incorporate the results of your big data analysis into your business process and real-time business actions.

Companies have high expectations for gaining real business value from big data analysis. In fact, many companies would like to begin a deeper analysis of internally generated big data, such as security log data, that was not previously possible due to technology limitations. Technologies for high-speed transport of very large and fast data are a requirement for integrating across distributed big data sources and between big data and operational data.

Unstructured data sources often need to be moved quickly over large geographic distances for the sharing and collaboration required in everything from major scientific research projects to development and delivery of content for the entertainment industry.

For example, scientific researchers typically work with very large data sets. Researchers share data and collaborate more easily than in the past by using a combination of big data analytics and the cloud. One example of a large data set shared by scientific researchers across the world is the 1000 Genomes Project. Disease researches study the human genome to identify and compile variations to help understand and treat diseases. The data for the 1000 Genomes Project — the largest and most detailed catalog of human genetic variation in the world — is maintained on Amazon Web Services (AWS). The data is made available to the international scientific research community. AWS is able to support the transfer of very large files at fast speeds over the Internet (700 megabytes per second) using technology by Aspera. Aspera provides high-speed file transport technology called fasp. This software transfers big data at speeds that are many times faster than TCP-based file transfer technologies like FTP and HTTP. This speed can be guaranteed with very large file sizes and long distances, and across geographic boundaries.

Linking traditional sources with big data is a multistaged process after you have looked at all the data from streaming big data sources and identified the relevant patterns. You may not have known what you were looking for when you started, but now you have some important information for your business. As you move from the exploratory stage and get closer to the real business problem, you need to begin thinking about metadata and rules and the structure of the data. After narrowing the amount of data you need to manage and analyze, now you need to think about integration.

A company that uses big data to predict customer interest in new products needs to make a connection between the big data and the operational data on customers and products to take action. If the company wants to use this information to buy new products or change pricing or manage inventory, it needs to integrate its operational data with the results of its big data analysis. The retail industry is one market where companies are beginning to use big data analytics to deepen its relationship with customers and create more personalized and targeted offers. Integration of big data and operational data is key to the success of these efforts. For example, consider a customer who registers on a retailer's website, providing her mobile number and e-mail address. Today, the customer receives e-mails about sales and coupon incentives to make purchases in the store or online. In the future, retailers are planning to use location-based services from the customer's mobile device to identify where the customer is located in the store and send a text message with a coupon for immediate use in that department. In other words, a customer might walk into the entertainment section of the store and receive a text message for a discount on the purchase of a Blu-ray disc player. To do this, the retailer needs real-time integration of big data feeds (location-based information) with operational data on customer history and in-store inventory. The analysis needs to take place immediately, and communication with the customer needs to happen at the same time. Even a delay of ten minutes may be too long, and the moment of customer interaction will be lost.

Understanding the Fundamentals of Big Data Integration

The elements of the big data platform manage data in new ways as compared to the traditional relational database. This is because of the need to have the scalability and high performance required to manage both structured and unstructured data. Components of the big data ecosystem ranging from Hadoop to NoSQL DB, MongoDB, Cassandra, and HBase all have their own approach for extracting and loading data. As a result, your teams may need to develop new skills to manage the integration process across these platforms. However, many of your company's data management best practices will become even more important as you move into the world of big data.

While big data introduces a new level of integration complexity, the basic fundamental principles still apply. Your business objective needs to be focused on delivering quality and trusted data to the organization at the right time and in the right context. To ensure this trust, you need to establish common rules for data quality with an emphasis on accuracy and completeness of data. In addition, you need a comprehensive approach to developing enterprise metadata, keeping track of data lineage and governance to support integration of your data.

At the same time, traditional tools for data integration are evolving to handle the increasing variety of unstructured data and the growing volume and velocity of big data. While traditional forms of integration take on new meanings in a big data world, your integration technologies need a common platform that supports data quality and profiling.

To make sound business decisions based on big data analysis, this information needs to be trusted and understood at all levels of the organization. While it will probably not be cost or time effective to be overly concerned with data quality in the exploratory stage of a big data analysis, eventually quality and trust must play a role if the results are to be incorporated in the business process. Information needs to be delivered to the business in a trusted, controlled, consistent, and flexible way across the enterprise, regardless of the requirements specific to individual systems or applications. To accomplish this goal, three basic principles apply:

✔ **You must create a common understanding of data definitions.** At the initial stages of your big data analysis, you are not likely to have the same level of control over data definitions as you do with your operational data. However, once you have identified the patterns that are most relevant to your business, you need the capability to map data elements to a common definition. That common definition is then carried forward into operational data, data warehouses, reporting, and business processes.

✔ **You must develop of a set of data services to qualify the data and make it consistent and ultimately trustworthy.** When your unstructured and big data sources are integrated with structured operational data, you need to be confident that the results will be meaningful.

✔ **You need a streamlined way to integrate your big data sources and systems of record.** In order to make good decisions based on the results of your big data analysis, you need to deliver information at the right time and with the right context. Your big data integration process should ensure consistency and reliability.

To integrate data across mixed application environments, you need to get data from one data environment (source) to another data environment (target). Extract, transform, and load (ETL) technologies have been used to accomplish this in traditional data warehouse environments. The role of ETL is evolving to handle newer data management environments like Hadoop. In a big data environment, you may need to combine tools that support batch integration processes (using ETL) with real-time integration and federation across multiple sources. For example, a pharmaceutical company may need to blend data stored in its Master Data Management (MDM) system with big data sources on medical outcomes of customer drug usage. Companies use MDM to facilitate the collecting, aggregating, consolidating, and delivering of consistent and reliable data in a controlled manner across the enterprise. In addition, new tools like Sqoop and Scribe are used to support integration of big data environments. You also find an increasing emphasis on using extract, load, and transform (ELT) technologies. These technologies are described next.

Defining Traditional ETL

ETL tools combine three important functions required to get data from one data environment and put it into another data environment. Traditionally,

ETL has been used with batch processing in data warehouse environments. Data warehouses provide business users with a way to consolidate information across disparate sources (such as enterprise resource planning [ERP] and customer relationship management [CRM]) to analyze and report on data relevant to their specific business focus. ETL tools are used to transform the data into the format required by the data warehouse. The transformation is actually done in an intermediate location before the data is loaded into the data warehouse. Many software vendors, including IBM, Informatica, Pervasive, Talend, and Pentaho, provide ETL software tools.

ETL provides the underlying infrastructure for integration by performing three important functions:

- **Extract:** Read data from the source database.
- **Transform:** Convert the format of the extracted data so that it conforms to the requirements of the target database. Transformation is done by using rules or merging data with other data.
- **Load:** Write data to the target database.

However, ETL is evolving to support integration across much more than traditional data warehouses. ETL can support integration across transactional systems, operational data stores, BI platforms, MDM hubs, the cloud, and Hadoop platforms. ETL software vendors are extending their solutions to provide big data extraction, transformation, and loading between Hadoop and traditional data management platforms. ETL and software tools for other data integration processes like data cleansing, profiling, and auditing all work on different aspects of the data to ensure that the data will be deemed trustworthy. ETL tools integrate with data quality tools, and many incorporate tools for data cleansing, data mapping, and identifying data lineage. With ETL, you only extract the data you will need for the integration.

ETL tools are needed for the loading and conversion of structured and unstructured data into Hadoop. Advanced ETL tools can read and write multiple files in parallel from and to Hadoop to simplify how data is merged into a common transformation process. Some solutions incorporate libraries of prebuilt ETL transformations for both the transaction and interaction data that run on Hadoop or a traditional grid infrastructure.

Data transformation

Data transformation is the process of changing the format of data so that it can be used by different applications. This may mean a change from the format the data is stored in into the format needed by the application that will use the data. This process also includes *mapping* instructions so that applications are told how to get the data they need to process.

The process of data transformation is made far more complex because of the staggering growth in the amount of unstructured data. A business application such as a customer relationship management or sales management system typically has specific requirements for how the data it needs should be stored. The data is likely to be *structured* in the organized rows and columns of a relational database. Data is *semi-structured* or *unstructured* if it does not follow these very rigid format requirements. The information contained in an e-mail message is considered unstructured, for example. Some of a company's most important information is in unstructured and semi-structured forms such as documents, e-mail messages, complex messaging formats, customer support interactions, transactions, and information coming from packaged applications like ERP and CRM.

Data transformation tools are not designed to work well with unstructured data. As a result, companies needing to incorporate unstructured information into its business process decision making have been faced with a significant amount of manual coding to accomplish the required data integration. Given the growth and importance of unstructured data to decision making, ETL solutions from major vendors are beginning to offer standardized approaches to transforming unstructured data so that it can be more easily integrated with operational structured data.

Understanding ELT — Extract, Load, and Transform

ELT stands for extract, load, and transform. It performs the same functions as ETL, but in a different order. Early databases did not have the technical capability to transform the data. Therefore, ETL tools extracted the data to an intermediary location to perform the transformation before loading the data to the data warehouse. However, this restriction is no longer a problem, thanks to technology advances such as massively parallel processing systems and columnar databases. As a result, ELT tools can transform the data in the source or target database without requiring an ETL server. Why use ELT with big data? The performance is faster and more easily scalable. ELT uses structured query language (SQL) to transform the data. Many traditional ETL tools also offer ELT so that you can use both, depending on which option is best for your situation.

Prioritizing Big Data Quality

Getting the right perspective on data quality can be very challenging in the world of big data. With the majority of big data sources, you need to assume that you are working with data that is not clean. In fact, the overwhelming abundance of seemingly random and disconnected data in streams of social media data is one of the things that make it so useful to businesses. You start by searching petabytes of data without knowing what you might find after you start looking for patterns in the data. You need to accept the fact that a lot of noise will exist in the data. It is only by searching and pattern matching that you will be able to find some sparks of truth in the midst of some very dirty data. Of course, some big data sources such as data from RFID tags or sensors have better-established rules than social media data. Sensor data should be reasonably clean, although you may expect to find some errors. It is always your responsibility when analyzing massive amounts of data to plan for the quality level of that data. You should follow a two-phase approach to data quality:

> **Phase 1:** Look for patterns in big data without concern for data quality.

> **Phase 2:** After you locate your patterns and establish results that are important to the business, apply the same data quality standards that you apply to your traditional data sources. You want to avoid collecting and managing big data that is not important to the business and will potentially corrupt other data elements in Hadoop or other big data platforms.

As you begin to incorporate the outcomes of your big data analysis into your business process, recognize that high-quality data is essential for a company to make sound business decisions. This is true for big data as well as traditional data. The quality of data refers to characteristics about the data, including consistency, accuracy, reliability, completeness, timeliness, reasonableness, and validity. Data quality software makes sure that data elements are represented in the same way across different data stores or systems to increase the consistency of the data.

For example, one data store may use two lines for a customer's address and another data store may use one line. This difference in the way the data is represented can result in inaccurate information about customers, such as one customer being identified as two different customers. A corporation might use dozens of variations of its company name when it buys products. Data quality software can be used to identify all the variations of the company name in your different data stores and ensure that you know everything that this customer purchases from your business. This process is called *providing a single view of customer or product.* Data quality software matches data across different systems and cleans up or removes redundant data. The data quality process provides the business with information that is easier to use, interpret, and understand.

Data profiling tools are used in the data quality process to help you to understand the content, structure, and condition of your data. They collect information on the characteristics of the data in a database or other data store to begin the process of turning the data into a more trusted form. The tools analyze the data to identify errors and inconsistencies. They can make adjustments for these problems and correct errors. The tools check for acceptable values, patterns, and ranges and help identify overlapping data. The data-profiling process, for example, checks to see whether the data is expected to be alpha or numeric. The tools also check for dependencies or to see how the data relates to data from other databases.

Data-profiling tools for big data have a similar function to data-profiling tools for traditional data. Data-profiling tools for Hadoop will provide you with important information about the data in Hadoop clusters. These tools can be used to look for matches and remove duplications on extremely large data sets. As a result, you can ensure that your big data is complete and consistent. Hadoop tools like HiveQL and Pig Latin can be used for the transformation process.

Using Hadoop as ETL

Many organizations with big data platforms are concerned that ETL tools are too slow and cumbersome to use with large volumes of data. Some have found that Hadoop can be used to handle some of the transformation process and to otherwise improve on the ETL and data-staging processes. You can speed up the data integration process by loading both unstructured data and traditional operational and transactional data directly into Hadoop, regardless of the initial structure of the data. After the data is loaded into Hadoop, it can be further integrated using traditional ETL tools. When Hadoop is used as an aid to the ETL process, it speeds the analytics process.

The use of Hadoop as an integration tool is a work in progress. Vendors with traditional ETL solutions, such as IBM, Informatica, Talend, Pentaho, and Datameer, are incorporating Hadoop into their integration offerings. By relying on the capabilities of Hadoop as a massively parallel system, developers can perform data quality and transformation functions that were not previously possible. However, Hadoop does not stand on its own as a replacement for ETL.

Best Practices for Data Integration in a Big Data World

You find a lot of potential in using big data to look at a range of business and scientific problems in new ways, find answers to unanswered questions, and begin to take immediate action that delivers significant results. Many companies are exploring big data problems and coming up with some innovative solutions. Chapters 21 and 22 present some interesting case examples. The future is exciting. However, now is the time to pay attention to some basic principles that will serve you well as you begin your big data journey.

In reality, big data integration fits into the overall process of integration of data across your company. Therefore, you can't simply toss aside everything you have learned from data integration of traditional data sources. The same rules apply whether you are thinking about traditional data management or big data management. So keep these key issues at the top of your priority list:

- ✔ **Keep data quality in perspective.** Your emphasis on data quality depends on the stage of your big data analysis. Don't expect to be able to control data quality when you do your initial analysis on huge volumes of data. However, when you narrow down your big data to identify a subset that is most meaningful to your organization, this is when you need to focus on data quality. Ultimately data quality becomes important if you want your results to be understood in context with your historical data. As your company relies more and more on analytics as a key planning tool, data quality can mean the difference between success and failure.

- ✔ **Consider real-time data requirements.** Big data will bring streaming data to the forefront. Therefore, you will have to have a clear understanding of how you integrate data in motion into your environment for predictable analysis.

- ✔ **Don't create new silos of information.** While so much of the emphasis around big data is focused on Hadoop and other unstructured and semi-structured sources, remember that you have to manage this data in context with the business. You will therefore need to integrate these sources with your line of business data and your data warehouse.

Chapter 16

Dealing with Real-Time Data Streams and Complex Event Processing

....

In This Chapter

▶ Streaming data

▶ Exploring complex event processing

▶ Understanding how streaming data and complex event processing impact big data

▶ Using streaming data and complex event processing in the real world

▶ Streaming data in action

....

*B*ig data is offering new and exciting approaches to providing a different level of insight and operational sophistication to data management. In many of the examples discussed in the preceding chapters, big data is analyzed in batch mode. Often the most important issues for organizations are that the amount of data is huge and it needs to be processed and managed at the right speed to impact outcomes. But most of this analysis is related to large-scale analysis and decision making. Analyzing the massive amount of data from multitudes of sources can help the organization understand the meaning of data, plan for the future, and anticipate market changes and unanticipated customer requirements.

In many situations, you may need to react to the current state of data. You might need to react to sensor data that indicates a problem with a medical monitoring device. You might want to send a customer a coupon at the time of purchase. Or you may need to adjust the placement of equipment based on changing weather conditions. The list of possibilities goes on. But the common element is that you are analyzing data that is in motion. One executive stated the issue clearly: "We need to be able to process and analyze streaming data from sensors in real time, while that data is still moving."

In this chapter, we combine two techniques for managing the flow of data. Streaming technology is closely tied to the volume of the data, while complex event processing of the volume of data is secondary to the capability to match data to rules. Streaming data and complex event processing are increasingly important across industries. These technologies are the most important in the trenches of an organization, where reaction time to a condition or situation will make the difference between success and failure. In this chapter, we look at the impact and importance of streaming data and complex event processing to big data.

Explaining Streaming Data and Complex Event Processing

So what is streaming data and how is that different from complex event processing? This is not a simple question to answer because a continuum of data management exists. Streaming computing is designed to handle a continuous stream of a large amount of unstructured data. In contrast, Complex Event Processing (CEP) typically deals with a few variables that need to be correlated with a specific business process. In many situations, CEP is dependent on data streams. However, CEP is not required for streaming data. Like streaming data, CEP relies on analyzing streams of data in motion. In fact, if data is at rest, it does not fit into the category of streaming data or CEP. In the next section, we discuss streaming data and its application in organizations and industries.

Using Streaming Data

So far, we have talked about collecting massive amounts of data from many different sources and processing that information to gain insights. In general, this is considered data at rest. Before we give you an example, what is data that is *not* at rest? This would be systems that are managing active transactions and therefore need to have persistence. In these cases, the data will be stored in an operational data store. However, in other situations, those transactions have been executed, and it is time to analyze that data typically in a data warehouse or data mart. This means that the information is being processed in batch and not in real time. When organizations are planning for their future, they need to be able to analyze all sorts of data, ranging from information about what customers are saying to what they are buying and why. It is important to understand the leading indicators of change. In other words, what is changing? If customer buying preferences are changing, how will that impact what products and services an organization will offer next year or even in three years? Many research organizations are using this type of big data analytics to discover new medicines. An insurance company may want to compare the patterns of traffic accidents across a broad geographic area with weather statistics. In these use cases, no benefit exists to manage this information at real-time speed. Clearly, the analysis has to be fast enough to be practical. In addition, organizations will often analyze the data multiple times to see whether new patterns emerge.

But when a significant amount of data needs to be quickly processed in near real time to gain insights, data in motion in the form of streaming data is the best answer.

Data streaming

Streaming data is an analytic computing platform that is focused on speed. This is because these applications require a continuous stream of often unstructured data to be processed. Therefore, data is continuously analyzed and transformed in memory before it is stored on a disk. Processing streams of data works by processing "time windows" of data in memory across a cluster of servers. This is similar to the approach when managing data at rest leveraging Hadoop, covered in Chapter 9. The primary difference is the issue of velocity. In the Hadoop cluster, data is collected in batch mode and then processed. Speed matters less in Hadoop than it does in data streaming. Some key principles define when using streams is most appropriate:

- When it is necessary to determine a retail buying opportunity at the point of engagement, either via social media or via permission-based messaging

- Collecting information about the movement around a secure site

- To be able to react to an event that needs an immediate response, such as a service outage or a change in a patient's medical condition

- Real-time calculation of costs that are dependent on variables such as usage and available resources

Streaming data is useful when analytics need to be done in real time while the data is in motion. In fact, the value of the analysis (and often the data) decreases with time. For example, if you can't analyze and act immediately, a sales opportunity might be lost or a threat might go undetected.

The following are a few examples that can help explain how this is useful.

A power plant needs to be a highly secure environment so that unauthorized individuals do not interfere with the delivery of power to customers. Companies often place sensors around the perimeter of a site to detect movement. But a problem could exist. A huge difference exists between a rabbit that scurries around the site and a car driving by quickly and deliberately. Therefore, the vast amount of data coming from these sensors needs to be analyzed in real time so that an alarm is sounded only when an actual threat exists.

A telecommunications company in a highly competitive market wants to make sure that outages are carefully monitored so that a detected drop in service levels can be escalated to the appropriate group. Communications systems generate huge volumes of data that have to be analyzed in real time to take the appropriate action. A delay in detecting an error can seriously impact customer satisfaction.

An oil exploration company drilling at sea needs to know exactly where the sources of oil are and what other environmental factors might impact their operations. Therefore, it needs to know details such as water depth, temperature, ice flows, and so on. This massive amount of data needs to be analyzed and computed so that mistakes are avoided.

A medical diagnostic group was required to be able to take massive amounts of data from brain scans and analyze the results in real time to determine where the source of a problem is and what type of action needed to be taken to help the patient.

Needless to say, we are dealing with a lot of data that needs to be processed and analyzed in real time. Therefore, the physical environment that supports this level of responsiveness is critical. Streaming data environments typically require a clustered hardware solution, and sometimes a massively parallel processing approach will be required to handle the analysis. One important factor about streaming data analysis is the fact that it is a single-pass analysis. In other words, the analyst cannot reanalyze the data after it is streamed. This is common in applications where you are looking for the absence of data. In telecommunication networks, the loss of a heartbeat needs to be addressed as soon as possible. If several passes are required, the data will have to be put into some sort of warehouse where additional analysis can be performed. For example, it is often necessary to establish context. How does this streaming data compare to historical data? This correlation can tell you a lot about what has changed and what that change might mean to your business.

The need for metadata in streams

Most data management professionals are familiar with the need to manage metadata in structured database management environments. These data sources are strongly typed (for example, the first ten characters are the first name) and designed to operate with metadata. You might assume that metadata is nonexistent in unstructured data, but that is not true. Typically you find structure in any kind of data. Take the example of video. Although you might not be able to know exactly the content of a specific video, a lot of structure exists in the format of that video-based data. If you are looking at unstructured text, you know that the words are written in the English language and that if you apply the right tools and algorithms, you can interpret the text. Managing unstructured data is covered in Chapter 13.

Because of this implicit metadata from unstructured data, it is possible to parse the information using eXtensible Markup Language (XML). XML is a technique for presenting unstructured text files with meaningful tags. The underlying technology is not new and was one of the foundational technologies for implementing service orientation.

Examples of products for streaming data include IBM's InfoSphere Streams, Twitter's Storm, and Yahoo's S4.

IBM InfoSphere Streams

InfoSphere Streams provides continuous analysis of massive data volumes. It is intended to perform complex analytics of heterogeneous data types, including text, images, audio, voice, VoIP, video, web traffic, e-mail, GPS data, financial transaction data, satellite data, and sensors. Infosphere Streams can support all data types. It can perform real-time and look-ahead analysis of regularly generated data, using digital filtering, pattern/correlation analysis, and decomposition as well as geospacial analysis.

Twitter's Storm

Twitter's Storm is an open source real-time analytics engine developed by a company called BackType that was acquired by Twitter in 2011 partially because Twitter uses Storm internally. It is still available as open source and has been gaining significant traction among emerging companies. It can be used with any programming language for applications such as real-time analytics, continuous computation, distributed remote procedure calls (RPCs), and integration. Storm is designed to work with existing queuing and database technologies. Companies using Storm in their big data implementations include Groupon, RocketFuel, Navisite, and Oolgala.

Apache S4

The four *S*'s in S4 stand for Simple Scalable Streaming System. Apache S4 was developed by Yahoo! as a general-purpose, distributed, scalable, partially fault-tolerant, pluggable platform that allows programmers to easily develop applications for processing continuous streams of data. The core platform is written in Java and was released by Yahoo! in 2010. A year later, it was turned over to Apache under the Apache 2.0 license. Clients that send and receive events can be written in any programming language. S4 is designed as a highly distributed system. Throughput can be increased linearly by adding nodes into a cluster. The S4 design is best suited for large-scale applications for data mining and machine learning in a production environment.

Using Complex Event Processing

Both streams and Complex Event Processing (CEP) are intended to manage data in motion. But the uses of these two technologies are quite different. While streams are intended to analyze large volumes of data in real time, Complex Event Processing is a technique for tracking, analyzing, and processing data as an event happens. This information is then processed and communicated based on business rules and processes. The idea behind CEP is to be able to establish the correlation between streams of information and match the resulting pattern with defined behaviors such as mitigating a threat or seizing an opportunity.

CEP is an advanced approach based on simple event processing that collects and combines data from different relevant sources to discover events and patterns that can result in action.

Here is an example. A retail chain creates a tiered loyalty program to increase repeat sales — especially for customers who spend more than $1,000 a year. It is important that the company creates a platform that could keep these critical customers coming back and spending more. Using a CEP platform, as soon as a high-valued customer uses the loyalty program, the system triggers a process that offers the customer an extra discount on a related product. Another process rule could give the customer an unexpected surprise — an extra discount or a sample of a new product. The company also adds a new program that links the loyalty program to a mobile application. When a loyal customer walks near a store, a text message offers the customer a discounted price. At the same time, if that loyal customer writes something negative on a social media site, the customer care department is notified and an apology is issued. It is quite likely that we are dealing with a huge number of customers with a significant number of interactions. But it would not be enough to simply stream the data and analyze that data. To achieve the business goals the retailer wanted to achieve would require executing a process to respond to the results of the analysis.

Many industries take advantage of CEP. Credit card companies use CEP to better manage fraud. When a pattern of fraud emerges, the company can shut off the credit card before the company experiences significant losses. The underlying system will correlate the incoming transactions, track the stream of event data, and trigger a process. CEP is also implemented in financial-trading applications, weather-reporting applications, and sales management applications, to name a few. What all these applications have in common is that the applications have a predefined norm for temperature, pressure, size of transaction, or value of the sale. A change in state will trigger an action. If you drive a late-model car, you probably have noticed that when a tire's pressure has dropped, the car will trigger a dashboard indicator that notifies the driver to take action (getting the tire inflated or fixed).

Many vendors offer CEP solutions. Many of the CEP tools on the market allow the creation of real-time, event-driven applications. These applications might ingest data from streams, but they can also ingest data from traditional database sources. Most of the offerings include common capabilities, including a graphical development environment that is typically Eclipse-based, connectivity to real-time data flows, as well as APIs to historical data sources. Most of these products include a graphical event flow language and support SQL. Key vendors in this space include Esper (open source vendor), IBM with IBM Operational Decision Manager, Informatica with RulePoint, Oracle with its Complex Event Processing Solution, Microsoft's StreamInsights, and SAS DataFlux Event Stream Processing Engine, and Streambase's CEP. Numerous startups are emerging in this market.

Differentiating CEP from Streams

So, what is the difference between CEP and streaming data solutions? While stream computing is typically applied to analyzing vast amounts of data in real time, CEP is much more focused on solving a specific use case based on events and actions. However, a streaming data technique is often used as an integral part of a CEP application. As discussed earlier in the chapter, streaming data applications typically manage a lot of data and process it at a high rate of speed. Because of the amount of data, it is typically managed in a highly distributed clustered environment.

CEP, on the other hand, typically will not manage as much data, so it is often run on less complex hardware. In addition, the type of analysis will be different. It is critical that CEP applications be able to connect to key systems of record such as customer relationship management (CRM) systems or transaction management environments. It is not uncommon for CEP environments to deal with only a few variables that are applied to very complex models and processes. While relying on complex mining or statistical models, CEP systems are designed around a rules engine so that when an event takes place, the rules engine triggers an action.

Understanding the Impact of Streaming Data and CEP on Business

Both streaming data and CEP have an enormous impact on how companies can make strategic use of big data. With streaming data, companies are able to process and analyze this data in real time to gain an immediate insight. It often requires a two-step process to continue to analyze the key findings that might have gone unnoticed in the past. With CEP approaches, companies can stream data and then leverage a business process engine to apply business rules to the results of that streaming data analysis. The opportunities to gain insights that lead to new innovation and new action are the foundational value of streaming data approaches.

Chapter 17

Operationalizing Big Data

*T*he benefits of big data to business are significant. But the real question is how do you make big data part of your overall business process so that you can operationalize big data? What if you can combine the traditional decision making process with big data analysis? How do you make big data available to decision makers so that they get the benefit from the myriad data sources that transform business processes? To make big data a part of the overall data management process requires that you put together a plan. In this chapter, we talk about what it takes to combine the results of big data analysis with your existing operational data. The combination can be a powerful approach to transforming your business.

Making Big Data a Part of Your Operational Process

The best way to start making big data a part of your business process is to begin by planning an integration strategy. The data — whether it is a traditional data source or big data — needs to be integrated as a seamless part of the inner workings of the processes.

Can big data be ancillary to the business process? The answer is yes, but only if little or no dependency exists between transactional data and big data. Certainly you can introduce big data to your organization as a parallel activity. However, if you want to get the most from big data, it needs to be integrated into your existing business operating processes. We take a look at how to accomplish this task. In the next section, we discuss the importance of data integration in making big data operational.

Integrating big data

Just having access to big data sources is not enough. Soon there will be petabytes of data and hundreds of access mechanisms for you to choose from. But which streams and what kinds of data do you need? The identification of the "right" sources of data is similar to what we have done in the past:

- ✔ Understand the problem you are trying to solve
- ✔ Identify the processes involved
- ✔ Identify the information required to solve the problem
- ✔ Gather the data, process it, and analyze the results

This process may sound familiar because businesses have been doing a variation of this algorithm for decades. So is big data different? Yes, even though we have been dealing with large amounts of operational data for years, big data introduces new *types* of data into people's professional and personal lives. Twitter streams, Facebook posts, sensor data, RFID data, security logs, video data, and many other new sources of information are emerging almost daily. As these sources of big data emerge and expand, people are trying to find ways to use this data to better serve customers, partners, and suppliers. Organizations are looking for ways to use this data to predict the future and to take better actions. We look at an example to understand the importance of integrating big data with operating processes.

Healthcare is one of the most important and complex areas of investment today. It is also an area that increasingly produces more data in more forms than most industries. Therefore, healthcare is likely to greatly benefit by new forms of big data. The healthcare providers, insurers, researchers, and healthcare practitioners often make decisions about treatment options with data that is incomplete or not relevant to specific illnesses. Part of the reason for this disparity is that it is very difficult to effectively gather and process data for individual patients. Data elements are often stored and managed in different places by different organizations. In addition, clinical research that is being conducted all over the world can be helpful in determining the context for how a specific disease or illness might be approached and managed. Big data can help change this problem.

So, we apply our algorithm to a standard data healthcare scenario:

1. Understand the problem we are trying to solve:

   a. Need to treat a patient with a specific type of cancer

2. Identify the processes involved:

   a. Diagnosis and testing

       b. Results analysis including researching treatment options

       c. Definition of treatment protocol

       d. Monitor patient and adjust treatment as needed

  3. Identify the information required to solve the problem:

       a. Patient history

       b. Blood, tissue, test results, and so on

       c. Statistical results of treatment options

  4. Gather the data, process it, and analyze the results:

       a. Commence treatment

       b. Monitor patient and adjust treatment as needed

Figure 17-1 illustrates the process.

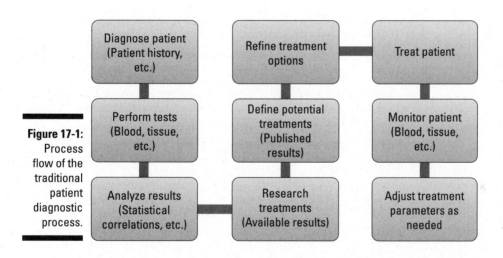

Figure 17-1:
Process flow of the traditional patient diagnostic process.

This is how medical practitioners work with patients today. Most of the data is local to a healthcare network, and physicians have little time to go outside the network to find the latest information or practice.

Incorporating big data into the diagnosis of diseases

Across the world, big data sources for healthcare are being created and made available for integration into existing processes. Clinical trial data, genetics and genetic mutation data, protein therapeutics data, and many other new sources of information can be harvested to improve daily healthcare processes. Social media can and will be used to augment existing data and processes to provide more personalized views of treatment and therapies. New medical devices will control treatments and transmit telemetry data for real-time and other kinds of analytics. The task ahead is to understand these new sources of data and complement the existing data and processes with the new big data types.

So, what would the healthcare process look like with the introduction of big data into the operational process of identifying and managing patient health? Here is an example of what the future might look like:

1. Understand the problem we are trying to solve:

   a. Need to treat a patient with a specific type of cancer

2. Identify the processes involved:

   a. Diagnosis and testing (identify genetic mutation)

   b. Results analysis including researching treatment options, clinical trial analysis, genetic analysis, and protein analysis

   c. Definition of treatment protocol, possibly including gene or protein therapy

   d. Monitor patient and adjust treatment as needed using new wireless device for personalized treatment delivery and monitoring. Patient uses social media to document overall experience.

3. Identify the information required to solve the problem:

   a. Patient history

   b. Blood, tissue, test results, and so on

   c. Statistical results of treatment options

   d. Clinical trial data

   e. Genetics data

   f. Protein data

   g. Social media data

4. Gather the data, process it, and analyze the results:

   a. Commence treatment

   b. Monitor patient and adjust treatment as needed

Figure 17-2 identifies the same operational process as before, but with big data integrations.

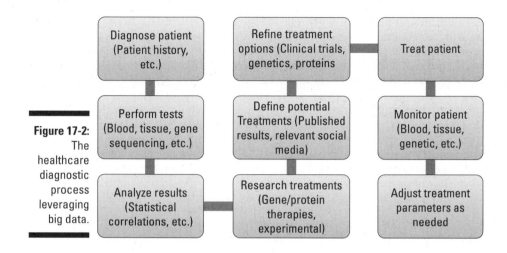

Figure 17-2:
The
healthcare
diagnostic
process
leveraging
big data.

This represents the optimal case where no new processes need to be created to support big data integrations. While the processes are relatively unchanged, the underlying technologies include the applications that will need to be altered to accommodate the impact of characteristics of big data, including the volume of data, the variety of data sources, and the speed or velocity required to process that data.

The introduction of big data into the process of managing healthcare will make a big difference in effectiveness to diagnosing and managing healthcare in the future. This same operational approach process can be applied to a variety of industries, ranging from oil and gas to financial markets and retail, to name a few. What are the keys to successfully applying big data to operational processes? Here are some of the most important issues to consider:

✔ Fully understand the current process.

✔ Fully understand where gaps exist in information.

✔ Identify relevant big data sources.

✔ Design a process to seamlessly integrate the data now and as it changes.

✔ Modify analysis and decision-making processes to incorporate the use of big data.

Understanding Big Data Workflows

To understand big data workflows, you have to understand what a process is and how it relates to the workflow in data-intensive environments. Processes tend to be designed as high level, end-to-end structures useful for decision making and normalizing how things get done in a company or organization. In contrast, workflows are task-oriented and often require more specific data than processes. Processes are comprised of one or more workflows relevant to the overall objective of the process.

In many ways, big data workflows are similar to standard workflows. In fact, in any workflow, data is necessary in the various phases to accomplish the tasks. Consider the workflow in the preceding healthcare example. One elementary workflow is the process of "drawing blood." Drawing blood is a necessary task required to complete the overall diagnostic process. If something happens and blood has not been drawn or the data from that blood test has been lost, it will be a direct impact on the veracity or truthfulness of the overall activity.

What happens when you introduce a workflow that depends on a big data source? Although you might be able to use existing workflows with big data, you cannot assume that a process or workflow will work correctly by just substituting a big data source for a standard source. This may not work because standard data-processing methods do not have the processing approaches or performance to handle the variety of complexity of the big data.

Workload in context to the business problem

The healthcare example focuses on the need to conduct an analysis after the blood is drawn from the patient. In the standard data workflow, the blood is typed and then certain chemical tests are performed based on the requirements of the healthcare practitioner. It is unlikely that this workflow understands the testing required for identifying specific biomarkers or genetic mutations. If you supplied big data sources for biomarkers and mutations, the workflow would fail. It is not big data aware and will need to be modified or rewritten to support big data.

The best practice for understanding workflows and the effect of big data is to do the following:

✔ Identify the big data sources you need to use.

✔ Map the big data types to your workflow data types.

✔ Ensure that you have the processing speed and storage access to support your workflow.

   ✔ Select the data store best suited to the data types.

   ✔ Modify the existing workflow to accommodate big data or create new big data workflow.

After you have your big data workflows, it will be necessary to fine-tune these workflows so that they won't overwhelm or contaminate your analysis. For example, many big data source do not include well-defined data definitions and metadata about the elements of those sources. In some cases, these data sources have not been cleaned. You need to make sure that you have the right level of knowledge about the big data sources that you are going to use.

Ensuring the Validity, Veracity, and Volatility of Big Data

High volume, high variety, and high velocity are the essential characteristics of big data. These characteristics are covered in detail in Chapter 1. But other characteristics of big data are equally important, especially when you apply big data to operational processes. This second set of "V" characteristics that are key to operationalizing big data includes

   ✔ **Validity:** Is the data correct and accurate for the intended usage?

   ✔ **Veracity:** Are the results meaningful for the given problem space?

   ✔ **Volatility:** How long do you need to store this data?

Data validity

It stands to reason that you want accurate results. But in the initial stages of analyzing petabytes of data, it is likely that you won't be worrying about how valid each data element is. That initial stream of big data might actually be quite dirty. In the initial stages, it is more important to see whether any relationships exist between elements within this massive data source than to ensure that all elements are valid.

However, after an organization determines that parts of that initial data analysis are important, this subset of big data needs to be validated because it will now be applied to an operational condition. When the data moves from exploratory to actionable, data must be validated. The validity of big data sources and subsequent analysis must be accurate if you are to use the results for decision making or any other reasonable purpose. Valid input data followed by correct processing of the data should yield accurate results. With big data, you must be extra vigilant with regard to validity. For example, in healthcare, you may have data from a clinical trial that could be related to a patient's disease symptoms. But a physician treating that person cannot simply take the clinical trial results as though they were directly related to the patient's condition without validating them.

A considerable difference exists between a Twitter data stream and telemetry data coming from a weather satellite. Why would you want to integrate two seemingly disconnected data sources? Imagine that the weather satellite indicates that a storm is beginning in one part of the world. How is that storm impacting individuals who live in the path of that storm? With about half a billion users, it is possible to analyze Twitter streams to determine the impact of a storm on local populations. Therefore, using Twitter in combination with data from a weather satellite could help researchers understand the veracity of a weather prediction.

Just because you have data from a weather satellite, that doesn't mean the data is a truthful representation of the weather on the ground in a specific geography. If you want to get a truthful representation of the weather, you might correlate a social media stream (like Twitter) with the satellite data for a specific area. If people within the area publish observations about the weather and they align with the data from the satellite, you have established the veracity of the current weather. While veracity and validity are related, they are independent indicators of the efficacy of data and process.

Data volatility

If you have valid data and can prove the veracity of the results, how long does the data need to "live" to satisfy your needs? In a standard data setting, you can keep data for decades because you have, over time, built an understanding of what data is important for what you do with it. You have established rules for data currency and availability that map to your work processes. For example, some organizations might only keep the most recent year of their customer data and transactions in their business systems. This will ensure rapid retrieval of this information when required. If they need to look at a prior year, the IT team may need to restore data from offline storage to honor the request. With big data, this problem is magnified.

If storage is limited, you must look at the big data sources to determine what you need to gather and how long you need to keep it. With some big data sources, you might just need to gather data for a quick analysis. For example, if you are interested in the experiences of hybrid car owners, you might want to tap into Facebook and Twitter feeds to collect all the posts/tweets about hybrid cars. You could then store the information locally for further processing. If you do not have enough storage for all this data, you could process the data "on the fly" (as you are gathering it) and only keep relevant pieces of information locally. How long you keep big data available depends on a few factors:

✔ How much data is kept at the source?

✔ Do you need to process the data repeatedly?

✔ Do you need to process the data, gather additional data, and do more processing?

✔ Do you have rules or regulations requiring data storage?

✔ Do your customers depend on your data for their work?

✔ Does the data still have value or is it no longer relevant?

Due to the volume, variety, and velocity of big data, you need to understand volatility. For some sources, the data will always be there; for others, this is not the case. Understanding what data is out there and for how long can help you to define retention requirements and policies for big data.

Big data and analytics can open the door to all kinds of new information about the things that are most interesting in your day-to-day life. As a consumer, big data will help to define a better profile for how and when you purchase goods and services. As a patient, big data will help to define a more customized approach to treatments and health maintenance. As a professional, big data will help you to identify better ways to design and deliver your products and services. This will only happen when big data is integrated into the operating processes of companies and organizations.

Chapter 18

Applying Big Data within Your Organization

*A*fter it is gathered and analyzed, big data will provide insights into existing challenges and also open the door to solving new problems. While organizations see the potential for leveraging big data to solve many previously unsolvable problems, the process comes at a cost. Operational processes, discussed in Chapter 17, will need to change to accommodate big data. New types of data will need to be added into the environment. Also, new kinds of analysis will emerge to help understand the implications of big data and how it relates (or doesn't relate) to existing data. Finally, new technologies will need to be employed to address the requirements of big data.

Understanding some of the economics of big data, especially how to implement and integrate big data in your environment, will decide

✔ What is the best use of big data for your organization?

✔ How can you create a flexible, cost-effective big data implementation?

✔ How do you get going with big data?

✔ How do you minimize the disruption of a disruptive technology?

Figuring the Economics of Big Data

The best way to understand the economics of big data is to look at the various methods for putting big data to work for your organization. While specific costs may vary due to the size of your organization, its purchasing power, vendor relationships, and so on, the classes of expense are fairly consistent. Big data economics should be analyzed in the following areas:

- Identification of data types and sources
- Business process modifications or new process creation
- Technology changes or new technologies for big data
- New talent acquisition and upgrades to existing talent
- ROI potential of big data investments

Given the growing popularity of big data, it is best to consider the economics from two perspectives: getting started and steady-state. We look at these areas and try to understand the economic impacts and advantages of big data.

Identification of data types and sources

As big data matures, you will need to consider new and evolving data types and data sources. Some of these you may be able to control; others will control some of what you do. The most important decisions you need to make with respect to types and sources are

- What data will be necessary to address your business problem?
- Where can you source the data?
- What can you do with the data?
- How often do you need to interact with the data?
- Who maintains ownership of the data and the work products?
- How long do you need to keep the data?
- Can you trust the data and its source?

Now look at an example to help you understand the practical aspects of the related economics. If you are a brand manager in a consumer products company, you are likely to want to use big data to better understand your customers' needs, habits, buying patterns, and loyalty. Given these requirements, you will need to find data about sentiment, experience, usability, competitive alternatives, and so on. Some of this data will be available in traditional forms like customer relationship management (CRM) systems and existing data warehouses. More than likely, this brand manager is looking for more than the traditional data and will need to understand where to get different perspectives.

Analyzing big data to anticipate what's next

The brand manager really wants to be able to go beyond asking questions. That brand manager wants to be able to anticipate changes in customer requirements or habits. Often hints are available within existing data. However, without enough data to analyze, these hints will be ignored because that data may look like an outlier or even an error. But being able to anticipate even the most subtle change could give the brand manager an early warning signal. That early notification of a changing requirement could enable the brand manager to test new services and new packaging that could become important — before a competitor knows that anything is changing.

Finding the right data sources

Sourcing the data is the next step. It is not just about where to get the data, but also the form or type of the data as well as the quality or trustworthiness of the data. Good sources of sentiment data are found in social web properties like Facebook, foursquare, Yelp, Pinterest, and Twitter. The sources you select may be determined by the habits of your customers. For example, your ideal customer may be very active in social media. However, you might be a company that only does business-to-business selling. Will social media sites really help you serve your customers more proactively? You may find important business-to-business (B2B) sites that should be part of your analysis. The amount of data is vast and sometimes you are looking for the proverbial needle in the haystack: the few bits of sentiment about your product or brand hidden in the vastness of the social web. In addition, the structure and types of this data vary from site to site, adding additional complexity and perhaps costs as well. The brand manager is going to need to understand the value of sourcing and sifting through this data to get the supporting insights. Some of these sources can be easily and inexpensively examined, while others will require deeper ROI analysis to determine the potential value of information on the site.

What can you do with the data?

After identifying the sources and types of data, the brand manager must then understand what can be done with the data. Can it be modified? Can it be stored locally for subsequent use? Is there a limit on how much data can be gathered in a given time period? How often can the data be sourced? Is a "throttle" limiting the speed of the data movement? How often does the data change at the source? How long is the data stored at the source? Answering these questions can help the brand manager understand the economic impacts of big data usage. For example, your analysis might require unrestricted access to a certain source. This level of access might be quite expensive. How important is constant access? If you use this data source every week, will it impact revenue or future product direction? If the answer is yes, you will need to spend the money.

Understanding how often the data is used by internal systems can help to control costs. If the requirements are to analyze customer sentiment in real time across several social properties, the costs will be very high. If the analysis can be performed more leisurely or with fewer data sources, the costs can be lower and more controllable (that is, only pay when you need to use the data). Data usage and currency are key contributors to big data economics.

Some big data source suppliers will want to maintain ownership of their data, licensing it for specific, nondestructive uses. Others will be open with little or no access costs or overbearing usage requirements. The brand manager in the example will need to look at each source and ensure that proper care is taken with respect to who owns the data and who owns work products using the data. Some data licensing will limit the usage to compute and destroy. You can use the data as part of an analytics process but must then expunge the data at the completion of the computations. Others may allow you to use the data, but require you to "give it back" when your analysis or computations are complete, enhancing the data source for other, future users. Care must be taken to protect company information and work products as you integrate big data into your work environment.

In the example, it is likely that the brand manager will also want to understand sentiment over a given time period. Has customer sentiment changed in the past month? Six months? A year? How about customer sentiment about competitive offerings in the same time periods? Knowing how often you need to access the data can help to predict the costs associated with data capacity, accessibility, and currency.

Big data economics should be understood from two dimensions: getting started and managing the steady state. Startup costs can be contained by finding open data or freely accessible data sources. If more data center resources are required, you should consider cloud-based services where you can "pay by the drink." It is much easier to experiment when employing this open source or cloud services strategy. After you decide on the approach that will best help you achieve your business goals, you can begin to operationalize your approach. The capability to operationalize the approach to leveraging big data will allow you to move to predictable steady-state economics. Of course, you must also plan for the fact that costs may rise and new issues become important. However, you will start with the right foundation.

Business process modifications or new process creation

After the brand manager in the example has vetted the data sources, she then needs to understand what processes are affected. For example, identifying new customers from big data sources and adding them (as prospects) to existing customer databases will have a minimal impact. In other cases, you may need to create new processes to understand how the big data sources can be utilized to create new understandings about your brand or drive deeper understandings of customer loyalty and retention. In any case, it is important to model the costs required to change existing work process or create new ones. The true economic impact of big data will need to balance the costs of these changes with the potential benefit.

The technology impact of big data workflows

So far, the brand manager has identified types and sources of big data and has scoped the required changes to business processes. Now she needs to understand the technology impacts of these discoveries. In an ideal world, it will be possible to use a lot of existing technologies and applications when big data is applied to workflows. However, it is much more likely that new technologies will need to be employed to extract maximum economic value from big data investments.

As discussed in Chapters 8, 9, and 10, many new and different tools are available for big data. If a brand manager needs to gather data from several different social sites, each with different data types, she will need to work with the IT teams to select what technology best fits the business and cost requirements. For example, if a MapReduce engine is required, can Hadoop be used or is a commercial implementation better suited to the tasks? Can existing data warehouses be used or is it necessary to implement Apache Hive? Can an RDBMS store the big data or will a different data store be required? You will certainly have implementations of products that will incorporate elements of Hadoop and Hive to take advantage of this hot new trend. However, it is most likely that this approach isn't going to take you far enough to solve the different situations that you will be applying to big data.

It is safe to say that new technologies *will* be required as you introduce big data into your work environments. The existing technologies are too brittle or because they are designed for a specific task, they are too simplistic or underpowered to address the stress of big data applications. This means that costs will be associated with taking your company to the next level with big data. This is why your economic analysis will be so important.

Finding the talent to support big data projects

In the example, the brand manager's needs will create new processes and technologies. Each of these requirements, in turn, will drive the need for new skills and upgrading existing skills in many departments, but most visibly in the IT and business analyst areas.

The business analysts will need to consider augmenting their ranks with data scientists. This can be accomplished with consulting relationships in the startup phases, but should transition to permanent staffing as the direction and benefits become more clear. A single data scientist is not likely to be the answer unless you are in a small- to medium-size enterprise or organization. The most leverage will be realized by creating a team of data scientists who are charged with discovering big data sources, analytical processes, and business process impacts.

For the IT team, knowledge of new big data technologies will need to be introduced to existing team members through training and mentoring. It is fair to assume that new talent will need to be hired as your organization approaches steady state. Consulting resources can and should be employed to help your organization get jump-started with its big data initiatives. While you should look at consulting companies as well as independent data scientists, many universities and colleges have begun to offer courses that should help fill the gap in the short term. In the long term, vendors providing solutions will have to create more usable big data solutions that abstract the complexity.

Calculating the return on investment (ROI) from big data investments

In the example, the brand manager needs to create an ROI case for the big data to better understand and predict new ways of growing the customer base. All the costs discussed must be balanced with the potential outcomes of the investments. How long will it take to recoup an investment in a big data initiative? Like many things, the answer is "it depends." If the brand manager is building out a solution unique to her area of responsibility, the ROI may not be as attractive as building a generic approach to using big data across many areas of the business. If other brand managers, customer support, or salespeople can leverage the enhancements, the ROI can look very attractive, perhaps even compelling. The most important part of building the ROI model is to fully bake in the economics across all the areas examined earlier in this chapter to ensure more complete coverage and better predictability of the outcomes.

Now that you have a better understanding about *what* you need to do to introduce big data in your organization, consider *how* you might accomplish it.

Enterprise Data Management and Big Data

Enterprise Data Management (EDM) is an important process for understanding and controlling the economics of data in your enterprise or organization.
Although EDM is not required for big data, the proper application of EDM will
help to ensure better integration, control, and usability of big data.

Defining Enterprise Data Management

EDM is a comprehensive approach to defining, governing, securing, and
maintaining the quality of all data involved in the business processes of an
organization. EDM establishes policy about and ownership of key data types
and sources as well as helping to create a strategic context for the technology underpinnings of data life cycle management. The primary object of EDM
processes is to sustain a single version of the "truth." Figure 18-1 depicts the
core components of EDM.

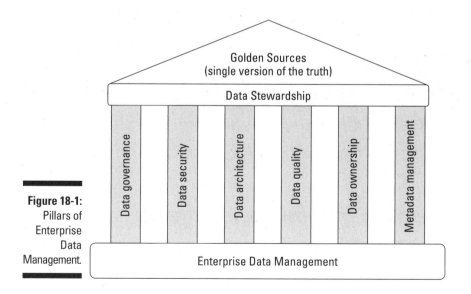

Figure 18-1:
Pillars of
Enterprise
Data
Management.

While your organization's version of EDM may vary slightly from what is shown in Figure 18-1, the tenets remain true: Data must be modeled, managed, and secured so that you can trust the processing results as part of your decision-making activities. It should also be noted that the absence of EDM in your organization is not a barrier to adopting big data. While not as effective, Enterprise Data Management can be performed at a departmental or even a project level. With that in mind, you need to examine where adoption of big data can impact enterprise data management practices. After you begin thinking about using big data in combination with your systems of record, you must have a good handle on the governance and stewardship of the overall data management environment. After all, you will be making decisions about business strategy, so it is critical that the data elements that you are comparing or analyzing are accurate, meaningful, and secure. We talk further about governance and compliance in Chapter 19.

Creating a Big Data Implementation Road Map

Big data implementation plans will be different depending on your business goals, the maturity of your data management environment, and the amount of risk your organization can absorb. So, begin your planning by taking into account all the issues that will allow you to determine an implementation road map. Here are a few of the factors that you need to consider:

- ✔ Business urgency
- ✔ Projected capacity
- ✔ Preferred software development methodology
- ✔ Available budgets and skill sets
- ✔ Appetite for risk

Now look at these factors and some example road maps you can use as guidelines for your big data implementations.

Understanding business urgency

Many ambitious organizations always seem to need the latest and greatest technologies immediately. In some situations, an organization can demonstrate that the availability of important big data sources can lead to new strategies. In these cases, it makes sense to create a strategy and plan. It is a mistake to assume that big data adoption and implementation are a defined project. The adoption of big data has broad implications for the company's overall data management strategy. So, independent of some of the other factors involved, the time required to design your big data solutions should be clearly noted on any road map. In addition, the design tasks should never be glossed over or eliminated. Doing so will reduce the value of any big data initiative. For example, new data sources may need to be acquired. New equipment and software may be required. In addition, you may need to sign up for cloud services. These services need to have the service level and security guarantees that conform to your company's requirements.

Projecting the right amount of capacity

Because the introduction of big data into your environment is a necessity, you must be able to answer the questions "How much data do you need?" and "How fast do you need to analyze it?" The answers will provide a context for the design, implementation, and testing phases of your road map. For example, if you expect to need to gather 200GB of data and only keep it until your analysis is complete, you should expect to set up this big data solution in two to four weeks. On the other hand, if you expect to require 2 petabytes of initial data, with a growth projection of 0.5 petabytes per month, and you need to keep all the data for years, you should plan on an implementation taking several months. In either case, if you need to perform the gathering and analysis in or near real time, you should expect your implementation time to increase by 50 percent.

Selecting the right software development methodology

Most companies and organizations have IT teams that follow prescribed development processes and practices. Some of these development methodologies are well suited to big data implementations, while others, sadly, are not.

Big data projects are best suited for an agile and interactive development process. Iterative methodologies use short time cycles with rapid results and constant user involvement to incrementally deliver a business solution. Therefore, it is not surprising that an iterative process is the most effective development methodology for big data implementations.

Balancing budgets and skill sets

It is always difficult to anticipate the budgetary requirements for a new type of project like big data. The best practice is to clearly understand the expected costs and downstream benefits of your big data implementation and then secure an appropriate budget for the initiative. An iterative approach will do the best job of determining the best approach to project budgeting. Therefore, budget can be allocated up front and then released as milestones as the progress of the project is achieved.

Getting the right skill sets for any project is another challenge. Often the most sought-after individuals are stretched thin across several initiatives. Staff augmentation is often the answer to resource challenges, but in an emerging, high-growth area, this is harder than usual. Big data skills are somewhat nascent as the market evolves. Over time, you will find more training and more qualified professionals. In the meantime, the best practice is to identify and acquire some data science skills for design and planning, Hadoop and NoSQL skills for implementation, and parallel/cluster computing skills for operations. You can also test products and build skill by conducting a pilot or proof-of-concept implementation in a cloud environment. Getting these skills in-house as quickly as possible will help to ensure success with your big data adoption.

Determining your appetite for risk

Every organization has a culture that will determine how much risk management it is willing to assume. If you are in a highly competitive market, you may be forced to take more risks on potential market innovation than a company whose products are required by customers and where fewer competitors exist. Even companies in highly competitive markets may be cautious before assuming risk. So, you have to understand the dynamics of your organization before you embark on a big data project. For example, you might want to create a bounded pilot project that demonstrates to management what is possible. In other cases, your organization may want to establish an ambitious plan based on predictive analytics of big data that could transform the customer experience.

If your organization is risk averse, the best you can hope to do is watch the evolution of big data and bring proposals to the table as it emerges. Identifying successes in other organizations can help to reduce the anxiety of introducing new technologies into your environment.

Even organizations with an appetite for high risk must also be wary as they adopt big data. It is all too easy to oversell the benefits or set very high expectations about working with big data. The development and acculturation of any new technology or solution can be fraught with failures. Using agile methodologies to help to explicate fast successes and fast failures is the best practice for setting proper expectations in a trailblazing organization.

Starting Your Big Data Road Map

The next two diagrams can help you to form a framework for creating road maps that are best suited to your organization's capability to adopt big data.

These are just examples of how other new technologies have been introduced successfully during their early emergence into daily use. You should think of these as starting points for how you can get the ball rolling with big data.

Figure 18-2 is an example of a road map you can adopt for your first big data initiative. It assumes that little or no process or technology is in place that is capable of meeting the requirements of big data volume, variety, and velocity. The desire is to keep the project moving, but not at a breakneck pace. One sure way to impugn big data as a key enabler for the next generation of your business decision making is to rush the process.

Deploy business application, deploy
new/modified IT operations practices,
refine big data requirements for veracity
and volatility, deploy analytics and
visualizations, tune infrastructure
and applications for best performance,
perform after-action assessment
(6-8 weeks)

Identify business owners, define
strategy, establish goals, build
team, establish or integrate into
EDM, research best practices,
secure funding
(4-6 weeks)

Identify big data sources, identify
affected business processes, create
technology and IT operating requirements,
define desired business outcomes,
begin technology implementation, iterate
with key business stakeholders
(12-15 weeks)

Deploy business application, deploy
new/modified IT operations practices,
refine big data requirements for veracity
and volatility, deploy analytics and
visualizations, tune infrastructure
and applications for best performance,
perform after-action assessment
(6-8 weeks)

Identify business owners, define
strategy, establish goals, build
team, establish or integrate into
EDM, research best practices,
secure funding
(4-6 weeks)

Figure 18-2:
Major
phases of
an inaugural
big data
implementa-
tion.

Identify big data sources, identify
affected business processes, create
technology and IT operating requirements,
define desired business outcomes,
begin technology implementation, iterate
with key business stakeholders
(12-15 weeks)

If your organization has experience with business intelligence applications and analytics, has relatively mature data management practices, and has established a high-capacity infrastructure and operations, the task of adopting big data is a bit easier. This does not imply guaranteed success or reduced risk. The existence of these capabilities is an indicator of the overall maturity of your company and its willingness to ingest new information, technology, and skills. The road map for a more experienced approach might look like what is shown in Figure 18-3.

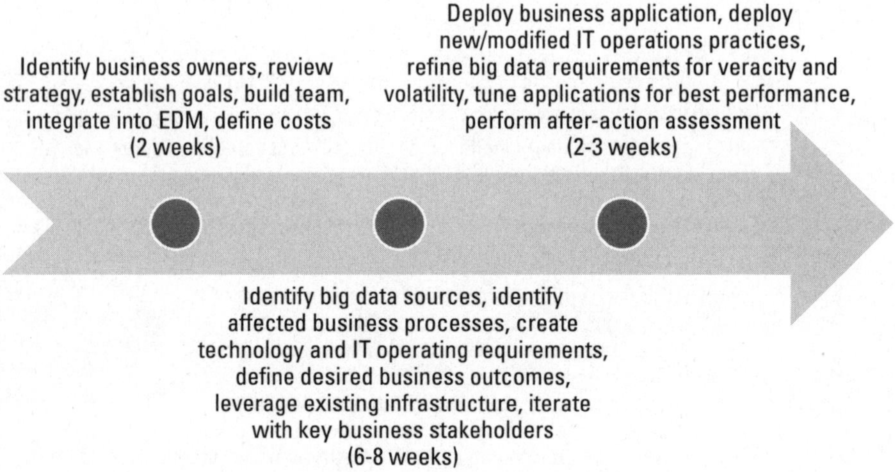

Figure 18-3: Major phases of a mature big data implementation.

Identify business owners, review strategy, establish goals, build team, integrate into EDM, define costs (2 weeks)

Deploy business application, deploy new/modified IT operations practices, refine big data requirements for veracity and volatility, tune applications for best performance, perform after-action assessment (2-3 weeks)

Identify big data sources, identify affected business processes, create technology and IT operating requirements, define desired business outcomes, leverage existing infrastructure, iterate with key business stakeholders (6-8 weeks)

Most of the activities are the same and very often can be run in parallel, depending again on organizational maturity. The good news is that everyone can achieve similar results. If you are diligent with after-action analysis and you incorporate improvements based on the lessons learned from the first or second project, you should be able to reduce the time to design, develop, test, implement, and deploy big data initiatives.

Getting started is always easier if some of the people involved have done it before. With new disruptive business and technology like big data, you won't find many people who have "been there, done that." Here are a few tips to consider as you contemplate bringing big data into your company or organization:

- **Get some help.** Don't be adverse to hiring an expert or two as consultants. Be sure that they know their "stuff" and ensure that they are capable of mentoring people in your organization. They should be willing to work themselves out of a job.

- **Get training.** Take classes, buy and read books (like this one!), do research on the Internet, ask questions, and attend a conference or two. Getting a better grounding can help with all the subsequent decision making.

✔ **Experiment.** Plan to fail. Fast failure is becoming de rigueur for contemporary technology-driven organizations. The best lessons learned often come from failures. Study other people's experiences as well.

✔ **Set proper expectations.** Some say that the key to happiness is low expectations. In the business world, properly set expectations can mean the difference between success and failure. A successful project may be viewed as a failure if the business benefits are overstated or if it takes 50 percent longer to deliver. Big data offers huge potential to your business, but only if you accurately represent the value, costs, and time to implement.

✔ **Be holistic.** Try to look at all the dimensions to any given big data initiative. If the project is delivered on time and on budget, but the end users weren't trained or ready to use it, the project may fall into failure. Most successful project managers understand that it's about people, process, and technology, at a very detailed level.

Chapter 19

Security and Governance for Big Data Environments

*I*n many areas of data management, an assumption exists that the data being leveraged for analysis and planning has been well vetted and secure. It has typically been through a data-cleansing and -profiling process so that the data can be trusted. The world of big data offers a new set of challenges and obstacles that make security and governance a challenge. Many individuals and organizations working with big data assume that they do not have to worry about security or governance. Therefore, little thought or planning is done. This all changes, however, when those big data sources become operational. In this chapter, we present the issues that you need to think about and plan for when you begin to leverage big data sources as part of your analysis and planning process.

Security in Context with Big Data

While companies are very concerned about the security and governance of their data in general, they are unprepared for the complexities that are presented by the management of big data.

Information governance is the capability to create an information resource that can be trusted by employees, partners, and customers, as well as government organizations.

Often big data analysis is conducted with a vast array of data sources that might come from many unvetted sources. Additionally, your organization needs to be aware of the security and governance policies that apply to various big data sources. Your organization might be looking to determine the importance of large amounts of new data culled from many different unstructured or semi-structured sources. Does your newly sourced data contain personal health information (PHI) that is protected by the Health Insurance Accountability and Portability Act (HIPAA) or personal identifiable information (PII) such as names and addresses? Once you acquire the data, you will subject your company to compliance issues if it is not managed securely. Some of this data will not be needed and must be properly disposed of. The data that remains will need to be secured and governed. Therefore, whatever your information management strategy is, you will have to have a well-defined security strategy.

Security is something you can never really relax about because the state of the art is constantly evolving. Hand in hand with this security strategy needs to be a governance strategy. The combination of security and governance will ensure accountability by all parties involved in your information management deployment. Managing the security of information needs to be viewed as a shared responsibility across the organization. You can implement all the latest technical security controls and still face security risks if your end users don't have a clear understanding of their role in keeping all the data that they are working with secure.

Assessing the risk for the business

Big data is becoming critical to business executives who are trying to understand new product direction and customer requirements or understand the health of their overall environment. However, if the data from a variety of sources introduces security risks into the company, unintended consequences can endanger the company. You have a lot to consider, and understanding security is a moving target, especially with the introduction of big data into the data management landscape. Ultimately, education is key to ensuring that everyone in the organization has an understanding of his or her roles and responsibilities with regard to security.

Risks lurking inside big data

While security and governance are corporate-wide issues that companies have to focus on, some differences are specific to big data that you need to remember. For example, if you are collecting data from unstructured data sources such as social media sites, you have to make sure that viruses or bogus links are not buried in the content. If you take this data and make it part of your analytics system, you could be putting your company at risk. Also, keep in mind what the original source of this data might be. An unstructured data source that might have interesting commentary about the type of customer you are trying to understand may also include extraneous noise. You need to know the nature of this data source. Has the data been verified? Is it secure and vetted against intrusion? The more reputable social media sites, for example, will watch closely for patterns of malicious behavior and delete those accounts before they cause damage. This requires a level of sophisticated big data analysis that not all sites are capable of. Your organization may have discovered a wonderful site, but that site has been hacked and you have selected that data as part of your big data platform. The consequences can be serious. Not all security threats are deliberate. You don't want to incorporate a big data source that includes sensitive personally identifiable information that could put your customers and your company's reputation at risk.

Understanding Data Protection Options

Some experts believe that different kinds of data require different forms of protection and that, in some cases in a cloud environment, data encryption might, in fact, be overkill. You could encrypt everything. You could encrypt data, for example, when you write it to your own hard drive, when you send it to a cloud provider, and when you store it in a cloud provider's database. You could encrypt at every layer.

Encrypting everything in a comprehensive way reduces your exposure; however, encryption poses a performance penalty. For example, many experts advise managing your own keys rather than letting a cloud provider do so, and that can become complicated. Keeping track of too many keys can be a nightmare. Additionally, encrypting everything can create other issues. For example, if you're trying to encrypt data in a database, you will have to examine the data as it's moving (point-to-point encryption) and also while it's being stored in the database. This procedure can be costly and complicated. Also, even when you think you've encrypted everything and you're safe, that may not be the case.

One of the long-standing weaknesses with encryption strategies is that your data is at risk before and after it's encrypted. For example, in a major data breach at Hannaford Supermarkets in 2008, the hackers hid in the network for months and were able to steal payment data when customers used their credit card at the point of sale. This breach took place before the data was encrypted.

Maintaining a large number of keys can be impractical, and managing the storing, archiving, and accessing of the keys is difficult. To alleviate this problem, generate and compute encryption keys as needed to reduce complexity and improve security.

Here are some other available data-safeguarding techniques:

- ✓ **Data anonymization:** When data is anonymized, you remove all data that can be uniquely tied to an individual (such as a person's name, Social Security number, or credit card number). Although this technique can protect some personal identification, hence privacy, you need to be really careful about the amount of information you strip out. If it's not enough, hackers can still figure out whom the data pertains to.

- ✓ **Tokenization:** This technique protects sensitive data by replacing it with random tokens or alias values that mean nothing to someone who gains unauthorized access to this data. This technique decreases the chance that thieves could do anything with the data. Tokenization can protect credit card information, passwords, personal information, and so on. Some experts argue that it's more secure than encryption.

- ✓ **Cloud database controls:** In this technique, access controls are built into the database to protect the whole database so that each piece of data doesn't need to be encrypted.

The Data Governance Challenge

Data governance is important to your company no matter what your data sources are or how they are managed. In the traditional world of data warehouses or relational database management, it is likely that your company has well-understood rules about how data needs to be protected. For example, in the healthcare world, it is critical to keep patient data private. You may be able to store and analyze data about patients as long as names, Social Security numbers, and other personal data is masked. You have to make sure that unauthorized individuals cannot access private or restricted data. What happens when you flood your environment with big data sources that come from a variety of sources? Some of these sources will come from commercial third-party vendors that have carefully vetted the data and masked out sensitive data.

However, it is quite likely that the big data sources may be insecure and unprotected, and include a lot of personal data. During initial processing of this data, you will probably analyze lots of data that will not turn out to be relevant to your organization. Therefore, you don't want to invest resources to protect and govern data that you do not intend to retain. However, if sensitive personal data passes across your network, you may expose your company to unanticipated compliance requirements. For data that is truly exploratory, with unknown contents, it might be safer to perform the initial analysis in a "walled" environment that is internal but segmented, or in the cloud.

Finally, after you decide that a subset of that data is going to be analyzed more deeply so that results may be incorporated into your business process, it is important to institute a process of carefully applying governance requirements to that data.

What issues should you consider when you incorporate these unvetted sources into your environment? Consider the following:

✔ Determine beforehand who is allowed to access new data sources initially as well as after the data has been analyzed and understood.

✔ Understand how this data will be segregated from other companies' data.

✔ Understand what your responsibility is to leverage the data. If the data is privately owned, you have to make sure that you are adhering to contracts or rules of use. Some data may be linked to a usage contract with a vendor.

✔ Understand where your data will be physically located. You may include data that is linked to customers or prospects in specific countries that have strict privacy requirements. You need to be aware of the details of these sources to avoid violating regulations.

✔ Understand how your data needs to be treated if it is physically moved from one location to another. Are you going to store some of this data with a cloud provider? What type of promises will that provider offer in terms of where the data will be stored, and how well it will be secured?

Just because you have created a security and governance process for your traditional data sources doesn't mean that you can assume that employees and partners will expand those rules to new data sources. You need to consider two key issues: visibility of the data and the trust of those working with the data.

✔ **Visibility:** While business analysts and partners you are working with may be eager to use these new data sources, you may not be aware of how this data will be used and controlled. In other words, you may not have control over your visibility into your resources that are running outside of your control. This situation is especially troublesome if you need to ensure that your provider is following compliance regulations or laws. This is also true when you are using a cloud provider to manage that data because the storage may be very inexpensive to manage.

✔ **Unvetted employees:** Although your company may go through an extensive background check on all of its employees, you're now trusting that no malicious insiders work in various business units outside of IT. You also have to assume that your cloud provider has diligently checked its employees. This concern is real because close to 50 percent of security breaches are caused by insiders (or by people getting help from insiders). If your company is going to use these new data sources in a highly distributed manner, you need to have a plan to deal with inside as well as outside threats.

You have a responsibility to make sure that your new big data sources do not open your company to unanticipated threats or governance risks. It is your responsibility to have good security, governance processes, and education in place across your entire information management environment.

As with any technology life cycle, you need to have a process for assessing the capability of your organization to meet the readiness of all constituents to follow security and governance requirements. You may already have processes for data security, privacy, and governance in place for your existing structured databases and data warehouses. These processes need to be extended for your big data implementation.

For example, is the chief security officer of the company aware of the new data sources being used in the various businesses? Is it clear how you are allowed to use third-party data sources? If you begin to incorporate proprietary data into your big data environment, your company may be violating copyright rules. When you create a big data environment that brings in a lot of new data sources, have you exposed private data that should be masked? At the same time, are you adhering to the data privacy policies of the different countries that you are operating in?

Auditing your big data process

At the end of the day, you have to be able to demonstrate to internal and external auditors that you are meeting the rules necessary to support the operations of the business. You will need a way to show logs or other evidence that the data you are using is secure and clean. You will need to explain the sources of that data. Will you be able to validate the results so that you minimize the risk to the company? You may have to prove that you have archived the data that you are using to make decisions and run the business. This may be well-managed for your traditional databases and your data warehouse, but your unstructured big data sources have not been added to this process.

Although external auditors may not analyze the accuracy of the data warehouse–based data with external big data sources, your internal process will dictate that these sources be well synchronized. For example, the data warehouse will have a clear set of master data definitions, but the big data sources may not have documented metadata. Therefore, it is important that external data sources be managed in a way that metadata definitions are codified so that you can have a set of consistent metadata across these sources. Thinking through this process can make the difference between business success and failure.

Identifying the key stakeholders

One of the characteristics of big data is that it is typically tied to specific business initiatives. For example, the Marketing organization wants to be able to use the huge volumes of data generated by social media sites such as Facebook, Twitter, and so on. Operations teams will want to manage their supply chain leveraging RFID data. The Human Resources department will be eager to keep track of what employees are publishing on social media sites to make sure that they are not violating internal and external regulations. A medical claims department will want to keep track of the regulations determining how patient claim information within health insurance records is managed so that privacy rules are not violated. All of these constituents may reside within the same company, so it is critical that everyone has a common understanding of what the rules are and that the infrastructure is in place to keep the company consistently safe.

Putting the Right Organizational Structure in Place

Typically, companies begin their journey to big data by starting with an experiment to see whether big data can play an important role in defining and impacting business strategy. However, after it becomes clear that big data will have a strategic role as part of the information management environment, you have to make sure that the right structure is in place to support and protect the organization.

Before you establish policies, you first have to know what you are dealing with. For example, are you going to involve transactional systems, social media data, or machine-generated data? Do you intend to combine information from these different sources as part of your data analytics strategy? If you are planning to move forward with more than an isolated experiment, you will need to update your governance strategy so that you are prepared to manage a new variety of data in ways that are safe.

Preparing for stewardship and management of risk

No matter what your information management strategy is, you need to make sure that you have the right level of oversight. This is simply a best practice in general and does not change when you add big data to the mix. However, you may need to implement data stewardship differently with the addition of big data sources. For example, you might need to have a different individual monitor social media data because it has a different origin and different structure than traditional relational data. This new data steward role needs to be carefully defined so that the individual selected can work across the business units that find this type of data most relevant to how they are analyzing the business. For example, the data steward needs to understand or have access to the right people who understand the company's data retention policy as well as the requirements for masking out personal data no matter where that data originates.

Setting the right governance and quality policies

The way that an organization deals with big data is an ongoing cycle and not a one-time project. The potential for causing risk to the business can be serious if consistent rules and processes are not applied consistently. Data quality should also be approached from a governance standpoint. When you think about policy, here are some of the key elements that need to be codified to protect your organization:

- ✔ Determine best practices that your peers have implemented to have consistent polices documented so that everyone has the same understanding of what is required.

- ✔ Compare your policies with the governance requirements for your own business and your industry. Update your policies if you find oversights.

- ✔ Do you have a policy about the length of time that you must hold on to information? Do these policies apply to the data you are collecting from external sources, such as customer discussion groups and social media sites?

- ✔ What is the importance of the data sources that you are bringing into the business? Do you have quality standards in place so that a set of data is only used for decision making if it is proven to be clean and well documented? It is easy to get caught up in the excitement of leveraging big data to conduct the type of analysis that was never achievable before. But if that analysis leads to incorrect conclusions, your business will be at risk. Even data coming from sensors could be impacted by extraneous data that will cause an organization to come to the wrong conclusion.

Developing a Well-Governed and Secure Big Data Environment

A thoughtful approach to security can succeed in mitigating against many security risks. You need to develop a secure big data environment. One thing that you can do is to evaluate your current state.

In a big data environment, security starts with assessing your current state. A great place to begin is by answering a set of questions that can help you form your approach to your data security strategy. Here are a few important questions to consider:

- Have you evaluated your own traditional data security approach?

- How do you control access rights to the data in your applications, your databases, and your warehouse both those within your company and those from third-party sources? Who has the right to access existing data resources as well as the new big data sources you are introducing? How do you ensure that only the right identities gain access to your applications and information?

- Can you identify data vulnerabilities and risks and then correct any weaknesses?

- Do you have a way of tracking your security risk over time so that you can easily share updated information with those who need it?

- Is your overall infrastructure protected at all times from external security threats? If not, this could be the weak link that could seriously impact the security of your data.

- Do you maintain your own keys if you are using encryption, or do you get them from a trusted, reliable provider? Do you use standard algorithms? Have you applied this standard to new data sources that you have determined are critical to your business?

- Are you able to monitor and quantify security risks in real time?

- Can you implement security and governance policies consistently across all types of data sources, including ones that reside in a cloud environment?

- Can you protect all your data no matter where it's stored?

- Can you satisfy auditing and reporting requirements for data wherever it resides?

- Can you meet the compliance requirements of your industry?

- What are your disaster and recovery plans? How do you ensure service continuity for all your critical data sources?

Part VI
Big Data Solutions in the Real World

Use Big Data as a Business Planning Tool

✔ Stage 1: Plan with Data

✔ Stage 2: Do the analysis

✔ Stage 3: Check the results

✔ Stage 4: Act on the plan

✔ Stage 5: Monitor in real time

✔ Stage 6: Adjust the impact

✔ Stage 7: Enable experimentation

web extras

Explore the big data planning stages online at www.dummies.com/extras/bigdata.

In this part . . .

- ✔ Review big data utilization models.
- ✔ Use big data in fraud detection.
- ✔ Integrate social media feedback into corporate decision making.
- ✔ Improve healthcare diagnoses with big data.

Chapter 20

The Importance of Big Data to Business

*T*he idea of managing data to transform business is nothing new. As long as organizations have been capturing information about their business processes, their customers, their prospects, and their products, a big data problem has existed. It was simply not economical or practical for companies to be able to effectively manage all the data across their organizations. Therefore, for the past 30 years, companies have had to make compromises. Either data management professionals would have to compromise by saving only snapshots of data or they would have to create separate databases to store segments of data. Companies have tried complex work-arounds to try to integrate data together to improve business decision making. This often required programmers to develop complex programs to create the right business view of data.

The gating factors keeping businesses from being able to get the most business value from their data were varied and complicated. These factors included

✔ The expense of purchasing enough systems and storage to physically contain the data

✔ The problem of managing a database that was too big to be managed, backed up, or queried

✔ The immaturity of available technology to manage the variety of the data at the right speed

> ✔ The difficulty of programming to integrate data elements and then maintain that code
>
> ✔ The complexity of keeping data up to date and relevant to emerging business requirements

In this chapter, we explore the business imperative behind the movement to big data and describe how companies leverage big data to affect business outcomes.

Big Data as a Business Planning Tool

What does the business hope to achieve by leveraging big data? This is not an easy question to answer. Different companies in different industries need to manage their data differently. But some common business issues are at the center of the way that big data is being considered as a way to both plan and execute for business strategy. While most businesses have mechanisms in place to track customer interactions, it is much more difficult to determine the relationships among a lot of data sources to understand changing customer requirements.

The greatest challenge for the business is to be able to look into the future and anticipate what might change and why. Companies want to be able to make informed decisions in a faster and more efficient manner. The business wants to apply that knowledge to take action that can change business outcomes. Leaders also need to understand the nuances of the business impacts that are across product lines and their partner ecosystem. The best businesses take a holistic approach to data. Four stages are part of the planning process that applies to big data: planning, doing, checking, and acting.

Stage 1: Planning with data

With the amount of data available to the business, dangers exist in making assumptions based on a single view of data. The only way to make sure that business leaders are taking a balanced perspective on all the elements of the business is to have a clear understanding of how these data sources are related. But companies typically only have a small amount of the data they will need to make informed decisions. The business needs a road map for determining what data is needed to plan for new strategies and new directions.

For example, if your company needs to expand the type of services it can offer to existing customers, you need to analyze as much data as possible about what customers are buying and how that is changing. What do customers like and dislike about products? What are competitors offering? What new macro trends are emerging that will change customer requirements? And how are your customers reacting to your products and those from your competitors? If you find ways to effectively manage the data, you may be able to have a powerful planning tool. While the data may confirm your existing strategy, it might send you in new unexpected directions. Part of your planning process requires that you use a variety of data to test assumptions and think differently about the business.

Stage 2: Doing the analysis

After your organization understands the business objectives, it is time to begin analyzing the data itself as part of the planning process. This is not a stand-alone process. Executing on big data analysis requires learning a set of new tools and new skills. Many organizations will need to hire some big data scientists who can understand how to take this massive amount of disparate data and begin to understand how all the data elements relate in the context of the business problem or opportunity.

The big data analytics market is very immature, so you find few highly abstracted and easy-to-use tools to support analysis. So right now, it will be necessary to find highly skilled professionals within consulting organizations who can help you make progress. Big data analytics is a dynamic area that is experiencing very rapid change. Combining the immaturity of the analytics with the needs of business to continually add new data sources that need to be added into the analytics approach will put a lot of pressure on the business to push the boundaries of what is possible. The businesses that are able to get a handle on applying big data analytics to their business planning will be able to identify business nuances and changes that can impact the bottom line. For example, if your company is in the e-commerce market, you will want to analyze the results of new partnerships to see whether they are generating both customer interest and new sales. You may want to see the reaction to the new services on social media sites. At the same time, you want to have a clear understanding of what your closest competitors are offering that could impact revenue.

Stage 3: Checking the results

It is easy to get caught up in the process of analyzing data and forget to do a reality check. Does the analysis reflect business outcomes? Is the data you are using accurate enough or do problems exist? Are the data sources going to truly help with planning? This is the time to make sure that you are not relying on data sources that will take you in the wrong direction. Many companies will use third-party data sources and may not take the time to vet the quality of the data. When you are planning and making business decisions based on analysis, you have to make sure that you are on a strong foundation.

Stage 4: Acting on the plan

After this cycle of analysis is complete, it is time to put the plan into action. But actions have to be part of an overall planning cycle that is repeated — especially as markets become more dynamic. Each time a business initiates a new strategy, it is critical to constantly create a big data business evaluation cycle. This approach of acting based on results of big data analytics and then testing the results of executing business strategy is the key to success. Big data adds the critical element of being able to leverage real results to verify that a strategy is working as intended. Sometimes the results of a new strategy do not match expectations. In some cases, this will mean resetting the strategy. In other situations, the unintended consequences will lead a company in a new direction that might have a better outcome.

Adding New Dimensions to the Planning Cycle

With the advent of big data, some changes can impact the way you approach business planning. As more businesses begin to use the cloud as a way to deploy new and innovative services to customers, the role of data analysis will explode. You might want to therefore think about another part of your planning process. After you make your initial road map and strategy, you may want to add three more stages to your data cycle: monitoring, adjusting, and experimenting.

Stage 5: Monitoring in real time

Big data analytics enables you to monitor data in near real time proactively. This can have a profound impact on your business. If you are a pharmaceutical company conducting a clinical trial, you may be able to adjust or cancel a trial to avoid a lawsuit. A manufacturing company may be able to monitor the results of sensors on equipment to fix a flaw in the manufacturing process before it has a greater impact.

Stage 6: Adjusting the impact

When your company has the tools to monitor continuously, it is possible to adjust processes and strategy based on data analytics. Being able to monitor quickly means that a process can be changed earlier and result in better overall quality. This type of adjustment is something new for most companies. In the past, analysts often were able to analyze the results of monitoring processes, but typically after a problem had already become apparent. Therefore, this type of analysis was used to find out why a problem happened and why a product failed or why a service did not meet customer expectations. While understanding the cause of failure is important, it is always better to be able to avoid mistakes in the first place.

Stage 7: Enabling experimentation

Being able to try out new product and service offerings is important in an increasingly real-time data world. But it is not without risk. Experimentation without the capability to understand the outcome quickly will only confuse customers and partners. Therefore, combining experimentation with real-time monitoring and rapid adjustment can transform a business strategy. You have less risk with experimentation because you can change directions and outcomes more easily if you are armed with the right data.

Keeping Data Analytics in Perspective

Big data is beginning to have an important impact on business strategy. As companies are putting a big data strategy in place, management is beginning to realize that they can begin leveraging data throughout the planning cycle rather than at the end. As the big data market begins to mature, companies will be able to run their business based on a data-centric view of the world. Predictive analytics, for example, is making it possible for companies to understand the small and subtle changes in customer buying patterns so that they can make changes in strategy earlier. For example, Walmart uses social media data to determine what new products customer are starting to demand earlier in the cycle. It is difficult for a retail company to change the products already on store shelves. If a company can predict changes in customer buying preferences six months in advance, it can have a huge impact on the bottom line.

It is easy to assume that all a company needs is to create a big data platform and the strategy will just happen. The reality, of course, is much more complicated. While big data will be an important business tool, a danger exists in relying too much on data alone. Business leaders need to make sure that they do not trust the results of big data analytics in isolation from other factors that cannot easily be codified into an algorithm. You find subtle issues such as what strategies are practical in light of changing business conditions. You'll see emerging trends or a changing competitive landscape that isn't showing up in the analysis. Senior leaders also bring intuition and knowledge to the table. So before you assume that big data is the panacea for all business strategy issues, make sure that you are taking a balanced approach.

Getting Started with the Right Foundation

So, how do you get started in your journey to creating the right environment so that you are ready to both experiment with big data and be prepared to expand your use of big data when you are ready? Will you have to invest in new technologies for your data center? Can you leverage cloud computing services? The answer to these questions is yes. You will have to make changes to support big data. First, you need to make sure that you understand the various types of data that are important to your organization. You also need to understand the new types of data management environments that are available. Each of these new options could be helpful in different types of situations.

For example, if you need to process data quickly, you might want to evaluate in-memory databases. If you have a lot of data that needs to be processed in real time, streaming data offerings are worth evaluating. Many different products can handle spatial data. Chapters 1 and 4 give you a good idea of some of the products and architectures that will support a variety of different data structures and different analytic processes. In addition, you will want to evaluate the cloud-based offerings that allow you to store massive amounts of information inexpensively. Several cloud-based analytics services are changing the way that companies can access and use complicated tools that were never affordable in the past.

Getting your big data strategy started

While clearly a huge amount of technology is involved in building your big data strategy, you have to get started by building the right team of individuals with both technical and business knowledge. You will need business leaders who are involved in planning the strategy for the next generation of products and services. You need to understand the types of answers that they are looking for and the types of questions that they are asking.

Therefore, the best way to get started is to build a team. You may want to involve consultants who have experience working on big data implementations and can help you with best practices. You should understand that at this stage in the industry, you would be working with low-level tools that typically involve a lot of programming. But as new tools emerge, you should continue to experiment to take advantage of innovations. In some cases, you will discover that vendors and consultants have packaged best practices into product offerings that can be customized for your markets and your business model.

But to take advantage of the emerging technologies, it is important that you focus on the basics. You need to make sure that after you select the right data elements for your analysis, that it all makes sense. You have to be able to trust the data so that you minimize the risks. Each new data source will have its own structure. These sources may not be well-vetted. So, before these sources are brought into an analytics framework, you will have to make sure that metadata is consistent.

Getting started will mean taking things slowly. Most organizations do not jump in and start doing full-fledged, corporate-wide big data analytics. Rather, most companies continue to progress with the analytics they have always been doing. However, they are adding pilot projects or planning to add pilots based on areas where the business needs to leverage new types of data at greater speed than ever before.

Planning for Big Data

The ways that big data can be applied to business problems are almost endless. Virtually every industry has the capability or potential to collect and analyze data to improve business outcomes. Some use cases are more obvious than others. You find hundreds of examples of how companies might use social media data to improve business planning and execution. But the capability to leverage big data touches everything from monitoring manufacturing processes to the detection of diseases. In the insurance industry, executives are using big data to figure out what product offerings are the best for a certain customer with the least amount of risk.

Executives in almost every industry want to be able to analyze patterns in all different types of structured and unstructured data to be able to predict outcomes. Companies are leveraging information from customer service notes and information collected from sensors and system logs to understand their businesses. Big data has the potential to help companies get a handle on both risk and opportunities in the best way. Chapters 21 and 22 list how big data is applied to specific industries.

Transforming Business Processes with Big Data

More and more organizations are discovering that they can take advantage of lots of different types of information in new ways. The maturation of the technology will coincide with business leaders' ability to push the envelope on business strategy. We have only touched on the potential value of big data. Companies can save money by identifying fraud before money is paid out. Companies can determine the next best action based on real-time access to customer actions — what they are buying and what they are asking. Healthcare practitioners can leverage massive amounts of best practice data to be better prepared to treat patients more quickly with better results at a lower cost. Needless to say, this is only an early indicator of what will be possible. Preparing for this new world requires your organization to gain knowledge about the potential for technology to transform business processes.

Chapter 21

Analyzing Data in Motion: A Real-World View

*I*f you want to be successful with big data, you need to begin by thinking about solving problems in new ways. Many of the previous limitations placed on problem-solving techniques were due to lack of data, limitations on storage or compute power, or high costs. The technology of big data is shattering some of the old concepts of what can't be done and opening new possibilities for innovation across many industries. The new reality is that an enormous amount of data is generated every day that may have some relevance to your business, if you can only tap into it.

Most likely, you have invested lots of resources to manage and analyze the structured data that you need to understand your customers, manage your operations, and meet your financial obligations. However, today you find huge growth in a very different type of data. The type of information you get from social media, news or stock market data feeds, and log files, and spatial data from sensors, medical-device data, or GPS data, is constantly in motion. These newer sources of data can add new insight to some very challenging questions because of the immediacy of the knowledge. Streaming data — data in motion — provides a way to understand an event at the moment it occurs.

In this chapter, you learn about organizations and entire industries that are changing the way they look at data that is constantly flowing across various interconnected channels of communication. We show you how the technology presented in previous chapters can be applied to solve business problems. Chapter 14 discusses in detail how stream computing technology is used to process and analyze these continuous streams of data. For information on how companies approach the integration of streaming data sources with other data sources — both structured and unstructured — refer to Chapter 15.

Understanding Companies' Needs for Data in Motion

To complete a credit card transaction, finalize a stock market transaction, or send an e-mail, data needs to be transported from one location to another. Data is at rest when it is stored in a database in your data center or in the cloud. In contrast, data is in motion when it is in transit from one resting location to another. Companies that must process large amounts of data in near real time to gain business insights are likely orchestrating data while it is in motion. You need data in motion if you must react quickly to the current state of the data.

Data in motion and large volumes of data go hand in hand. Many real-world examples of continuous streams of large volumes of data are in use today:

- Sensors are connected to highly sensitive medical equipment to monitor performance and alert technicians of any deviations from expected performance. The recorded data is continuously in motion to ensure that technicians receive information about potential faults with enough lead time to make a correction to the equipment and avoid potential harm to patients.

- Telecommunications equipment is used to monitor large volumes of communications data to ensure that service levels meet customer expectations.

- Point-of-sale data is analyzed as it is created to try to influence customer decision making. Data is processed and analyzed at the point of engagement — maybe in combination with location data or social media data.

- Messages, including details about financial payments or stock trades, are constantly exchanged between financial organizations. To ensure the security of these messages, standard protocols such as Advanced Message Queuing Protocol (AMQP) or IBM's MQSeries are often used. Both of these messaging approaches embed security services within their frameworks.

- Collecting information from sensors in a security-sensitive area so that an organization can differentiate between the movement of a harmless rabbit and a car moving rapidly toward a facility.

- Medical devices can provide huge amounts of detailed data about different aspects of a patient's condition and match those results against critical conditions or other abnormal indicators.

The value of streaming data

Data in motion, often in the form of streaming data, is becoming increasingly important to companies needing to make decisions when speed is a critical factor. If you need to react quickly to a situation, having the capability to analyze data in real time may mean the difference between either being able to react to change an outcome or to prevent a poor result. The challenge with streaming data is to extract useful information as it is created and transported before it comes to a resting location. Streaming data can be of great value to your business if you can take advantage of that data when it is created or when it arrives at your business.

You need to process and analyze the streaming data in real time so that you can react to the current state of the data — while in motion and before it is stored. You need to have some knowledge of the context of this data and how it relates to historical performance. And you need to be able to integrate this information with traditional operational data. The key issue to remember is that you need to have a clear understanding of the nature of that streaming data and what results you are looking for. For example, if your company is a manufacturer, it will be important to use the data coming from sensors to monitor the purity of chemicals being mixed in the production process. This is a concrete reason to leverage the streaming data. However, in other situations, it may be possible to capture a lot of data, but no overriding business requirement exists. In other words, just because you can stream data doesn't mean that you always should.

How can you use streaming data to change your business? In the following sections, we look at how organizations in several industries are finding ways to gain value from data in motion. In some situations, these companies are able to take data they already have and begin to use it more effectively. In other situations, they are collecting data that they were not able to collect before. Sometimes organizations can collect much more of the data that they had been only collecting snapshots of in the past. These organizations are using streaming data to improve outcomes for customers, patients, city residents, or perhaps for mankind. Businesses are using streaming data to influence customer decision making at the point of sale.

Streaming Data with an Environmental Impact

Scientists measure and monitor various attributes of lakes, rivers, oceans, seas, wells, and other water environments to support environmental research. Important research on water conservation and sustainability depends on tracking and understanding underwater environments and knowing how they change. Why is this work done? Changes in these natural environments can have an enormous impact on the economic, physical, and cultural well-being of individuals and communities throughout the world. To improve their ability to predict environmental impacts, researchers at universities and environmental organizations across the globe are beginning to include the analysis of data in motion in their research.

Scientific research includes the collection of large volumes of time-sensitive information about water resources and weather to help protect communities against risks and respond appropriately to disasters impacting these natural resources. Mathematical models are used to make predictions such as the severity of flooding in a particular location or the impact of an oil spill on sea life and the surrounding ecosystem. The type of data that can be used includes everything from measuring temperature, to measuring the chemicals in the water, to measuring the current flow. In addition, it is helpful to be able to compare this newly acquired data with historical information about the same bodies of water.

Many sophisticated research programs are in place to improve the understanding of how to protect natural water resources. Rivers and adjacent floodplains and wetlands, for example, need protection because they are important habitats for fish and wildlife. Many communities depend on rivers for drinking water, power generation, food, transportation, and tourism. In addition, the rivers are monitored to provide knowledge about flooding and to give communities advance warnings about floods. By adding a real-time component to these research projects, scientists hope to have a major impact on people's lives.

Using sensors to provide real-time information about rivers and oceans

At one research center in the United States, sensors are used to collect physical, chemical, and biological data from rivers. These sensors monitor spatial changes in temperature, pressure, salinity, turbidity, and the chemistry of water. Their goal is to create a real-time monitoring network for rivers and estuaries. Researchers expect that in the future, they will be able to predict changes in rivers in the same way that weather predictions are made today. Another research center based in Europe is using radio-equipped buoys containing sensors to collect data about the ocean, including measurements of wave height and wave action. This streaming data is combined with other environmental and weather data to provide real-time information on ocean conditions to fisherman and marine researchers.

In both examples, sensors are used to collect large volumes of data as events are taking place. Although infrastructure platforms vary, it is typical to include a middleware layer to integrate data collected by the sensor with data in a data warehouse. These research organizations are also using external sources like mapping databases and sensors coming from other locations as well as geographical information. The data is analyzed and processed as it streams in from these different sources. One organization is building an integrated network of sensors, robotics, and mobile monitoring. It is using this information to build complicated models such as real-time, multiparameter modeling systems. The models will be used to look at the dynamic interactions within local rivers and estuary ecosystems.

The benefits of real-time data

By incorporating real-time analysis of data into environmental research, scientists are advancing their understanding of major ecological challenges. Streaming technology opens new fields of research and takes the concept of scientific data collection and analysis in a new direction. They are looking at data they may have collected in the past in a new way and are also able to collect new types of data sources. Although you can learn a lot by monitoring change variables such as water temperature and water chemistry at set intervals over time, you may miss out on identifying important changes or patterns.

When you have the opportunity to analyze streaming data as it happens, it is possible to pick up on patterns you might have missed. Real-time data on river motion and weather is used to predict and manage river changes. Scientists are hoping to predict environmental impacts just like we report on and forecast weather. They are furthering research on the impact of global warming. They are asking what can be learned from watching the movements of migrating fish. How can watching how pollutants are transported help to clean up from future environmental contamination?

If data scientists are able to take data they have already collected, they can combine it with the real-time data in a much more efficient manner. They also have the capability to do more in-depth analysis and do a better job of predicting future outcomes. Because this analysis is completed, it allows other groups needing the same information to be able to use the findings in new ways to analyze the impact of different issues. This data could be stored in a data cloud environment so that researchers across the globe can have access, add new data into the mix, and solve other environmental problems.

Streaming Data with a Public Policy Impact

Almost every area of a city has the capability to collect data, whether in the form of taxes, sensors on buildings and bridges, traffic pattern monitoring, location data, and data about criminal activity. Creating workable policies that make cities safer, more efficient, and more desirable places to live and work requires the collection and analysis of huge amounts of data from a variety of sources. Much of the data that is pertinent to research on public policy improvements is collected by various city agencies and has historically taken months or years to analyze (such as annual census data, police records, and city tax records). Even within one specific agency, such as the police department, data may be collected by separate districts and not easily shared across the city and its surrounding communities.

As a result, city leaders have an abundance of information about how policies impacted people in their city in prior years, but it has been very challenging to share and leverage fast-changing data to make real-time decisions that can improve city life. What makes leveraging this data even more complicated is the fact that data is managed and stored in separate silos. This causes problems because a direct relationship can exist between different aspects of city operations. Policy makers are beginning to realize that change can only happen if they can use the available data and data from best practices to transform the current state of their environment. The more complex a city, the more a need exists to leverage data to change things for the better.

This is changing as policy makers, scientists, and technology innovators team up to implement policies based on data in motion. For example, to design and implement a program to improve city traffic congestion, you may need to collect data on population, employment figures, road conditions, and weather. Much of this data has been collected in the past, but it is stored in various silos and represents a static view of historical information. To make suggestions based on current streaming information, you need a new approach. Researchers at a technical university in Europe are collecting real-time traffic data from a variety of sources such as Global Positioning System (GPS) data from traveling vehicles, radar sensors on the roads, and weather data. They integrated and analyzed the streaming data to decrease traffic congestion and improve traffic flow. By analyzing both structured and unstructured data as events are taking place, the systems can assess current travel conditions and make suggestions on alternative routes that will cut down on traffic. Ultimately, the goal is to have a major impact on traffic flow in the city. Data in motion is evaluated in connection with historical data so that the recommendations make sense in context with actual conditions.

Streaming data can have a significant impact on lower crime rates in cities. For example, a police department uses predictive analytics to identify crime patterns by time and location. If a sudden change is found in an identified pattern to a new location, the police can dispatch officers to the right location at the right time. After the fact, this data can now be used to further analyze changes in criminal behavior patterns.

Streaming Data in the Healthcare Industry

Big data is of enormous significance to the healthcare industry — including its use in everything from genetic research to advanced medical imaging and research on improving quality of care. While conducting big data analysis in each of these areas is significant in furthering research, a major benefit is applying this information to clinical medicine. If enough data is captured, this data can be applied practically and quickly at the right time to help save lives. Medical clinicians and researchers are using streaming data to speed decision making in hospital settings and improve healthcare outcomes for patients.

Doctors make use of large amounts of time-sensitive data when caring for patients, including results of lab tests, pathology reports, X-rays, and digital imaging. They also use medical devices to monitor a patient's vital signs such as blood pressure, heart rate, and temperature. While these devices provide alerts when the readings go out of normal range, in some cases, preventive action could take place if doctors were able to receive an early warning. Subtle changes in a patient's condition are often hard to pick up with a physical exam, but could be picked up by monitoring devices if a way existed to have more immediate access to the data.

Monitoring devices used in intensive care units generate thousands of readings every second. In the past, these readings have been summarized into one reading every 30–60 minutes. These devices were monitoring very large volumes of data, but because of technology limitation, much of that data was not available for analysis.

Capturing the data stream

Using streaming technology, a hospital university research team is able to capture the data stream from bedside monitors and process it using algorithms designed to look for early warning signs of serious infections. The data is used in real time to provide early warnings of changes in a patient's condition. In some situations, doctors are finding that they are able to take corrective action to help a patient almost 24–36 hours earlier than without the data-streaming technology. Another benefit is the ability of doctors to compare the analysis to a database of patient outcomes that could provide additional insight.

Streaming Data in the Energy Industry

Reducing energy consumption, finding new sources of renewable energy, and increasing energy efficiency are all important goals for protecting the environment and sustaining economic growth. Large volumes of data in motion are increasingly being monitored and analyzed in real time to help achieve these goals.

Many large organizations are using a variety of measures to ensure that they have the energy resources they need now and in the future. Nontraditional sources of energy, such as wind turbines, solar farms, and wave energy, are becoming more realistic options as the price and scarcity of fossil fuels continue to be of concern. These organizations are generating and storing their own energy and need good real-time information to match the supply to demand. They use streaming data to measure and monitor energy demand and supply to improve their understanding of their energy requirements and to make real-time decisions about energy consumption.

Using streaming data to increase energy efficiency

Organizations are beginning to use streaming data to increase energy efficiency, as highlighted by the following two examples:

- ✔ A large university monitors streaming data on its energy consumption and integrates it with weather data to make real-time adjustments in energy use and production.

- ✔ Members of a business community collectively share and analyze streaming energy use data. This enables the companies in this community to consume energy more efficiently and reduce energy costs. Streaming data enables them to monitor supply and demand and ensure that changes in demand are anticipated and kept in balance with supply.

Using streaming data to advance the production of alternative sources of energy

Organizations are also beginning to use streaming data to help advance research and efficient production of alternative energy sources, as demonstrated by the following two examples:

✔ A research institution is using streaming data to understand the viability of using wave energy as source of renewable energy. Many different parameters, such as temperature, geospatial data, and moon and tide data, need to be collected. The organization uses monitoring devices, communications technology, cloud computing, and stream analytics to monitor and analyze the noise made by wave energy technology. The group is studying the impact of the noise levels on fish and other marine life.

✔ A wind-farm company uses streaming data to create hourly and daily predictions about energy production. The company collects turbine data, temperature, barometric pressure, humidity, precipitation, wind direction, and velocity from ground level up to 300 feet. The data comes for thousands of meteorological stations around the world and from its own company's turbines. What does the company do with the data? It creates a model of wind flow to improve the understanding of wind patterns and turbulence near existing turbines. The resulting analytics are used to select the best location for its wind turbines and to reduce cost per kilowatt-hour of energy produced.

Connecting Streaming Data to Historical and Other Real-Time Data Sources

The examples in this chapter demonstrate how companies can gain value from streaming data. The most important aspect of these types of outcomes requires the ability to understand the context of the situation. A doctor might see analysis that points to a particular disease. However, further analysis of other patients with similar symptoms and test results shows that other possible diagnoses may exist. In a complicated world, data is valuable in taking action only in the context of how it is applied to a problem.

Chapter 22

Improving Business Processes with Big Data Analytics: A Real-World View

*I*t is becoming clearer every day that business decision makers need to be able to interpret data differently if businesses expect to keep up with rapid market changes. C-level executives know that future success depends on innovation and building more predictive, responsive, and personalized customer experiences. Success also depends on reducing risk and making governance and security a priority. Meeting these changing business requirements demands that the right information be available at the right time. Many companies see big data analytics as central to their business strategy to increase the level of partner and customer engagement and to decrease the time to decision.

In this chapter, you find out about organizations and entire industries that are changing the way they manage and analyze structured and unstructured data that is increasing in volume, velocity, variety, and veracity. We show how the technology presented in previous chapters can be applied to solve real-world business problems.

Understanding Companies' Needs for Big Data Analytics

The data that can make a difference in how companies satisfy their customers and partners is not necessarily in traditional databases any more. The value of unstructured data from nontraditional sources has become apparent. Business leaders have discovered that if they can quickly analyze information that is unstructured — either in the form of text from customer support systems or social media sites — they can gain important insights. When companies can analyze massive collections of data and compare those results in real time to the customer decision-making process, businesses can gain huge revenue increases. Therefore, leveraging a combination of unstructured and structured data as part of a business process can transform a business's capability to be agile and nimble, and most importantly, profitable.

Improving the Customer Experience with Text Analytics

Many companies accumulate huge amounts of unstructured data that have been underutilized as sources of information about their customer experience. Unstructured data is the text found in e-mails, text messages, call center notes, comments in survey responses, tweets, and blogs. This type of data represents about 80 percent of the data available to companies, and it is continuing to grow. Unstructured data has typically taken many manual hours to review, and in many companies, it has never have been adequately analyzed. Companies recognize that if this data is analyzed at the right time, it may help to identify patterns of customer dissatisfaction or a potential product defect so that corrective action can be taken before it is too late. The increasing sophistication of text analytics is viewed by companies as a major benefit, enabling the deep analysis of large volumes of unstructured data in real or near real time so that the results can be used in decision making. Text analytics is the process of analyzing unstructured text, extracting relevant information, and transforming it into structured information that can be leveraged in various ways. (Text analytics is covered in more detail in Chapter 13.)

How would this work in the real world? Look at an example of a car rental company that was experiencing huge pressures from emerging companies that didn't have the same high overhead. How could the existing company compete? Improving responsiveness seemed to be the key to success. Therefore, the company was able to use text analytics to begin making significant improvements in its customer service. The company encouraged its customers to provide feedback on its services in online surveys or by e-mail or text. Customers used these communication methods to provide comments about service issues such as longer-than-expected wait times, poor agent service, or not getting the car they ordered. However, the company's response and interpretation of these comments had been inconsistent. The company was taking the right approach, but the response was too slow and the analysis was inconsistent. Agency managers read the e-mails and comments in web surveys and text messages. Managers read the comments online and placed them in categories for future attention. Unfortunately, this approach took a long time, and each manager followed a different approach to categorizing comments. It was too easy to miss patterns of dissatisfaction or concern that might show up if you were able to look across a large number of comments at one time.

What managers wanted to do was analyze feedback from customers faster so that they could identify potential issues in real time and address problems at the outset before they become bigger problems. Managers implemented a text analytics solution that allowed them to quickly analyze text for insight across all types of sources, including structured and unstructured data. They also implemented a sentiment analysis solution that enabled an automated approach to identifying forms of communication that might need immediate attention. They were able to capture large volumes of information about the customer experience in real time and quickly analyze and take action.

The business value to the big data analytics implementation

The company was able to make major improvements in customer satisfaction. It is able to keep better track of car and equipment rental performance levels and find problems and fix them early. It now has a more accurate understanding of where problems are located and can recognize them much faster. The new analysis provided managers with an early identification of problems at one location. As a result, they were able to make changes and improve customer satisfaction at this location.

Using Big Data Analytics to Determine Next Best Action

Today the customer is in the driver's seat when it comes to making a choice about how to interact with a service provider. This is true across many industries, including telcos, insurance companies, banks, and retailers. The buyer has many more channel options and is increasingly researching purchase decisions and making buying decisions from a mobile device. You need to manage your customer interactions armed with in-depth and customized knowledge about each individual customer to compete in a fast-paced, mobile-driven market. What does it take to provide the right offer to a buyer while he is making a purchasing decision? How do you ensure that your customer service representatives are armed with customized knowledge about your customer's value to the company and her specific requirements? How can you integrate and analyze multiple sources of structured and unstructured information so that you can offer customers the most appropriate action at the time of engagement? How do you quickly assess the value of a customer and determine what sort of offer that customer needs so that you can keep the customer satisfied and make a sale?

Company executives are increasingly viewing big data analytics as the secret weapon they need to take the next best action in highly competitive environments. Using analytics to understand customer requirements on a more personal level is seen as an important capability when dealing with the increased pressures of an empowered consumer. Companies are expanding their use of social media and mobile computing environments and want to reach their customers at the right time through their channel of choice. To deliver successful customer outcomes in a mobile world, offers need to be as targeted and personal as possible. Companies are using their analytics platform combined with big data analysis with fast processing of real-time data to achieve competitive advantage. Some of the key goals they wish to achieve include

- ✔ Increase their understanding of each customer's unique needs. Provide these in-depth customer insights at the right time to make them actionable.

- ✔ Improve responsiveness to customers at the point of interaction.

- ✔ Integrate real-time purchase data with large volumes of historical purchase data and other sources of data to make a targeted recommendation at the point of sale.

- ✔ Provide customer service representatives with the knowledge to recommend the next best action for the customer.

- ✔ Improve customer satisfaction and customer retention.

- ✔ Deliver the right offer so that it is most likely to be accepted by the customer.

What does a next best action solution look like? Companies are integrating and analyzing large volumes of unstructured and streaming data from e-mails, text messages, call center notes, online surveys, voice recordings, GPS units, and social media. In some situations, companies are able to find new uses for data that was too large, too fast, or of the wrong structure to be incorporated into analytics and predictive models before. The models that companies are able to build are more advanced and can incorporate real-time data from a variety of sources. Company analysts are looking for patterns in the data that will provide additional insight into customer opinions and behavior. Speed is a top priority. Your model needs to predict the next best action very quickly if you want to be successful in this fast-paced mobile world.

...y is helping companies to generate actionable informa-
...ad of days or weeks. Predicting the next best action
...e of sophisticated machine-learning algorithms from a
...environment like IBM's Watson. Watson can be used to
...es of data and analyze data in motion and to understand
...nt an immediate response, using cognitive computing to
...efer to Chapter 13 for information on Watson.)

...al-world examples of companies in the financial services
...sting heavily in new ways to understand and respond to

...y wants to increase the efficiency and effectiveness
...esentatives. Agents could not quickly identify the full
...s mix of business, and therefore, it was hard to identify
...eeded special attention. In addition, agents found it very
...arch for call notes captured during previous calls with
...and found that information that might have helped
...was not located until it was too late. Unfortunately, a
...stomer interactions resulted in dissatisfied customers.
...ents a solution that transforms conversations from
...t. Keywords are identified and analyzed. This data is
...cal data about the customer to identify high-priority
...e immediate attention and to deliver a more timely and
...to all customers.

...ned about the length of time it takes to access customer
...o provide call center representatives with more infor-
mation about customers and to have a better understanding of the network of customer relationships (family, business, and social networks). Executives have large volumes of structured and unstructured information about customers, including e-mails, letters, call center notes, chats, and voice recordings. The bank implemented a big data analytics solution that improves the way its representatives support customers by providing them with an early indication of each customer's needs before they got on the phone. The platform uses social media data to understand relationships and can determine whom the customer connected to. The solution combines multiple sources of data, both internal and external. Some indication may exist of major life events that are taking place for this customer. As a result, agents are able to take the

next best action. For example, a customer may have a child ready to graduate from high school, and this might be a good time to discuss a college loan.

A credit card company wants to increase its capability to monitor customer experience and take action based on each customer's unique situation. It wants to tailor its solution to the individual customer and not to a demographic. As a response, the company developed a big data analytics solution that integrates information from traditional structured sources, such as customer transaction information, with unstructured and streaming data such as click-stream data, Twitter feeds, and other social media data. Its immediate goal is to create detailed microsegmentations of customers to be able to provide targeted offers. The solution provides the company with an effective approach to analyzing lots of information quickly to identify customer intent to buy and create a personalized next best offer for that customer.

Preventing Fraud with Big Data Analytics

By many estimates, at least 10 percent of insurance company payments are for fraudulent claims, and the global sum of these fraudulent payments amounts to billions or possibly trillions of dollars. While insurance fraud is not a new problem, the severity of the problem is increasing and perpetrators of insurance fraud are becoming increasingly sophisticated. Fraud occurs in all lines of the insurance business, including automobile, health, workers' compensation, disability, and business insurance. Fraud may be committed by an individual who falsifies a claim of a broken arm after staging a fall in a shopping mall or by any number of business workers who have some association with the process of repairing damage from accidents, treating medical injuries, or dealing with other aspects of the claims process. The practice of insurance fraud is widespread and may include organized crime groups involved in car repairs, medical treatment, legal work, home repairs, or other functions related to the claim.

What is the role for big data analytics in helping insurance companies find ways to detect fraud? Insurance companies want to stop fraud early before they get involved in the processing of the claim. By developing predictive models based on both historical and real-time data on wages, medical claims, attorney costs, demographics, weather data, call center notes, and voice recordings, companies are in a better position to identify suspected fraudulent claims in the early stages of interaction. For example, a personal injury claim could potentially include fake medical claims or a staged accident. Companies have seen an increase in sophisticated crime rings to perpetrate auto insurance or medical fraud. These rings may have similar methods of operation that are enacted in different regions of the country or using different aliases for the claimants. Big data analysis can quickly look for patterns in historical claims and identify similarities or bring up questions in a new claim before the process gets too far along.

Risk and fraud experts at insurance companies, along with actuarial and underwriting executives and insurance business managers, all see big data analytics as having the potential to deliver a huge benefit by helping to anticipate and decrease attempted fraud. The goal is to identify fraudulent claims at the first notice of loss — at the first point where you need an underwriter or actuary.

Consider the following real-world example. An insurance company wants to improve its ability to make real-time decisions when deciding how to process a new claim. The company's cost outlay including litigation payments related to fraudulent claims has been rising steadily. The company has extensive policies in place to help underwriters evaluate the legitimacy of claims, but the underwriters often did not have the data they needed at the right time to make an informed decision. The company implemented a big data analytics platform to provide the integration and analysis of data from multiple sources. The platform incorporates extensive use of social media data and streaming data to help provide a real-time view. Call center agents are able to have a much deeper insight into possible patterns of behavior and relationships between other claimants and service providers when a call first comes in.

For example, an agent may receive an alert about a new claim that indicates the claimant was a previous witness on a similar claim six months ago. After uncovering other unusual patterns of behavior and presenting this information to the claimant, the claim process may be halted before it really gets going. In other situations, social media data may indicate that conditions described in a claim did not take place on the day in question. For example, a claimant indicated that his car was totaled in a flood, but documentation from social media showed that the car had actually been in another city on the day the flood occurred.

Insurance fraud is such a huge cost for companies that executives are moving quickly to incorporate big data analytics and other advanced technology to address the problem of insurance fraud. Insurance companies not only feel the impact of these high costs, but the costs also have a negative impact on customers who are charged higher rates to account for the losses. By using big data analytics to look for patterns of fraudulent behavior in enormous amounts of unstructured and structured claims-related data, companies are detecting fraud in real time. The return on investment for these companies can be huge. They are able to analyze complex information and accident scenarios in minutes as compared to days or months before implementing a big data platform.

The Business Benefit of Integrating New Sources of Data

Big data analytics is providing companies with a new way to provide answers to some age-old questions. Businesses have traditionally focused on how to improve customer service, provide the right offer to the right customer at the right time, and reduce risk and fraud. So what's changed? By integrating new sources of unstructured data such as web logs, call center notes, e-mails, log data, and geospatial data with traditional sources of transaction, customer, and operational data, companies can look at their businesses much differently. They can gather data they were not able to collect previously and use this data to look for patterns of behavior that provide a great insight to the business. Integrating all these sources of data provides a way for companies to deepen their understanding of customers, products, and risk.

Part VII

Find out what the top ten big data trends are at www.dummies.com/extras/bigdata.

In this part . . .

- ✔ Find out best practices for big data.
- ✔ Understand big data resources.
- ✔ Follow big data industry standards.
- ✔ Track big data conferences.
- ✔ Predict emerging data trends in the big data arena.

Chapter 23

Ten Big Data Best Practices

*W*hile we are at an early stage in the evolution of big data, it is never too early to get started with good practices so that you can leverage what you are learning and the experience you are gaining. As with every important emerging technology, it is important to understand why you need to leverage the technology and have a concrete plan in place. In this chapter, we provide you with the top-ten best practices you need to understand as you begin the journey to manage big data.

Understand Your Goals

Many organizations start their big data journey by experimenting with a single project that might provide some concrete benefit. By selecting a project, you have the freedom of testing without risking capital expenditures. However, if all you end up doing is a series of one-off projects, you will likely not have a good plan in place when you begin to understand the value of leveraging big data in the company. Therefore, after you conclude some experiments and have a good initial understanding of what might be possible, you need to set some goals — both short- and long-term. What do you hope to accomplish with big data? Could parts of your business be more profitable with the infusion of more data to predict customer behavior or buying patterns? It is important to have a collaboration between IT and business units to come up with well-defined goals.

After you understand the goals you have for leveraging big data, your work is just beginning. You now need to get to the meat of the issues. You need to involve all the stakeholders in the business. Big data affects every aspect of your organization, including the historical data that you already store, the information sources managed by different business units. New data sources may be considered in some business areas that few managers are even aware of. Getting a task force together is a great way to get representatives of the business together so that they can see how their data management issues are related. This team can evolve into a team that can help various business units with best practices. The task force should have representatives from upper-management leaders who are setting business strategy and direction.

Establish a Road Map

At this stage, you have experimented with big data and determined your company's goals and objectives. You have a good understanding of what upper management and business units need to accomplish. It is time to establish a road map. Your road map is your action plan. You clearly can't do all the projects and meet all the demands from your company simultaneously. Your road map needs to begin with the set of foundational services that can help your company get started. Part of your road map should include the existing data services. Make sure that your road map has benchmarks that are reasonable and achievable. If you take on too much, you will not be able to demonstrate to management that you are executing well. Therefore, you don't need a ten-year road map. Begin with a one- to two-year road map with well-defined goals and outcomes. You should include both business and technical goals as part of the road map.

Discover Your Data

No company ever complains that it has too little data. In reality, companies are swimming in data. The problem is that companies often don't know how to use that data pragmatically to be able to predict the future, execute on important business processes, or simply gain new insights. The goal of your big data strategy and plan should be to find a way to leverage data for more predictable business outcomes. But you need to walk before you run. We recommend that you start by embarking on a discovery process. You need to get a handle on what data you already have, where it is, who owns and controls it, and how it is currently used. What are the third-party data sources that your company relies on? This process will give you a lot of insights. For example, it will let you know how many data sources you have and how much overlap exists. This process will also help you to understand the gaps in knowledge about those sources. You might discover that lots of duplicate data exists in one area of the business and almost no data exists in another area. You might discover that you are dependent on third-party data that isn't as accurate as it should be. Spend the time you need to do this discovery process because it will be the foundation for your planning and execution of your big data strategy.

Figure Out What Data You Don't Have

Now that you have discovered what data you have, it is time to think about what is missing. Take advantage of the task force you have set up. Business leaders are your best source of information. These leaders will understand better than anyone else what is keeping them from making even better decisions. When you start this process of determining what you need and what is missing, it is good to encourage people to think out of the box. For example, you might want to ask something like this: "If you could have any information at any speed to support the business and cost were no issue, what would you want?" This doesn't mean that cost isn't an issue. Rather, you are looking for management to think out of the box about what could really change the business. With the innovation happening in the data space, some of these wild ideas and hopes are actually possible.

Understand the Technology Options

At this point, you understand your company's goals, you have an understanding of what data you have, and you know what data is missing. But how do you take actions to execute your strategy? You have to know what technologies are available and how they might be able to assist your company to produce better outcomes. Therefore, do your homework. Begin to understand the value of technologies such as Hadoop, streaming data offerings, and complex event-processing products. You should look at different types of databases such as in-memory databases, spatial databases, and so on. You should get familiar with the tools and techniques that are emerging as part of the big data ecosystem. It is important that your team has enough of an understanding of the technology available to make well-informed choices.

Plan for Security in Context with Big Data

While companies always list security of data as one of the most important issues they need to manage, they are often unprepared for the complexities involved in managing data that is highly distributed and highly complex. In the early stages of big data analytics, the analyst will not secure the data, because only a small portion of that data will be saved for further analysis. However, when an analyst selects an amount of data that will be brought into the company, the data has to be secured against internal and external risk. Some of this data will have private information that must be masked so that no one without authorization has access. For security to be effective in the context of big data, you need to have a well-defined plan.

Plan a Data Governance Strategy

Information governance is the ability to create an information resource that can be trusted by employees, partners, and customers. A governance strategy is the joint responsibility of IT and the business. It is key that concrete rules exist that dictate how big data will be governed. For example, rules exist that determine how data must be protected depending on the circumstance and governmental requirements. Healthcare data must be stored so that the identity and personal data remain private. Financial markets have their own set of data governance requirements that have to be adhered to. Problems can develop when an analyst collects and analyzes huge volumes of information and does not remember to implement the right governance to protect that data. In addition, data sources themselves may be proprietary. When these sources are used within an organization, restrictions may exist on how much data is used and for what purposes. Accountability for managing data in the right way is the heart of a good data governance strategy.

Plan for Data Stewardship

It is easy to fall into the trap of assuming that the results of data analytics are correct. Management likes numbers and likes to make decisions based on what the numbers say. But hazards can occur if the data isn't managed in the right way. For example, you might be using data from five or six different data sources. In a situation where a company is determining which customers are potentially the best targets for a new product offering, a company might want to analyze 10 or 15 different sources of data to come up with the results. Do you have common metadata across these data sources? If not, is a process in place to vet the viability of that source to make sure that it is accurate and usable? Using data sources that are based on different metadata and different assumptions can send a company off on the wrong direction. So, be careful and make sure that when you collect data that might be meaningful that it can execute in a way that helps the company make the most informed and accurate decisions. This also means understanding how to integrate these new data sources with historical data systems, such as the data warehouse.

Continually Test Your Assumptions

You will begin to find that making use of new data sources and massive amounts of data that could never be processed in the past can help make your company much better at anticipating the future. You will be able to determine the best actions to take in near real time based on what your data tells you about a customer or a decision you need to make. Even if you have all the processes in place to ensure that you have the right controls and the right metadata defined, it is still important to test continuously. What types of outcomes are you getting from your analysis? Do the results seem accurate? If you are getting results that seem hard to believe, it is important to evaluate outcomes. After you have more accurate data, you will be able to achieve better and more accurate outcomes. However, in some cases, you may see a problem that wasn't apparent. Therefore, don't just assume that the data is always right. Test your assumptions and what you know about your business.

Study Best Practices and Leverage Patterns

As the big data market matures, companies will gain more experience with best practices or techniques that are successful in getting the right results. You can access best practices in several different ways. You can meet with peers who are investigating the ways to leverage big data to gain business results. You can also look to vendors and systems integrators who have codified best practices into patterns that are available to customers. It is always better to find ways to learn from others rather than to repeat a mistake that someone else made and learned from. As the big data market begins to mature, you will be able to leverage many more codified best practices to make your strategy and execution plan more successful.

Chapter 24

Ten Great Big Data Resources

You will find lots of resources that can help you start making sense of the big data world. Standard organizations are tackling some of the key emerging issues with getting data resources to work together effectively. Open source offerings can help you experiment easily so that you can better understand what is possible with big data. Lots of big data conferences and research groups are out there. Of course, all the vendors in the market have research, white papers, and best practices that they are happy to share. In this chapter, we offer you some ideas of the resources that are out there to help you.

Hurwitz & Associates

www.hurwitz.com

The authors of this book are partners and associates at Hurwitz & Associates. We're happy to help you with your questions about big data. We provide training, strategy guidance, blogs, and research services. If you're a big data vendor, we can help you understand customer requirements so that you can position your company and offer products that will meet customer needs. We invite you to subscribe to our blogs and visit our website.

Standards Organizations

For big data to mature, standards are required. A number of organizations are working hard to bring vendors together to help move the process forward. The following sections describe some of these organizations.

The Open Data Foundation

www.opendatafoundation.org

The Open Data Foundation (ODaF) is a nonprofit organization that is organized to help promote the adoption of global metadata standards as well as the development of open source for the use of statistical data. The organization focuses on improving metadata in the fields of economics, finance, healthcare, education, labor, social science, technology, agriculture, development, and the environment.

The Cloud Security Alliance

https://cloudsecurityalliance.org/research/big-data

The Cloud Security Alliance (CSA) was established to promote the use of best practices for providing and ensuring security within cloud computing and to educate people about the uses of cloud computing to help secure all other forms of computing. The organization has established the Big Data Working Group (BDWG) to help identify the scalable techniques for data-centric security and privacy problems in big data.

National Institute of Standards and Technology

www.nist.gov/itl/ssd/is/big-data.cfm

The National Institute of Standards and Technology (NIST) is a U.S. government agency that focuses on emerging standards efforts. This organization has done a considerable amount of work defining and providing good information on everything from cloud computing to big data. In March 2012, NIST started a big data initiative. The focus of the new initiative is to help transform the capability of organizations to use big data for scientific discovery, environmental and biomedical research, education, and national security. It will collaborate with the National Science Foundation (NSF) Center for Hybrid Multicore Productivity Research (CHMPR) in convening a big data workshop. The issues to be addressed include

- State-of-the-art core technologies needed to collect, store, preserve, manage, analyze, and share big data that could benefit from standardization

- Potential measurements to ensure the accuracy and robustness of methods that harness these technologies

Apache Software Foundation

http://hadoop.apache.org

The Apache Software Foundation provides organizational, legal, and financial support for a broad range of open source software projects. It was founded in 1999 as a membership-based, not-for-profit corporation to ensure that the Apache projects continue to exist beyond the participation of individual volunteers. One of the organization's key projects is its management of Hadoop. It offers an open source software library that is a standards-based framework for processing large data sets across clusters of computers.

OASIS

www.oasis-open.org

One of the most important standards organizations is OASIS, the Organization for the Advancement of Structured Information Standards. It is a nonprofit organization that has started to focus on big data standards. This process is at an early stage, but we expect that the organization will begin to focus on creating big data standards.

Vendor Sites

All the major data management vendors offer great resources online. We recommend that you check out vendors such as

Google: http://research.google.com/

Amazon: http://aws.amazon.com/big-data/

IBM: http://bigdatauniversity.com/ and http://www-01.ibm.com/software/data/bigdata/

Oracle: http://www.oracle.com/us/technologies/big-data/index.html

Microsoft: http://research.microsoft.com/en-us/projects/bigdata/

Cloudera: http://www.cloudera.com/content/cloudera/en/why-cloudera/hadoop-and-big-data.html

SAS Institute: http://www.sas.com/

Teradata: http://www.teradata.com/business-needs/Big-Data-Analytics/

This is only a partial list. Hundreds of companies are lining up to provide great big data information. Make sure to check out the blogs of some of these companies' thought leaders.

Online Collaborative Sites

Many emerging groups encourage online collaboration around the topic of big data. LinkedIn has a number of groups worth checking out at `http://www.linkedin.com/groups/Big-Data-Analytics-Strategy-FP-1814785?home=&gid=1814785&trk=anet_ug_hm`. In addition, look at the forums sponsored by the Apache Hadoop Initiative at `http://hadoop.apache.org/`.

Big Data Conferences

Lots of data conferences are out there, and many of them are either initiating new conferences on big data or have big data tracks at their meetings. Here are some examples of the big data conferences that are springing up every day:

- **The Data Warehousing Institute (TDWI):** Sponsors many conferences, seminars, and educational forums on data warehouses and big data

- **Big Data Conference:** Provides analytics and applications for big data

- **Big Data Retail Forum:** A conference for companies looking to retailers and consumer goods manufacturers needing to analyze real-time information

- **Hadoop World:** Sponsored by O'Reilly

- **O'Reilly Strata and StrataRx:** Visit `http://strataconf.com`.

- **StructureData:** Visit `http://event.gigaom.com/structuredata`.

Chapter 25

Ten Big Data Do's and Don'ts

Many companies that are beginning their exploration of big data are in the early stages of execution. Most companies are experimenting with pilots to see whether they can leverage big data sources to transform decision making. It is easy to make mistakes that can cause disruptions in your business strategy. In this chapter, we give you some ideas about what you should do and what you should avoid as you begin your journey to big data.

Do Involve All Business Units in Your Big Data Strategy

Big data is not an isolated activity. Rather, it is the way that the business can leverage huge volumes of data to learn more about customers, processes, and events than would be possible with snapshots of data. If executed properly, a big data strategy can have a huge impact on the effectiveness of a business strategy. Companies that assume that data that is out of the norm is wrong may suddenly discover some new emerging patterns of customer requirements. The business units can gain significant value when they are brought into the process early.

Do Evaluate All Delivery Models for Big Data

It is natural to assume that if you are dealing with petabytes of data, the only way to store and manage that data is in the data center. However, technology is evolving so that it is possible and necessary to use cloud computing storage and compute resources to manage big data. Therefore, evaluate the type of services that are cloud based and determine which ones have the performance that you will need for certain tasks.

Do Think about Your Traditional Data Sources as Part of Your Big Data Strategy

Many companies that have found value in big data analytics assume that they no longer have to think about the traditional data warehouse. This is not true. In fact, it is critical that you plan to use the results of your big data analytics in conjunction with your data warehouse. The data warehouse includes the information about the way your company operates. Therefore, being able to compare the big data results against the benchmarks of your core data is critical for decision making.

Do Plan for Consistent Metadata

When you complete the analysis of a massive data set, it is quite possible that you will come up with data that all matches a pattern. This set of data now can lead your organization to begin analyzing a new issue in depth. Keep in mind that this data might come from customer service sites or social media environments that have not been cleansed. Therefore, before you trust the data, you have to make sure that you are dealing with a consistent set of metadata so that you can bring this information into your organization and analyze it in concert with the data from your systems of record.

Do Distribute Your Data

When you are dealing with big data, don't assume that you will be able to manage all this information within a single server. Find out how to use distributed computing techniques such as Hadoop to effectively manage the size, variety, and required speed to manage your data.

Don't Rely on a Single Approach to Big Data Analytics

So much hype exists in the market around technologies such as Hadoop and MapReduce that you might lose sight of what you are actually trying to accomplish. A lot of important technologies are available, such as text analytics, predictive analytics, streaming data environments, and spatial data analysis, that may be important for the job you are trying to accomplish. Spend the time to investigate the variety of technologies that can support you. Experiment and investigate the technology solutions that can make you successful.

Don't Go Big Before You Are Ready

You are right to be excited about the potential that big data offers your company. Big data can mean the difference between jumping into an exciting new market before your competitors or being left behind. But walk before you run. You need to start with pilot projects that can allow you to gain some experience. You need to work with experts who can keep you from making huge mistakes because of inexperience.

Don't Overlook the Need to Integrate Data

Your big data sources will not be effective if they live in isolation from each other. Good technologies in the market are focused on making it easier to integrate the results of big data analytics with other data sources. Therefore, be prepared not just to analyze but also to integrate.

Don't Forget to Manage Data Securely

When companies embark on big data analysis, they often forget to maintain the same level of data security and governance that is assumed in traditional data management environments. When you begin doing analysis of several petabytes or more of data, you typically won't mask out private information at the outset. However, when you have a subset of that initial data set that is now critical to determining your next best action or your approach to a new market, you need to first secure that data so that it doesn't put your business at risk. Some of this data will now become corporate intellectual property that has to be secured. You may also need to manage privacy requirements. This security has to become part of your big data life cycle. In addition, some of the data sources that you are using may come from third-party data sources that require licenses. Make sure that you are allowed to use this data and that you haven't violated governance rules.

Don't Overlook the Need to Manage the Performance of Your Data

Big data demonstrates that we are able to make use of more data than ever before at a faster rate of speed than was possible in the past. This capability to gain more insights is a huge benefit. However, if that data isn't managed in an effective way, it will cause huge problems for the company. Therefore, you need to build manageability into your road map and plan for big data.

Glossary

· ·

A

abstraction: The idea of minimizing the complexity of something by hiding the details and just providing the relevant information. It's about providing a high-level specification rather than going into lots of detail about how something works. In the cloud, for instance, in an IaaS delivery model, the infrastructure is abstracted from the user.

access control: Determining who or what can go where, when, and how.

ACID: An acronym for *atomicity, consistency, isolation,* and *durability,* which are the main requirements for guaranteed transaction processing.

advanced analytics: Algorithms for complex analysis of either structured or unstructured data. It includes sophisticated statistical models, machine learning, neural networks, text analytics, and other advanced data-mining techniques Advanced analytics does not include database query and reporting and OLAP cubes.

API (application programming interface): A defined protocol that allows computer programs to use functionality and data from other software systems.

application life cycle: The process of maintaining a piece of code so that it's consistent and predictable as it's changed to support business requirements.

architecture: In information processing, the design approach taken in developing a program or system.

archiving: The process by which a database or file data that's seldom used or outdated, but that's required for historical or audit reasons, is copied to a cheaper form of storage. The storage medium may be online, tape, or optical disc. Companies are using the cloud as a means of archiving data.

asset management: Software that allows organizations to record all information about their hardware and software. Most such applications capture cost information, license information, and so on. Such information belongs in the configuration management database. See also *CMDB*.

audit: A check on the effectiveness of a task or set of tasks, and how the tasks are managed and documented. Auditing is also a process that is used within organizations to ensure that the data is secure and in compliance with regulatory organizations.

audit trail: A trace of a sequence of events in a clerical or computer system. This audit usually identifies the creation or modification of any element in the system, who did it, and (possibly) why it was done.

authentication: The process by which the identity of a person or computer process is verified.

B

backup: A utility that copies databases, files, or subsets of databases and files to a storage medium. This copy can be used to restore the data in case of system failure.

bandwidth: Technically, the range of frequencies over which a device can send or receive signals. The term is also used to denote the maximum data transfer rate, measured in bits per second, that a communications channel can handle.

batch: A noninteractive process that runs in a queue, usually when the system load is lowest, and generally used for processing batches of information in a serial and usually efficient manner. Early computers were capable of only batch processing.

best practice: An effective way of doing something. It can relate to anything from writing program code to IT governance.

big data: The capability to manage a huge volume of disparate data, at the right speed and within the right time frame, to allow real-time analysis and reaction. Big data is typically broken down by three characteristics, including volume (how much data), velocity (how fast that data is processed), and variety (the various types of data).

Bigtable: Developed by Google to be a distributed storage system intended to manage highly scalable structured data. Data is organized into tables with rows and columns. Unlike a traditional relational database model, Bigtable is a sparse, distributed, persistent, multidimensional sorted map. It is intended to store huge volumes of data across commodity servers.

binding: Making the necessary connections among software components so that they can interact.

biometrics: Using a person's unique physical characteristics to prove his identity to a computer — for example, by using a fingerprint scanner or voice analyzer.

black box: A component or device with an input and an output whose inner workings need not be understood by or accessible to the user.

BPaaS: See *Business Process as a Service.*

BPEL (Business Process Execution Language): A computer language based on WSDL (Web Services Description Language, an XML format for describing web services) and designed for programming business services. See also *XML.*

BPM (business process management): A technology and methodology for controlling the activities — both automated and manual — needed to make a business function.

broker: In computer programming, a program that accepts requests from one software layer or component and translates them into a form that can be understood by another layer or component.

bus: A technology that connects multiple components so they can talk to one another. In essence, a bus is a connection capability. A bus can be software (such as an enterprise service bus) or hardware (such as a memory bus).

business process: The codification of rules and practices that constitute a business.

Business Process as a Service (BPaaS): A whole business process is provided as a service involving little more than a software interface, such as a parcel delivery service.

business process modeling: A technique for transforming how business operates into a codified source so that it can be translated into software.

business rules: Constraints or actions that refer to the actual commercial world but may need to be encapsulated in service management or business applications.

business service: An individual function or activity that is directly useful to the business.

C

cache: An efficient method of storing data in memory so that future requests for that data can be achieved more quickly.

center of excellence: A group of key people from all areas of the business and operations that focus on best practices. A center of excellence provides a way for groups within the company to collaborate. This group also becomes a force for change, because it can leverage its growing knowledge to help business units benefit from experience.

change management: The management of change in operational processes and applications. Change management is critical when IT organizations are managing software infrastructure in conjunction with new development processes. All software elements have to be synchronized so that they work as intended.

cloud computing: A computing model that makes IT resources such as servers, middleware, and applications available as services to business organizations in a self-service manner.

CMDB (configuration management database): In general, a repository of service management data.

COBIT (Control Objectives for Information and Related Technology): An IT framework with a focus on governance and managing technical and business risks.

columnar or column-oriented database: A database that stores data across columns rather than rows. This is in contrast to a relational database that stores data in rows.

Complex Event Processing (CEP): A technique for tracking, analyzing, and processing data as an event happens. This information is then processed and managed based on a business rules and processes.

component: A piece of computer software that can be used as a building block in larger systems. Components can be parts of business applications that have been made accessible through web service–related standards and technologies, such as WSDL, SOAP, and XML. See also *web service*.

configuration: The complete description of the way in which the constituent elements of a software product or system interrelate, both in functional and physical terms.

configuration management: The management of configurations, normally involving holding configuration data in a database so that the data can be managed and changed where necessary.

container: In computer programming, a data structure or object used to manage collections of other objects in an organized way.

content management system: A system that provides methods and tools to capture, manage, store, preserve, and deliver content and documents related to organizational processes. The technologies include document management, records management, imaging, workflow management, web content management, and collaboration.

CRM (customer relationship management): Software designed to help you run your sales force and customer support operations.

D

data access: See *access control.*

data at rest: Data that is placed in storage rather than used in real time.

data cleansing: Software used to identify potential data-quality problems. If a customer is listed multiple times in a customer database because of variations in the spelling of her name, the data-cleansing software makes corrections to help standardize the data.

data federation: Data access to a variety of data stores, using consistent rules and definitions that enable all the data stores to be treated as a single resource.

data in motion: Data that is moving across a network or in memory for processing in real time.

data marts: A subset of a data warehouse that is designed to focus on a specific set of business information.

data mining: The process of exploring and analyzing large amounts of data to find patterns.

data profiling: A technique or process that helps you understand the content, structure, and relationships of your data. This process also helps you validate your data against technical and business rules.

data quality: Characteristics of data such as consistency, accuracy, reliability, completeness, timeliness, reasonableness, and validity. Data-quality software ensures that data elements are represented in a consistent way across different data stores or systems, making the data more trustworthy across the enterprise.

data transformation: A process by which the format of data is changed so that it can be used by different applications.

data warehouse: A large data store containing the organization's historical data, which is used primarily for data analysis and data mining. It is the data system of record.

database: A computer system intended to store large amounts of information reliably and in an organized fashion. Most databases provide users with convenient access to the data, along with helpful search capabilities.

database management system (DBMS): Software that controls the storage, access, deletion, security, and integrity of primarily structured data within a database.

directory: A term used in both computing and telephony to indicate an organized map of devices, files, or people.

distributed computing: The ability to process and manage the processing of algorithms across many different nodes in a computing environment.

E

early binding: Defining the connections among applications before processing to improve speed. This also limits flexibility. Also see *late binding*.

elasticity: The capability to expand or shrink a computing resource in real time, based on need.

ELT (extract, load, transform): Tools for locating and loading data into a business application so that it can be later transformed. This is similar to ETL (see its entry) but is associated with big data integration processes.

emulation: When hardware, software, or a combination of both duplicates the functionality of a computer system in a different, second system. The behavior of the second system will closely resemble the original functionality of the first system. See also *virtualization*.

Entity Relationship (ER) model: A data management approach that graphically represents relationships between data. This allows developers to create new relationships between data sources without complex programming.

ERP (enterprise resource planning): A packaged set of business applications that combines business rules, processes, and data management into a single integrated environment to support a business.

Enterprise Service Bus (ESB): A packaged set of middleware services that are used to communicate between business services in a secure and predictable manner.

ETL (extract, transform, and load): Tools for locating and accessing data from a data store (data extraction), changing the structure or format of the data so it can be used by the business application (data transformation), and applying the data to the business application (data load).

F

fault tolerance: The capability of a system to provide uninterrupted service despite the failure of one or more of the system's components.

federation: The combination of disparate things so that they can act as one — as in federated states, data, or identity management — and to make sure that all the right rules apply.

framework: A support structure for developing and managing software products.

G

governance: The ability to ensure that corporate or governmental rules and regulations are conformed with. Governance is combined with compliance and security issues across computing environments.

granularity: An important software design concept, especially in relation to components, referring to the amount of detail or functionality — from fine to coarse — provided in a service component. One software component can do something quite simple, such as calculate a square root; another has a great deal of detail and functionality to represent a complex business rule or workflow. The first component is fine-grained, and the second is coarse-grained. Developers often aggregate fine-grained services into coarse-grained services to create a business service.

grid computing: A step beyond distributed processing, involving large numbers of networked computers (often geographically dispersed and possibly of different types and capabilities) that are harnessed to solve a common problem. A grid computing model can be used instead of virtualization in situations that require real time where latency is unacceptable.

H

Hadoop: An Apache-managed software framework derived from MapReduce and Bigtable. Hadoop allows applications based on MapReduce to run on large clusters of commodity hardware. Hadoop is designed to parallelize data processing across computing nodes to speed computations and hide latency. Two major components of Hadoop exist: a massively scalable distributed file system that can support petabytes of data and a massively scalable MapReduce engine that computes results in batch.

Hadoop Distributed File System (HDFS): A versatile, resilient, clustered approach to managing files in a big data environment. HDFS is not the final destination for files. Rather, it is a data "service" that offers a unique set of capabilities needed when data volumes and velocity are high.

hardware partitioning: The act of subdividing and isolating elements of a physical server into fractions, each of which can run an operating system or an application.

hybrid cloud: A computing environment that includes the use of public and private clouds as well as data center resources in a coordinated fashion.

hypervisor: Hardware that allows multiple operating systems to share a single host. The hypervisor sits at the lowest levels of the hardware environment and uses a thin layer of code in software to enable dynamic resource sharing. The hypervisor makes it seem like each operating system has the resources all to itself.

1

IaaS: See *Infrastructure as a Service.*

identity management: Keeping track of a single user's (or asset's) identity throughout an engagement with a system or set of systems.

information integration: A process using software to link data sources in various departments or regions of the organization with an overall goal of creating more reliable, consistent, and trusted information.

infrastructure: The fundamental systems necessary for the ordinary operation of anything, be it a country or an IT department. The physical infrastructure that people rely on includes roads, electrical wiring, and water systems. In IT, infrastructure includes basic computer hardware, networks, operating systems, and other software that applications run on top of.

Infrastructure as a Service (IaaS): Infrastructure, including a management interface and associated software, provided to companies from the cloud as a service.

infrastructure services: Services provided by the infrastructure. In IT, these services include all the software needed to make devices talk to one another, for starters.

in-memory database: A database structure where information is managed and processed in memory rather than on disk.

interoperability: The capability of a product to interface with many other products; usually used in the context of software.

ISO (International Organization for Standardization): An organization that has developed more than 17,000 international standards, including standards for IT service management and corporate governance of information technology.

ITIL (Information Technology Infrastructure Library): A framework and set of standards for IT governance based on best practices.

L

LAMP (Linux, Apache, MySQL, PHP, Perl, or Python): An increasingly popular open source approach to building web applications. LAMP is a software bundle made up of the *L*inux operating system, the *A*pache web server, a *My*SQL database, and a scripting language such as *P*HP, *P*erl, or *P*ython.

late binding: Deferring the necessary connections among applications to when the connection is first needed. Late binding allows more flexibility for changes than early binding does, but it imposes some cost in processing time.

latency: The amount of time lag before a service executes in an environment. Some applications require less latency and need to respond in near real time, whereas other applications are less time-sensitive.

legacy application: Any application that is more than a few years old. When applications can't be disposed of and replaced easily, they become legacy applications. The good news is that they're still doing something useful when selected pieces of code can be turned into business services with new standardized interfaces.

Linux: An open source operating system based upon and similar to UNIX. In cloud computing, Linux is the dominant operating system, primarily because it is supported by a large number of vendors.

Linux web hosting: The vast majority of websites run on the Linux operating system managed by a Linux web hosting service using the LAMP (Linux, Apache, MySQL, PHP) software stack.

loose coupling: An approach to distributed software applications in which components interact by passing data and requests to other components in a standardized way that minimizes dependencies among components. The emphasis is on simplicity and autonomy. Each component offers a small range of simple services to other components.

M

MapReduce: Designed by Google as a way of efficiently executing a set of functions against a large amount of data in batch mode. The "map" component distributes the programming problem or tasks across a large number of systems and handles the placement of the tasks in a way that balances the load and manages recovery from failures. After the distributed computation is completed, another function called "reduce" aggregates all the elements back together to provide a result.

markup language: A way of encoding information that uses plain text containing special tags often delimited by angle brackets (< and >). Specific markup languages are based on XML to standardize the interchange of information between different computer systems and services. See also *XML*.

mashup: A program (possibly installed on a web page) that combines content from more than one source, such as Google Maps and a real estate listing service.

metadata: The definitions, mappings, and other characteristics used to describe how to find, access, and use the company's data and software components.

metadata repository: A container of consistent definitions of business data and rules for mapping data to its actual physical locations in the system.

middleware: Multipurpose software that lives at a layer between the operating system and application in distributed computing environments.

mission-critical: An application that a business cannot afford to be without at any time.

MOM (Message Oriented Middleware): A precursor to the enterprise service bus. See also Enterprise Service Bus *(ESB), a set of packaged middleware services.*

multitenancy: This refers to the situation where a single instance of an application runs on an SaaS vendor's servers, but serves multiple client organizations (tenants), keeping all their data separate. In a multitenant architecture, a software application partitions its data and configuration so that each customer has a customized virtual application instance.

MySQL: An open source option to SQL.

N

network: The connection of computer systems (nodes) by communications channels and appropriate software.

NoSQL (not only SQL): A set of technologies that created a broad array of database management systems that are distinct from relational database systems. One major difference is that SQL is not used as the primary query language. These database management systems are also designed for distributed data stores.

O

object-oriented database management system (OODBMS): A database management system where data is stored as an object that is closely aligned with an application.

open source: A movement in the software industry that makes programs available along with the source code used to create them so that others can inspect and modify how programs work. Changes to source code are shared with the community at large.

operationalized analytics: Making analytics part of a business process.

p

P2P (peer-to-peer): A networking system in which nodes in a network exchange data directly instead of going through a central server.

PaaS: See *Platform as a Service.*

persistence: A guarantee that data stored in a database won't be changed without permissions and it will available as long as it is important to the business.

Platform as a Service (PaaS): A cloud service that abstracts the computing services, including the operating software and the development and deployment and management life cycle. It sits on top of Infrastructure as a Service.

PostgreSQL: The most widely used open source relational database.

predictive analytics: A statistical or data-mining solution consisting of algorithms and techniques that can be used on both structured and unstructured data (together or individually) to determine future outcomes. It can be deployed for prediction, optimization, forecasting, simulation, and many other uses.

private cloud: As opposed to a public cloud, which is generally available, a private cloud is a set of computing resources within the corporation that serves only the corporation, but that is set up to operate in a cloud-like manner in regard to its management.

process: A high-level, end-to-end structure useful for decision making and normalizing how things get done in a company or organization. See also *workflow*.

protocol: A set of rules that computers use to establish and maintain communication among themselves.

provisioning: Making resources available to users and software. A provisioning system makes applications available to users and makes server resources available to applications.

public cloud: A resource that is available to any consumer either as a fee-per-transaction service or as a free service. It does not have deep security or a well-defined SLA.

R

real-time: A form of processing in which a computer system accepts and updates data at the same time, feeding back immediate results that influence the data source.

real-time event processing: A class of applications that demand timely response to actions that take place out in the world. Typical examples include automated stock trading and RFID. See also *RFID*.

registry: A single source for all the metadata needed to gain access to a web service or software component.

relational database management system (RDBMS): A database management system that organizes data in defined tables.

repository: A database for software and components, with an emphasis on revision control and configuration management (where they keep the good stuff, in other words).

resource pool: A set of compute, storage, or data services that are combined to be used across hybrid environments.

response time: The time from the moment at which a transaction is submitted by a user or an application to the moment at which the final result of that transaction is made known to the user or application.

REST (Representational State Transfer): Designed specifically for the Internet and is the most commonly used mechanism for connecting one web resource (a server) to another web resource (a client). A RESTful API provides a standardized way to create a temporary relationship (also called "loose coupling") between and among web resources.

RFID (radio frequency identification): A technology that uses small, inexpensive chips attached to products (or even animals) that then transmit a unique identification number over a short distance to a special radio transmitter/receiver.

RPC (remote procedure call): A way for a program running on one computer to run a subprogram on another computer.

S

SaaS: See _Software as a Service._

SAML (Security Assertion Markup Language): A standard framework for exchanging authentication and authorization information (that is, credentials) in an XML format called _assertions._

SAN (storage-area network): A high-speed network of interconnected storage devices. These storage devices might be servers, optical disc drives, or other storage media. The difference between a SAN and an NAS (Network Attached Storage) is that a SAN runs at a higher speed than an NAS, while an NAS is generally easier to install and provides a file system.

scalability: In regard to hardware, the capability to go from small to large amounts of processing power with the same architecture. It also applies to software products such as databases, in which case it refers to the consistency of performance per unit of power as hardware resources increase.

scripting language: A computer programming language that is interpreted and has access to all or most operating system facilities. Common examples include Perl, Python, Ruby, and JavaScript. It is often easier to program in a scripting language, but the resulting programs generally run more slowly than those created in compiled languages such as C and C++.

semantics: In computer programming, what the data means as opposed to the formatting rules (syntax).

service: A purposeful activity carried out for the benefit of a known target. Services are often made up of a group of component services, some of which may also have component services. Services always transform something, and they complete by delivering an output.

service catalog: A directory of IT services provided across the enterprise, including information such as service description, access rights, and ownership.

service desk: A single point of contact for IT users and customers to report any issues they may have with the IT service (or, in some cases, with IT's customer service).

service management: Monitoring and optimizing a service to ensure that it meets the critical outcomes that the customer values and the stakeholders want to provide.

silo: In IT, an application with a single narrow focus, such as human resources management or inventory control, with no intention or preparation for use by others.

SLA (service-level agreement): A document that captures the understanding between a service user and a service provider regarding quality and timeliness.

SOA (service-oriented architecture): An approach to building applications that implements business processes or services by using a set of loosely coupled black-box components orchestrated to deliver a well-defined level of service.

SOAP (Simple Object Access Protocol): A protocol specification for exchanging data. Along with REST, it is used for storing and retrieving data in the Amazon storage cloud. See also *REST*.

Software as a Service (SaaS): The delivery of computer applications over the Internet.

spatial database: A database that is optimized for data related to where an object is in a given space.

SQL (structured query language): The most popular computer language for accessing and manipulating databases.

SSL (Secure Sockets Layer): A popular method for making secure connections over the Internet, first introduced by Netscape.

standards: A core set of common, repeatable best practices and protocols that have been agreed on by a business or industry group. Typically, vendors, industry user groups, and end users collaborate to develop standards based on the broad expertise of a large number of stakeholders. Organizations can leverage these standards as a common foundation and innovate on top of them.

streaming data: An analytic computing platform that is focused on speed. Data is continuously analyzed and transformed in memory before it is stored on a disk. This platform allows the analyzing of large volumes of data in real time.

structured data: Data that has a defined length and format. Examples of structured data include numbers, dates, and groups of words and numbers called *strings* (for example, a customer's name, address, and so on).

T

text analytics: The process of analyzing unstructured text, extracting relevant information, and transforming it into structured information that can be leveraged in various ways.

throughput: The rate at which transactions are completed in a system.

TLS (Transport Layer Security): A newer name for SSL. See also *SSL*.

TQM (Total Quality Management): A popular quality-improvement program.

transaction: A computer action that represents a business event, such as debiting an account. When a transaction starts, it must either complete or not happen at all.

U

unstructured data: Data that does not follow a specified data format. Unstructured data can be text, video, images, and so on. Also see *structured data*.

utility computing: A metered service that acts like a public service based on payment for the use of a measured amount of a component or asset.

V

virtualization: Virtual memory is the use of a disk to store active areas of memory to make the available memory appear larger. In a virtual environment, one computer runs software that allows it to emulate another machine. This kind of emulation is commonly known as virtualization. See also *emulation*.

W

web service: A software component created with an interface consisting of a WSDL definition, an XML schema definition, and a WS-Policy definition. Collectively, components could be called a service contract — or, alternatively, an API. See also *API, WSDL (Web Standard Definition Language), WS (Web Standard), and XML (eXtended Markup Language).*

workflow: This is a sequence of task-oriented steps needed to carry out a business process. See also *process.*

WS (Web Standard): Policy framework that provides a way of expressing the capabilities, requirements, and characteristics of software components in a Web Services system.

WSDL (Web Service Definition Language): An XML (eXtended Markup Language) format for describing web services.

X

XML (eXtensible Markup Language): A way of presenting data as plain-text files that has become the lingua franca of SOA. In XML, as in HTML, data is delimited in tags that are enclosed in angle brackets (< and >), although the tags in XML can have many more meanings. See also *SOA.*

XML Schema: A language for defining and describing the structure of XML documents.

XSD (XML Schema Definition): The description of what can be in an XML document.

XSLT (eXtensible Stylesheet Language Transformation): A computer language, based on XML, that specifies how to change one XML document into another. See also *XML.*

Index

• C •

• E •

Math & Science

Algebra I For Dummies,
2nd Edition
978-0-470-55964-2

Anatomy and Physiology
For Dummies,
2nd Edition
978-0-470-92326-9

Astronomy For Dummies,
3rd Edition
978-1-118-37697-3

Biology For Dummies,
2nd Edition
978-0-470-59875-7

Chemistry For Dummies,
2nd Edition
978-1-1180-0730-3

Pre-Algebra Essentials
For Dummies
978-0-470-61838-7

Microsoft Office

Excel 2013 For Dummies
978-1-118-51012-4

Office 2013 All-in-One
For Dummies
978-1-118-51636-2

PowerPoint 2013
For Dummies
978-1-118-50253-2

Word 2013 For Dummies
978-1-118-49123-2

Music

Blues Harmonica
For Dummies
978-1-118-25269-7

Guitar For Dummies,
3rd Edition
978-1-118-11554-1

iPod & iTunes
For Dummies,
10th Edition
978-1-118-50864-0

Programming

Android Application
Development For
Dummies, 2nd Edition
978-1-118-38710-8

iOS 6 Application
Development For Dummies
978-1-118-50880-0

Java For Dummies,
5th Edition
978-0-470-37173-2

Religion & Inspiration

The Bible For Dummies
978-0-7645-5296-0

Buddhism For Dummies,
2nd Edition
978-1-118-02379-2

Catholicism For Dummies,
2nd Edition
978-1-118-07778-8

Self-Help & Relationships

Bipolar Disorder
For Dummies,
2nd Edition
978-1-118-33882-7

Meditation For Dummies,
3rd Edition
978-1-118-29144-3

Seniors

Computers For Seniors
For Dummies,
3rd Edition
978-1-118-11553-4

iPad For Seniors
For Dummies,
5th Edition
978-1-118-49708-1

Social Security
For Dummies
978-1-118-20573-0

Smartphones & Tablets

Android Phones
For Dummies
978-1-118-16952-0

Kindle Fire HD
For Dummies
978-1-118-42223-6

NOOK HD For Dummies,
Portable Edition
978-1-118-39498-4

Surface For Dummies
978-1-118-49634-3

Test Prep

ACT For Dummies,
5th Edition
978-1-118-01259-8

ASVAB For Dummies,
3rd Edition
978-0-470-63760-9

GRE For Dummies,
7th Edition
978-0-470-88921-3

Officer Candidate Tests,
For Dummies
978-0-470-59876-4

Physician's Assistant Exam
For Dummies
978-1-118-11556-5

Series 7 Exam
For Dummies
978-0-470-09932-2

Windows 8

Windows 8 For Dummies
978-1-118-13461-0

Windows 8 For Dummies,
Book + DVD Bundle
978-1-118-27167-4

Windows 8 All-in-One
For Dummies
978-1-118-11920-4

Available in print and e-book formats.

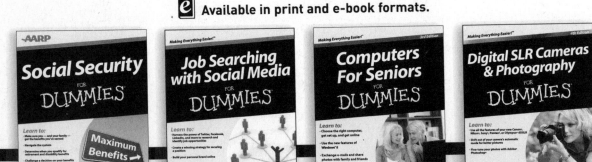